W9-AEP-386

Writing Fiction

TENTH EDITION

writing

A GUIDE TO NARRATIVE CRAFT

Tenth Edition

fiction

JANET BURROWAY

with ELIZABETH STUCKEY-FRENCH

and NED STUCKEY-FRENCH

THE UNIVERSITY OF CHICAGO PRESS Chicago and London

The University of Chicago Press, Chicago 60637
The University of Chicago Press, Ltd., London
© 2019 by Janet Burroway, Elizabeth Stuckey-French, and Ned Stuckey-French

Published 2019

Printed in the United States of America

28 27 26 25 24 23 22 21   4 5 6 7

ISBN-13: 978-0-226-61655-1 (cloth)
ISBN-13: 978-0-226-61669-8 (paper)
ISBN-13: 978-0-226-61672-8 (e-book)
DOI: https://doi.org/10.7208/chicago/9780226616728.001.0001

Library of Congress Cataloging-in-Publication Data

Names: Burroway, Janet, author. | Stuckey-French, Elizabeth, author. |
    Stuckey-French, Ned, author.
Title: Writing fiction : a guide to narrative craft / Janet Burroway ; with Elizabeth
    Stuckey-French and Ned Stuckey-French.
Other titles: Chicago guides to writing, editing, and publishing.
Description: Tenth edition. | Chicago ; London : The University of Chicago Press,
    2019. | Series: Chicago guides to writing, editing, and publishing | Includes index.
Identifiers: LCCN 2018050263 | ISBN 9780226616551 (cloth : alk. paper) |
    ISBN 9780226616698 (pbk. : alk. paper) | ISBN 9780226616728 (e-book)
Subjects: LCSH: Fiction—Technique. | Fiction—Authorship.
Classification: LCC PN3355 .B79 2019 | DDC 808.3—dc23
LC record available at https://lccn.loc.gov/2018050263

♾ This paper meets the requirements of ANSI/NISO Z39.48-1992
(Permanence of Paper).

In memory of David Daiches, mentor and friend

Contents

Preface

Writing Fiction came about by fluke. In 1972, I left England and Sussex University, where I had been teaching such things as Chaucer, Romantic Poetry, and Tragedy, and came to Florida State, where as a novelist and new hire in the embryonic Creative Writing Program I was assigned "Narrative Techniques," the first course in fiction.

I had no idea how to teach it. I was familiar with the form of the workshop from my undergraduate days at Barnard, but this was intended as an instructional first course, including lectures and the discussion of concepts. I inherited the subject from Michael Shaara, who was apparently very successful at it, but he had left as guidance no more than a couple of pages of cryptic notes. There were (it is difficult now to imagine) virtually no books to serve as guidance. Strunk and White's *Elements of Style* was a mainstay, but it took, as White notes, a barking tone toward its writer novices. I reread E. M. Forster's lovely *Aspects of the Novel*, but it was mostly too abstract and too advanced for my Florida eighteen-year-olds. I combed Eric Bentley's *The Life of the Drama* for clues to plot. I read another how-to, the name and author of which I no longer remember, but which memorably assured me that women use a lot of exclamation points but men should not.

For a few years I floundered toward coherence in the course, until it occurred to me that such concepts as *character, plot, point of view,* and *setting*—what we discussed in a literature class—were of necessity elements put there by the writer. If I could turn around and consider how the writer went about that *putting*—how do you develop a character, shape a plot, settle on a point of view, produce an atmosphere that is organic to the whole and not mere description?—I should be able to direct an intelligible and helpful classroom conversation. And, gradually, it worked. By the end of the seventies my students were learning how to ask about technique, critique each other's style and structure, and adopt the vocabulary of craft as their own.

My novels were at that point being published by Little, Brown in America, and my editor was friends with an editor in its textbook division who was headed to Tallahassee for a sales talk. My editor told Chuck Christensen to take me out to lunch, which he did, and over shrimp and hush puppies I described my dilemma and my solution. Now that the burgeoning of creative writing programs was well established in America, I asked, did he think there might be a market for a college text in fiction writing? He said, "I don't know, what do you think?" I said, "I don't know, what do you think?" By the end of the meal he said, "Let's try it"—which was all the contract I had when, the following year, as I guest-taught at the Iowa Writer's Workshop, I put together the first draft of a college textbook at first called *Narrative Techniques*.

The first edition of *Writing Fiction: A Guide to Narrative Craft* came out in 1982 and a second in 1987. Meanwhile, Little, Brown sold its textbook division to Scott Foresman and Scott Foresman to HarperCollins. By the time HarperCollins was bought by Addison Wesley Longman, sometime during the life of the fourth edition, the book had become a creative writing staple. By the sixth edition Addison had become Longman, which by the seventh became Pearson. For the sixth edition I took on one-time reviser Susan Weinberg, and for the seventh I engaged my colleague Elizabeth Stuckey-French to help with revision and especially with the onerous task of choosing new stories for the "anthology" section of the book. She was joined by her husband Ned Stuckey-French for the eighth and ninth editions, the latter published in 2014.

Elizabeth, Ned, and I continually worried about the price of the book, which augmented with every edition and every new publishing house. The cost of permissions added to the problem, increasing in spite of the growing availability of stories on the internet. Some teachers, we knew, made course packets of their own favorite examples; some chose other anthologies, which only raised the amount their students spent on books; some told us that they could not in conscience ask their students to pay the price of our text. We worried that the expense also made the book less accessible to developing writers who were not enrolled in courses but who might want a self-guided course in writing fiction. It was always our hope to find a way to make it more affordable.

So the tenth edition of *Writing Fiction* contains, rather than an anthology, a list of ten short stories at the end of each chapter, each of which could act as an exemplar of the contents of that chapter. Some of these are in the public domain and freely available online, some can be found in the archives of the literary magazines in which they appeared, and some will require a library search (a labor, perhaps, that students ought to learn). Of course, virtually all of the stories listed will demonstrate virtually all of the skills discussed in the book, as will virtually all of the stories teachers choose for themselves. Some teachers will prefer not to use any of them, or to use any at all, but to go directly to workshopping student work, in which case the lists remain a resource for the owners of the text.

Like its previous manifestations, the tenth edition attempts to guide the new writer from first impulse to final revision, employing concepts of fiction's elements familiar from literature study but shifting the perspective toward that of the practicing writer. I have wanted to address the student, however inexperienced, as a fellow artist, whose concerns are both frightening and, often, a question of understanding and developing technique. I have been aware that *Writing Fiction* is used by many instructors in both beginning and advanced writing courses and for students at very different levels of understanding, and I have tried to make it practical, comprehensive, and flexible, and to keep the focus on the student writer and the process of the writing.

The new edition contains the whole of the ninth edition text, minus the anthology, with, in addition to the lists of stories, many updated examples within the text, exercises new and culled from previous editions, new quotations of advice from successful authors, and new sections on distraction, appropriation, genre, young adult and middle-grade fiction, and white space.

As experienced instructors are aware, the idea of a text for writing fiction is itself problematic. Unlike such subjects as math and history, where a certain mass of information needs to be organized and conveyed, the writing of fiction is more often a process of trial and error—the learning is perpetual and, paradoxically, the writer needs to know everything at once. Over the years, my revisers and I have shuffled the chapters in a vain attempt to find the perfect sequence. In the new edition I have continued that effort, in some instances returning to an earlier order. At the same time, I have tried to keep the chapters sufficiently self-contained that teachers may assign them, and writers may consult them, in any order they prefer.

The institutional necessity of dividing the study of writing into its types—fiction, nonfiction, poetry, drama—runs the risk of forcing (or at least persuading) those enrolled in writing programs to specialize too early, before their nascent talents are fully formed. I have always encouraged my students to try, early and often, writing in every genre. Likewise, teachers and individual readers will find in these pages an occasional encouragement toward genre-busting, hybrid writing and the short-short, a form that bends toward poetry.

There has of late been a good deal of pushback against the explosion of creative writing as a college subject. The negative view has appeared in print, in both literary and glossy magazines and some full books, such as Mark McGurl's *The Program Era*; the answering and further-analyzing collection *After the Program Era*, edited by Loren Glass; and *MFA vs NYC*, edited by Chad Harbach. It comes from academics who think creative writing undeserving of university credit, from writers who disdain academia, from celebrity authors who count fame as the only true success, and from self-styled outliers who disdain the notion of a "degree" as inimical to the calling. Such polemics may argue that only fiction writers read fiction, only poets read poetry, and only writers for "little" or literary magazines read those magazines, assuming that such closed communities must be pointless. Like the parents of many of my former students, they may argue that writing is a dead end if you can't make a living or a fortune at it.

All this is in error. We are, I believe, at a point in history where, the computer and the internet having reintroduced writing as a constant activity, the elite again becomes the demotic, with both good and bad consequences. In the eighteenth century, education was not widespread, but all the educated in the Western world wrote. People "naturally" learned to write by reading, though it was universally assumed that the more specialized arts—music, painting, sculpture—required apprenticeships and conservatories. Women of means, locked out of the profession of writing altogether, wrote diaries and letters often and at length—luckily, since much of our sense of daily life is now retrieved from such of their manuscripts as have survived.

Over the last two centuries, society has experienced the increasing professionalization of authorship through agenting, marketing, and the takeover of the publishing industry by corporations not primarily concerned with literature. Film, television, and the internet have all had roles in promoting fame and fortune—or rather, celebrity and money—as the proper goals of authorship. At the same time and at the same pace, the respect with which society regards literature has declined. (Norman Mailer thought he could change the world. What contemporary author would make that claim?) Women of the fifties broke into the writing profession at just the moment when corporatization began to sour the industry. Movies and the sitcom became the major forms of storytelling. The popular authors of the *Saturday Evening Post* and the *Ladies Home Journal* became less popular, those sources of authorial income dried, and when some colleges and universities tried to teach their storytelling skills, the schools were decried as fostering pop and pap.

In the face of this, it amazed me, as a young teacher, to find that my (by and large poorly read) students were passionate about writing fiction. What was it that motivated them? Was it a superficial and selfish fantasy? Or did they somehow perceive that their passive absorption of the sitcom and the soap had left them wanting? Was this a lazy alternative to academia, or were we in fact the monks of the new dark ages, keeping the culture alive?

An answer is suggested in two interestingly contrasting articles that appeared in the *Atlantic* in December 2017: "What's College Good for?" by Bryan Caplan, and "The Desirability of Storytellers" by Ed Yong.

Caplan, a professor of economics, argues that college graduates earn more than non-college-educated people mainly because of the "signaling" of preexisting traits, not anything they've learned; a student who completes a PhD in philosophy, for example, has shown herself to be "brilliant, diligent, and willing to tolerate serious boredom," all eminently employable traits. That philosophy might be a passion, or a desirable study in itself, does not figure in Caplan's system of values. "Why do English classes focus on literature and poetry instead of business and technical writing?" he asks, not rhetorically. He complains that students spend twelve hours a week "socializing with friends." It does not occur to him that, for young adults living on their own for the first time, *socializing* represents the process of *socialization*.

Yong, on the other hand, recounts the experience of social scientists among preliterate societies of hunter-gatherers in the Philippines and Bolivia. Among the Tsimane of Bolivia, they showed that stories conveyed important information about food, weather, and animal behavior, as well as reinforcing norms and ethics. Among the Agta of the Philippines, they found to their surprise that storytellers were likely to be judged the most desirable living companions and mates, enjoying prestige greater than the best hunters and warriors. An analysis of the tales they told suggested that for nomadic people who had neither religion nor government, which rely on punitive methods of instilling good citizenship, it was the stories' function to promote cooperation, gender equality, and the cementing of social bonds.

A university has two distinct purposes. One is to get its students ready for life in the "real" world. The other is to keep, in a cool dry place, the knowledge and wisdom that the real world isn't buying at the moment. In a world of global capitalism, I would argue, the desire to write well is to be celebrated, and creative writing must remain a college subject because, like philosophy and history (and similarly unremunerative studies), it is neither taught nor learned without pedagogical effort.

People read a great deal, but they do not read skillfully written and edited text as a part of daily life. Of literary readers there may be precious few, but the computer and the internet have made writers of all the generations present and to come. To write emails, messages, posts, tweets, and blogs is all to the good. To write a grammatically accurate post, an alliterative tweet, a metaphorical blog entry, will salvage just a little of our culture. To recognize the tools of grammar, alliteration, and metaphor will salvage a little more.

In *Sapiens: A Brief History of Humankind*, Yuval Noah Harari points out that it is not language itself but the related capacity *to imagine what is not immediately present* that distinguishes the human species. To imagine what is not immediately present allows us spirituality, nationhood, commerce, and law, and it is of course the essence of story. To write better and better stories may promote cooperation, gender equality, and the cementing of social bonds. If an aspiring writer has natural talent, so much the better. If she gets published, even paid—wonderful. Her mother is probably right that she'll need a day job. She may even find one with her literary skills, in PR, marketing, or law. (My best friend in college, hoping to break into journalism, ended up as the first female chief justice of the Supreme Court of New York . . .) But in any case, it is good for a full-blooded life and good for the culture that human beings should continue to study the craft of fiction.

I hope *Writing Fiction* will aid that study for many years to come.

Janet Burroway

1: Whatever Works

THE WRITING PROCESS

You want to write. Why is it so hard?

There are a few lucky souls for whom the whole process of writing is easy, for whom the smell of fresh paper is better than air, whose minds chuckle over their own agility, who forget to eat, and who consider the world at large an intrusion on their good time at the keyboard. But you and I are not among them. We are in love with words except when we have to face them. We are caught in a guilty paradox in which we grumble over our lack of time, and when we have the time, we sharpen pencils, check email, or clip the hedges.

Of course, there's also joy. We write for the satisfaction of having wrestled a sentence to the page, for the rush of discovering an image, for the excitement of seeing a character come alive. Even the most successful writers will sincerely say that these pleasures—not money, fame, or glamour—are the real rewards of writing. Fiction writer Alice Munro concedes:

> It may not look like pleasure, because the difficulties can make me morose and distracted, but that's what it is—the pleasure of telling

the story I mean to tell as wholly as I can tell it, of finding out in fact what the story is, by working around the different ways of telling it.

Nevertheless, writers may forget what such pleasure feels like when confronting a blank page, like the heroine of Anita Brookner's novel *Look at Me*:

> Sometimes it seems like a physical effort simply to sit down at my desk and pull out the notebook. . . . Sometimes the effort of putting pen to paper is so great that I literally feel a pain in my head.

It helps to know that most writers share the paradox of least wanting to do what we most want to do. It also helps to know some of the reasons for our reluctance. Fear of what could emerge on the page, and what it may reveal about our inner lives, can keep us from getting started. "What's called writer's block," claims novelist Tom Wolfe, "is almost always ordinary fear." Indeed, whenever I ask a group of writers what they find most difficult, a significant number answer that they feel they aren't good enough, that the empty page intimidates them, that they are in some way afraid. Many complain of their own laziness, but laziness, like money, doesn't really exist except to represent something else—in this case fear, severe self-judgment, or what Natalie Goldberg calls "the cycle of guilt, avoidance, and pressure."

There's another impediment to beginning, expressed by a writer character in Lawrence Durrell's *Alexandria Quartet*. Durrell's Pursewarden broods over the illusory significance of what he is about to write, unwilling to begin in case he spoils it. Many of us do this: The idea, whatever it is, seems so luminous, whole, and fragile, that to begin to write about that idea is to commit it to rubble. Knowing in advance that words will never exactly capture what we mean or intend, we must gingerly and gradually work ourselves into a state of accepting what words can do instead. No matter how many times we find out that what words can do is quite all right, we still shy again from the next beginning. Against this wasteful impulse I have a motto over my desk that reads: "Don't Dread; Do." It's a fine motto, and I contemplated it for several weeks before I began writing this chapter.

The mundane daily habits of writers are apparently fascinating. No author offers to answer questions at the end of a public reading without being asked: Do you write in the morning or at night? Do you write every day? Do you compose longhand or on a computer? Sometimes such questions show a reverent interest in the workings of genius. More often, I think, they're a plea for practical help: Is there something I can do to make this job less horrific? Is there a trick that will unlock my words?

....

GET STARTED

The variety of authors' habits suggests that there is no magic to be found in any particular one. Donald Hall spent a dozen hours a day at his desk, moving back and forth between as many projects. Philip Larkin said that he wrote a poem only every eighteen months or so and never tried to write one that was not a gift. Gail Godwin goes to her workroom every day "because what if the angel came and I wasn't there?" Julia Alvarez begins the day by reading first poetry, then prose, by her favorite writers "to remind me of the quality of writing I am aiming for." Like Hemingway, Andre Dubus advised students to stop writing midsentence in order to begin the next day by completing the thought, thereby reentering the creative flow. Yelizaveta P. Renfro always begins with lists, "often in the margins or endpapers of books I'm reading." T. C. Boyle starts knowing "nothing. Nothing at all. The first line comes and I start." Shawn Wong wants "to hear the language in my ears before I start writing." Dickens could not deal with people when he was working: "The mere consciousness of an engagement will worry a whole day." Thomas Wolfe wrote standing up. Some writers can plop at the kitchen table without clearing the breakfast dishes; others need total seclusion, a beach, a cat, a string quartet.

There is something to be learned from all this, though. It is not an "open sesame" but a piece of advice older than fairy tales: Know thyself. The bottom line is that if you do not at some point write your story down, it will not get written. Having decided that you will write it, the question is not "How do you get it done?" but "How do *you* get it done?" Any discipline or indulgence that helps nudge you into position facing the page is acceptable and productive. If jogging after breakfast energizes your mind, then jog before you sit. If you have to pull an all-nighter on a coffee binge, do that. Some schedule, regularity, pattern in your writing day (or night) will always help, but only you can figure out what that pattern is for you.

But you don't have time! It's true, you don't. You have a job, six courses, two kids, a dying parent, a divorce. I know; I've gone through all those things. One truth is that these hour-eaters will never get any easier; obligations and pleasures accumulate, and if you're lucky, life is always too full. If you're not, it's worse. So it's not that there will be no better time to develop the writing habit; there will no other time.

Another really important part of my writing process is that I have a writing group. . . . You sit down, you're in a room, everyone has the experience together.
—Jennifer Egan

Yet I believe it is not really, or not mainly, a question of time. I used to fret that I never had time to write—yet I notice that I have time to read the morning op-eds, do some stretching exercises, put fresh flowers on the table, read one more chapter of fiction, have a glass of wine in front of the evening news, catch whatever late-night comic grabs my attention before I go to bed. What all those things have in common is that I don't make myself do them; I allow myself. The lesson is not that I should give up any of those pleasures in order to write. It's that I should allow myself also to write every day. It is not a duty; it's what I want to do and am willing to structure my life to do. Try—over and over again, if necessary—to think of that writing time, wherever it falls in your day, however short or long it is, as the time you allow yourself to indulge in this activity that is not an obligation but a choice.

Keeping a Journal
There are, though, a number of tricks you can teach yourself in order to free the writing self, and the essence of these is to give yourself permission to fail. The best place for such permission is a private place, and for that reason a writer's journal is an essential, likely to be the source of originality, ideas, experimentation, and growth.

Keep a journal. A journal is an intimate, a friend that will accept you as you are. Pick a notebook you like the look of, one you feel comfortable with. I find a bound blank book too elegant to live up to, preferring instead a loose-leaf because I write my journal mainly at the computer and can stick anything in at the flip of a three-hole punch. But you can glue scribbled napkins into a spiral, too, or take a picture and upload it, if you prefer to keep your journal entirely on the computer.

Keep the journal regularly, at least at first. It doesn't matter what you write and it doesn't matter very much how much, but it does matter that you make a steady habit of the writing. Keeping a journal regularly will put you in the habit of observing in words. If you know at dawn that you are committed to writing so many words before dusk, you will half-consciously tell the story of your day to yourself as you live it, finding phrases to catch whatever catches your eye. When that habit is established, you'll begin to find that whatever invites your sympathy or anger or curiosity may be the beginning of invention.

But before the habit is developed, you may find that even a blank journal page has the awesome aspect of a void, and you may need some tricks of permission to let yourself start writing there. The playwright Maria Irene Fornes says that there are two of you: one who wants to write and one who doesn't. The one who wants to write had better keep tricking the one who doesn't. Another way to think of this conflict is between your right brain and left brain—the playful, detail-loving creator, and the linear critic. The critic is an absolutely essential part of the writing process. The trick is to shut him or her up until there is something to criticize.

Freewriting and Freedrafting
Freewriting is a technique that allows you to take very literally the notion of getting something down on paper. It can be done whenever you want to write, or just to free up the writing self. The idea is to put . . .

anything on paper and I mena anything, it doesn't matter as long
as it's coming out of your head nad hte ends of your fingers,
down ont the page I wonder if;m improving, if this process gets
me going better now than it did all those—hoewever many years

ago? I know my typing is geting worse, deteriorating even as we
speak (are we speaking? to whom? IN what forM? I love it when
i hit the caps button by mistake, it makes me wonder whether
there isn;t something in the back or bottom of the brain that sez
PAY ATTENTION now, which makes me think of a number of
things, freud and his slip o tonuge, self-deception, the myriad
way it operates in everybody's life, no not everybody's but in my
own exp. llike Aunt Ch. mourniong for the dead cats whenevershe
hasn't got her way and can't disconnect one kind of sadness from
another, I wonder if we ever disconnect kinds of sadness, if the first
homesickness doesn;t operatfor everybody the same way it does for
me, grandma's house the site of it, the grass out the window and the
dog rolling a tin pie plate under the willow tree, great heavy hunger
in the belly, the empty weight of loss, loss, loss

That's freewriting. Its point is to keep going, and that is the only point.
When the critic intrudes and tells you that what you're doing is awful,
tell the critic to take a dive, or acknowledge her/him ("typing is geting
worse") and keep writing. If you work on a computer, try dimming the
screen so you can't see what you're doing. At times, you might find it liberating to freewrite to music, ran-
dom or selected. If you freewrite often, pretty soon you'll be bored with
writing about how you don't feel
like writing (though that is as good
a subject as any) and will find your
mind and your phrases running on
things that interest you. Fine. The
subject doesn't matter, nor does the
quality of the writing. Freewriting is
the literary equivalent of scales at the piano or a short gym workout. All
that matters is that you do it. The verbal muscles will develop of their
own accord.

*When I stare at a blank page
where I'm supposed to build
worlds and lives, I think that
maybe I shouldn't be doing
this after all. But if I start with
something, with one thing,
everything follows.
—Tabitha Chartos*

Though freewriting is mere technique, it can affect the freedom of
the content. Many writers feel themselves to be an instrument-through-

which, rather than a creator-of, and whether you think of this possibility as humble or holy, it is worth finding out what you say when you aren't monitoring yourself. Fiction is written not so much to inform as to find out, and if you force yourself into a mode of informing when you haven't yet found out, you're likely to end up pontificating or lying in some other way.

In *Becoming a Writer*, a book that only half-facetiously claims to do what teachers of writing claim cannot be done—to teach genius—Dorothea Brande advises that you rise each day, go directly to your desk (if you have to have coffee, put it in a thermos the night before), and begin writing whatever comes to mind, before you are quite awake, before you have read anything or talked to anyone, before reason has begun to take over from the dream-functioning of your brain. Write for twenty or thirty minutes and then put away what you have written without reading it over. After a week or two of this, pick an additional time during the day when you can salvage a half hour or so to write, and when that time arrives, write, even if you "must climb out over the heads of your friends" to do it. It doesn't matter what you write. What does matter is that you develop the habit of beginning to write the moment you sit down to do so.

Freedrafting, as you might expect, is a slightly more focused and directed way of getting the juices flowing. You've done a freewrite that suggests an interesting character, or you want to catch what that smell from the pantry reminds you of, or you're midway into a story and you haven't quite caught the dialogue between these two. Focus on the interest or the problem, jot a list, maybe, of whatever associations you may have, then take a breath, stare into space, and launch yourself forward, focusing on the subject at hand but making no corrections and no judgments. You're not expecting a piece that's polished or even well-spelled. You're giving your subconscious the best way it has of finding the way onward.

....

KEEP GOING

Prompts

Exercises, or prompts, can be helpful for writers at all stages. They help you get started, and they can give you focus—whether you are writing in your journal, doing those early morning pages Brande suggests, sneaking in a bit of freewriting during the day, or trying to get to that next scene in a story.

Prompts are another way to tap your unconscious. The process of writing does not proceed clearly and obviously from point A to point B, but if you've been thinking about your story—sleeping on it, puzzling over it, mulling about it, working on a draft—you may well have a solution waiting for you in your unconscious. Stories do not begin with ideas or themes or outlines so much as with images and obsessions, and they continue to be built by exploring those. Seemingly unrelated prompts can help you break loose that next page. Need to find out what should happen next with Nick and Ashley? Here's an exercise: write two pages about the two of them trying to decide what television show to watch. Pretty soon Nick and Ashley are fighting about the remote control, but more than that they're fighting about how Nick is remote and always wants control. Ashley is telling him that their relationship has got to change and he's acting like he doesn't have a clue. And you are off and running.

Gymnasts practice. Pianists practice. Artists sketch. Prompts are a form of writerly practice, a way to exercise your skills, develop them, hone them, make them stronger.

Each chapter of *Writing Fiction* will end with some prompts designed to help you get started and move further into the issues discussed along the way. You can also find books of exercises (*What If? Writing Exercises for Fiction Writers* by Anne Bernays and Pamela Painter has deservedly become a classic). *Glimmer Train* publishes a quarterly pamphlet of advice and perspectives called "Writers Ask." And there are numerous websites with prompts and exercises; one I especially like is published by *Poets and Writers* magazine. The online *Brevity* magazine has short and pithy craft essays. Internet help is also offered by LitHub, *Catapult*, and *Narrative Magazine*.

The Computer

I think it's important for a writer to try a pencil from time to time so as not to lose the knack of writing by hand, of jotting at the park or the beach without any source of energy but your own mind and muscle.

But for most writers, a computer is the tool of choice. Freewriting frees more freely on a computer. The knowledge that you can so easily delete makes it easier to quiet the internal critic and put down whatever comes. Darken the screen or ignore it, stare out the window into middle space. You can follow the thread of your thought without a pause.

Nobody, I think, denies that email and social media are enemies of concentration. The tricky question is not how those gremlins are best handled but, as with your writing habits in general, how *you* best handle them. Do you operate most efficiently by first clearing the petty distractions out of the way? Maybe. But it's countless writers' experience that whatever you start on absorbs you. "Do the most important thing first," says Warren Buffett, who, though not known for his fiction, gets a lot done. If the first thing you tackle is fiction, the emails recede to the end of the day. If it's Snapchat, you may find yourself, hours later, wondering where the time has gone. Maybe you're someone who can afford to check your email every half hour. Maybe. Or are you like the addict who deceives himself with the promise of *just one more . . . ?* Figure it out for yourself honestly, and then follow where honesty leads you. Allow yourself to do the thing you really want to do. That meme will wait. Today's Twitter will be gone tomorrow. Your work, your friends, and your family matter. That latest app? Not so much.

> *Forget inspiration.* **Habit** *is more* **dependable. Habit will sustain** *you whether you're inspired or not. Habit will help you finish and polish your stories. Inspiration won't. Habit is persistence in practice.*
> *—Octavia Butler*

The Critic: A Caution

The cautionary note that needs to be sounded regarding all the techniques and technology that free you to write is this: they are nourishing to inspiration, but they are only half the art. Revision—the heart of the writing process—will continue until you finally finish or abandon a piece of work. The revising process is continuous and begins as soon as you choose to let your critic in. Freewriting and prompts allow you to create before you criticize, to do the essential play before the essential work. But don't forget the essential work. The computer helps you to write a lot by making it easy to cut. Don't forget to do so.

Choosing a Subject

Some writers are lucky enough never to be faced with the problem of choosing a subject. The world presents itself to them in terms of conflict, crisis, and resolution. Ideas for stories pop into their heads day after day; their only difficulty is choosing among them. In fact, the habit of mind that produces stories is a habit and can be cultivated, so that the more and the longer you write, the less likely you are to run out of ideas.

But sooner or later you may find yourself faced with the desire (or the deadline necessity) to write a story when your mind is a blank. The sour and untrue impulse crosses your thoughts: Nothing has ever happened to me. The task you face then is to recognize among all the paraphernalia of your mind a situation, idea, perception, or character that you can turn into a story.

Some teachers and critics advise beginning writers to write only from their personal experience, but I feel that this is a misleading and demeaning rule. If your imagination never gets beyond your age group or moves off campus, never tackles issues larger than the local rivalries, then you are severely constricting its range. It is certainly true that you must draw on your own experience (including your experience of the shape of sentences). But the trick is to identify what is interesting, unique, and original in that experience (including your experience of the shape of sentences), which will therefore surprise and attract the reader.

The kind of "writing what you know" that is least likely to produce good fiction is trying to tell just exactly what happened to you at such and such a time. Probably all good fiction is "autobiographical" in some way, but the awful or hilarious or tragic thing you went through may offer as many problems as possibilities when you start to turn it into fiction. The first of these is that, to the extent you want to capture "what really happened," you remove your focus from what will work as narrative. Young writers, offended by being told that a piece is unconvincing, often defend themselves by declaring that it really happened. But credibility in words has almost nothing to do with fact. Aristotle went so far as to say that a "probable impossibility" makes a better story than an "improbable possibility," meaning that a skillful author can sell us glass mountains, UFOs, and hobbits, while a less skilled writer may not be able to convince us that Mary Lou has a crush on Sam.

The first step toward using autobiography in fiction is to accept this: Words are not experience. Even the most factual account of a personal experience involves choices and interpretations—your sister's recollection of the same event might be entirely different. If you are writing a memoir or personal essay, then it is important to maintain a basis in fact because, as Annie Dillard says, "that is the convention and the covenant between the nonfiction writer and his reader." But between fiction writer and reader, the revelation of meaning through the creation of character, the vividness of scene, and the effect of action take priority over ordinary veracity. The test of this other truth is at once spiritual and visceral; its validity has nothing to do with whether the things recounted did, or could, occur. Lorrie Moore says:

> The proper relationship of a writer to his or her own life is similar to a cook with a cupboard. What that cook makes from what's in the cupboard is not the same thing as what's in the cupboard.

Good. Now: what was it about this experience that made it matter to you? Try writing a very brief summary of what happened—no more than a hundred words. What are you going to cook? What kind of story might this be? Can the raw material of incident, accident, and choice be reshaped, plumped up, pared to the bone, refleshed, differently spiced? You experienced whatever it was chronologically—but is that the best way to tell it so as to bring out its meaning? Perhaps you watched events develop over a period of months or years; what is the smallest number of scenes in the least amount of time that could contain the action? If "you" are at the center of the action then "you" must be thoroughly characterized, and that may be difficult. Can you augment some aspect of yourself, change yourself so you are forced to see anew, even make someone else the central character? Try freewriting moments from your memory in no particular order. Or freedraft the last scene first. Describe a place and exaggerate the atmosphere: if it's cold, make it murderously

11

cold, if messy, then a disastrous mess. Describe the central character, and be at least partly unflattering. All of these are devices to put some distance between you and the raw experience so you can begin to shape the different thing that fiction is.

Eudora Welty suggests writing what you don't know about what you know—that is, exploring aspects of experience that remain puzzling or painful. In Making Shapely Fiction, Jerome Stern urges a broad interpretation of "writing what you know," recognizing that "the idea of you is complex in itself . . . your self is made up of many selves . . . not only persons you once were, but also persons you have tried to be, persons you have avoided being, and persons you fear you might be." John Gardner, in The Art of Fiction, argues that "nothing can be more limiting to the imagination" than the advice that you write only what you know. He suggests instead that you "write the kind of story you know and like best."

What you read is as important as what you write.
—Margaret Atwood

This is a useful idea, because the kind of story you know and like best has also taught you something about the way such stories are told, how they are shaped, what kind of conflict, surprise, and change they involve. Many beginning writers who are not yet avid readers have learned from television more than they realize about structure, the way characters behave and talk, how a joke is arranged, how a lie is revealed, and so forth. The trouble is that if you learn fiction from television, or if the kind of story you know and like best is genre fiction—science fiction, fantasy, romance, mystery—you may have learned about technique without having learned anything about the unique contribution you can make to such a story. The result is that you end up writing imitation soap opera or space odyssey, second-rate somebody else instead of first-rate you.

The essential thing is that you write about something you care about, and the first step is to find out what that is. Playwright Claudia Johnson advises her students to identify their real concerns by making a "menu" of them. Start with the big emotions and make lists in your journal: What makes you angry? What are you afraid of? What do you want? What hurts? Or consider the crucial turning points of your life: What really changed you? Who really changed you? Those will be the areas to look to for stories, whether or not those stories are autobiographical. Novelist Ron Carlson says, "I always write from my own experiences, whether I've had them or not."

Another journal idea is to jot down the facts of the first seven years of your life under several categories: Events, People, Your Body, Your Emotions, Your Relation to the Cosmos, Valued Things. What from those first seven years still occupies your mind? Underline or highlight the items that you aren't done with yet. Those items are clues to your concerns and a possible source of storytelling.

A related device for your journal might be borrowed from the *Pillow Book* of Sei Shōnagon. A courtesan in tenth-century Japan, she kept a diary of the goings-on at court and concealed it in her wooden pillow— hence its name. Sei Shōnagon made lists, inventories of things fitting specific, often quirky categories. This device is capable of endless variety and can reveal yourself to you as you find out what sort of things you want to list: Things I wish had never been said. Red things. Things more embarrassing than nudity. Things to put off as long as possible. Things to die for. Acid things. Things that last only a day.

Identifying what we care about is not always easy. We are surrounded by a constant barrage of information, drama, social media, theories, and judgments offered to us live, in print, and electronically. It is so much easier to know what we ought to think and feel than what we actually do. Worthy authorities constantly exhort us to care about worthy causes, only a few of which really touch us, whereas what we do care about at any given moment may seem trivial, egotistical, or self-serving.

This, I think, is in large part the value of Brande's first exercise, which forces you to write in the intuitively honest period of first light, when the half-sleeping brain is still dealing with its real concerns. Often what seems unworthy is precisely the thing that contains a universal, and by catching it honestly, then stepping back from it, you may achieve the authorial distance that is an essential part of significance. (All you really care about this morning is how you'll look at the dance tonight? This is a trivial obsession that can hit anyone, at any age, anywhere. Write about it as honestly as you can. Now who else might have felt this way? Someone you hate? Someone remote in time from you? Look out: You're on your way to a story.)

Eventually you will learn what sort of experience sparks ideas for your sort of story—and you may be astonished at how such experiences accumulate, as if your life were arranging itself to produce material for you. In the meantime, here are a half dozen suggestions for the kind of idea that may be fruitful.

The Dilemma, or Catch-22. You find yourself facing—or know someone who is facing—a situation that offers no solution. Any action taken would be painful and costly. You have no chance of solving the dilemma in real life, but you're a writer, and it costs nothing to explore it with imaginary people in an imaginary setting, even if the outcome is a tragic one. Some writers use newspaper stories to generate this sort of idea. The situation is there in the bland black and white of this morning's news. But who are these people, and how did they come to be in such a mess? Make it up, think it through.

The Incongruity. Something comes to your attention that is interesting precisely because you can't figure it out. It doesn't seem to make sense. Someone is breeding pigs in the backyard of a mansion. Who is it? Why is she doing it? Your inventing mind can find the motives and the meanings. An example from my own experience: Once when my phone was out of order (in the days before mobile phones), I went out very late at night to make a call from a public phone at a supermarket plaza. At something like two in the morning all the stores were closed, but the plaza was not empty. There were three women there, one of them with a baby in a stroller. What were they doing there? It was several years before I figured out a possible answer, and that answer was a short story.

The Connection. You notice a striking similarity in two events, people, places, or periods that are fundamentally unlike. The more you explore the similarity, the more striking it becomes. My novel *The Buzzards* came from such a connection: The daughter of a famous politician was murdered, and I found myself in the position of comforting the dead young woman's fiancé. At the same time I was writing lectures on the Aeschylus play *Agamemnon*. Two politicians, two murdered daughters—one in ancient Greece and one in contemporary America. The connection would not let go of me until I had thought it through and set it down.

The Memory. Certain people, places, and events stand out in your memory with an intensity beyond logic. There's no earthly reason you should remember the smell of Aunt K's rouge. It makes no sense that you still flush with shame at the thought of that ball you "borrowed" when you were in fourth grade. But for some reason these things remain vivid in your mind. That vividness can be explored, embellished, given form. Stephen Minot in *Three Genres* wisely advises, though, that if you are going to write from a memory, it should be a memory more than a year old. Otherwise you will likely be unable to distinguish between what happened and what must happen in the story or between what is in your mind and what you have conveyed on the page.

> *If you sit there long enough, you collect enough sentences to make a book. It's just chipping and chipping away.*
> *—D. B. C. Pierre*

The Transplant. You find yourself having to deal with a feeling that is either startlingly new to you or obsessively old. You feel incapable of dealing with it. As a way of distancing yourself from that feeling and gaining some mastery over it, you write about the feeling as precisely as you can, but giving it to an imaginary someone in an imaginary situation. What situation other than your own would produce such a feeling? Who would be caught in that situation? Think it through.

The Revenge. An injustice has been done, and you are powerless to do anything about it. But you're not really, because you're a writer. Reproduce the situation with another set of characters, in other circumstances or another setting. Cast the outcome to suit yourself. Punish whomever you choose. Even if the story ends in a similar injustice, you have righted the wrong by enlisting your reader's sympathy on the side of right. (Dante was particularly good at this: he put his enemies in the Inferno and his friends in Paradise.) Remember too that as human beings we are intensely, sometimes obsessively, interested in our boredom, and you can take revenge against the things that bore you by making them absurd or funny on paper.

A story idea may come from any source at any time. You may not know you have an idea until you spot it in the random jottings of your journal. Once you've identified the idea, the process of thinking it through begins and doesn't end until you finish (or abandon) the story. Most writing is done between the mind and the hand, not between the hand and the page. It may take a fairly competent typist about three hours to type a twelve-page story. It may take days or months to write it. It follows that, even when you are writing well, most of the time spent writing is not spent putting words on the page. If the story idea grabs hard hold of you, the process of thinking through may be involuntary, a gift. If not, you need to find the inner stillness that will allow you to develop your characters, get to know them, follow their actions in your mind—and it may take an effort of the will to find such stillness.

The metamorphosis of an idea into a story has many aspects, some deliberate and some mysterious. "Inspiration" is a real thing, a gift from the subconscious to the conscious mind. Perhaps influenced by the philosophy (although it was not always the practice) of the Beat authors, some new writers feel that "forcing" words is aesthetically false—and yet few readers can tell which story "flowed" from the writer's pen and which was set down one hard-won word at a time. Toni Morrison has said that she will frequently rewrite a passage eight times, simply to create the impression of an unbroken, inspired flow. Cynthia Ozick often begins with "simple forcing" until a breakthrough comes, and so bears with the "fear and terror until I've pushed through to joy."

Over and over again, successful writers attest that unless they prepare the conscious mind with the habit of work, the gift does not come. Writing is mind-farming. You have to plow, plant, weed, and hope for growing weather. Why a seed turns into a plant is something you are never going to understand, and the only relevant response when it does is gratitude. You may be proud, however, of having plowed.

Many writers have observed that it is ideal, having turned your story over in your mind, to write the first draft at one sitting, pushing on through the action to the conclusion, no matter how dissatisfied you are with this paragraph, that character, this phrasing, or that incident. There are two advantages to doing this. The first is that you are more likely to produce a coherent draft when you come to the desk in a single frame of mind, with a single vision of the whole, than when you write piecemeal, with altered ideas and moods. The second is that fast writing tends to make for fast pace in the story. It is always easier, later, to add and develop than it is to sharpen the pace. If you are the sort of writer who stays on page one for days, shoving commas around and combing the thesaurus for a word with slightly better connotations, then you should probably force yourself to try this method (more than once). A note of caution, though: If you write a draft at one sitting, it will not be the draft you want to show anyone, so schedule the sitting well in advance of whatever deadline you may have.

It may happen—keeping in mind that a single-sitting draft is the ideal—that as you write, the story takes off of its own accord in some direction other than you intended. You thought you knew where you were going and now you don't, and you know that unless you stop for a while and think it through again, you'll go wrong. You may find that although you are doing precisely what you had in mind, it doesn't work—Brian Moore called this "the place where the story gets sick," and often found he had to retrace his steps from an unlikely plot turn or unnatural character action. At such times, the story needs more imaginative mulching before it will bear fruit. Or you may find, simply, that your stamina gives out, and that though you have done your exercises, been steadfast and loyal, and practiced every writerly virtue known, you're stuck. You have writer's block.

Writer's block is not so popular as it used to be. I suspect people got tired of hearing or even talking about it—sometimes writers can be sensitive even to their own clichés. But it may also be that writers began to understand and accept their difficulties. Sometimes the process seems to require working yourself into a muddle and past the muddle to despair; until you have done this, it may be impossible suddenly to see what the shape of a thing ought to be. When you're writing, this feels terrible. You sit spinning your wheels, digging deeper and deeper into the mental muck. You decide you are going to trash the whole thing and walk away from it—only you can't, and you keep coming back to it like a tongue to an aching tooth. Or you decide you are going to sit there until you bludgeon it into shape—and as long as you sit there it remains recalcitrant. W. H. Auden observed that the hardest part of writing is not knowing whether you are procrastinating or must wait for the words to come.

I know a newspaper editor who says that writer's block always represents a lack of information. I thought this inapplicable to fiction until I noticed that I was mainly frustrated when I didn't know enough about my characters, the scene, or the action—when I had not gone to the imaginative depth where information lies.

Encouragement comes from the poet William Stafford, who advised his students always to write to their lowest standard. Somebody always corrected him: "You mean your highest standard." No, he meant your lowest standard. Jean Cocteau's editor gave him the same advice: "The thought of having to produce a masterpiece is giving you writer's cramp. You're paralysed at the sight of a blank sheet of paper. So begin any old way. Write: 'One winter evening . . .'" In *On Writer's Block: A New Approach to Creativity*, Victoria Nelson points out that "there is an almost mathematical ratio between soaring, grandiose ambition . . . and a severe creative block." More writers prostitute themselves "up" than "down"; more are false in their determination to write great literature than in their willingness to throw off a romance.

A rough draft is rough; that's its nature. Let it be rough. Think of it as making clay. The molding and the glaze come later.

And remember: Writing is easy. Not writing is hard.

Reading as a Writer

Learning to read as a writer means focusing on craft, the choices, methods, and techniques of the author. In *On Becoming a Novelist*, John Gardner urges young writers to read "the way a young architect looks at a building, or a medical student watches an operation, both devotedly, hoping to learn from a master, and critically alert for any possible mistake." T. S. Eliot's dictum was "Bad poets imitate; good poets steal."

Ask yourself as you read: What is memorable, effective, moving? Reread, watching for the techniques that produced those reactions in you. Why did the author choose to begin at this point? How does she engage my attention, make me wonder what will happen, make my heart race for the character? Why did she choose this image, this setting, this ending? You can also learn from stories that don't move you. How could you have handled the same material? What would you have changed, and how? Be greedy as an author: What can I learn from this story? What can I imitate, steal?

....

A WORD ABOUT THEME

The process of discovering, choosing, and revealing the theme of your story begins as early as a first freewrite and continues, probably, beyond publication. The theme is what your story is about and what you think about it, its core and the spin you put on it. John Gardner points out that theme "is not imposed on the story but evoked from within it—initially an intuitive but finally an intellectual act on the part of the writer."

What your story has to say will gradually reveal itself to you and to your reader through every choice you as a writer make—the actions, characters, setting, dialogue, objects, pace, metaphors and symbols, viewpoint, atmosphere, style, even syntax and punctuation, and in some cases typography.

And there are people who want to be writers because they love to write. . . . Because they love the process and . . . through that process they realize they become more intelligent and more honest and more imaginative than they can be in any other part of their life.
—Russell Banks

Because of the comprehensive nature of theme, I have placed the discussion of it at the end of the book, after the individual story elements have been addressed. But this is not entirely satisfactory, since each of those elements contributes to the theme as it unfolds. You may want to skip ahead and take a look at that chapter, or you may want to anticipate the issue by asking at every stage of your manuscript: What really interests me about this? How does this (image, character, dialogue, place) reveal what I care about? What connections do I see between one image and another? How can I strengthen those connections? Am I saying what I really mean, telling my truth about it?

SUGGESTED READINGS

What If? Writing Exercises for Fiction Writers
   Anne Bernays and Pamela Painter
Becoming a Writer
   Dorothea Brande
How to Write Short
   Roy Peter Clark
"Why I Write"
   Joan Didion
The Writing Life
   Annie Dillard
"Message from a Cloud of Flies: On Distraction"
   Bonnie Friedman
The Art of Fiction
   John Gardner
"Shitty First Drafts"
   Anne Lamott
The Subversive Copy Editor
   Carol Fisher Saller
One Writer's Beginnings
   Eudora Welty

WRITING PROMPTS

1. Keep a journal for two weeks. Then decide on a comfortable amount
   to write daily, and determine not to let a day slide. In addition to the
   journal suggestions in this chapter, you might try these:
   • Open any book and point at random. Take the noun nearest where
     your finger falls and make a quick list of anything it suggests to you.
     Freedraft a paragraph about it.
   • Take note of bumper stickers as you encounter them. When you
     have a half dozen or so, pick one and quickly list what you remem-
     ber about the car, its make, model, color, condition—or make it
     up. Then freedraft a portrait of the car's owner.

- Identify the kernel of a story from your experience of one of the following: first memory; angry parent; lost object; unfounded fear; haircut.

2. Every morning for a week, sit down before breakfast and freewrite a paragraph of whatever comes into your head. At the end of the week, read the pages over, circling any word, phrase, person, place, or thought that seems interesting to you. Pick one. Freedraft a page about it.

3. Make a list of a dozen things you know nothing about. Pick one at random and freedraft a paragraph about it.

4. Write a short memoir that has to do with reading or writing—the moment you discovered you could read or write your name, for example, or the class where you practiced making letters, or the person who inspired you to write. Is there the kernel of a story here?

5. Write a short passage about why you want to write. Write another about why it's so hard. Imagine someone radically different from yourself in some way. Write a page in which you attribute something of that desire and that difficulty to this other person.

6. Make a list of the first ten things that come into your head. Pick one. Make a list of the first ten things it brings to mind. Pick one. Write a paragraph about it.

7. Pick one of these phrases and, beginning with it, use it to freedraft a page:
   - After supper he would always . . .
   - In my favorite photo . . .
   - But why did she have to . . . ?
   - I took one look and . . .
   - That little space made me feel . . .
   - Then the door opened and . . .

2: Seeing Is Believing
SHOWING AND TELLING

Literature offers us feelings for which we do not have to pay. It allows us to love, condemn, condone, hope, dread, and hate without any of the risks those feelings ordinarily involve; for even good feelings—intimacy, power, speed, drunkenness, passion—have consequences, and powerful feelings may risk powerful consequences. Fiction also must contain ideas, which give significance to characters and events. If the ideas are shallow or untrue, the fiction will be correspondingly shallow or untrue. But the ideas must be experienced through or with the characters; they must be *felt* or the fiction will fail.

Much nonfiction writing, from editorials to advertising, tries to persuade us to feel one way rather than another, largely by means of logic and reasoning. Fiction, by contrast, tries to reproduce the emotional impact of experience. And this is a difficult task, because unlike the images of film and drama, which directly strike the eye and ear, written words are transmitted first to the mind, where they must be translated into images.

In order to move your reader, the standard advice runs, "Show, don't tell." This dictum can be confusing, considering that words are all a writer has to work with. What it means is that your job as a fiction writer is to focus attention not on the words, which are inert, nor on the thoughts these words produce, but through these to felt experience, where the vitality of understanding lies. There are techniques for accomplishing this—for making narrative vivid, moving, and resonant—which can be partly learned and always strengthened.

SIGNIFICANT DETAIL

In *The Elements of Style*, William Strunk Jr. writes:

> If those who have studied the art of writing are in accord on any
> one point, it is this: the surest way to arouse and hold the reader's
> attention is by being specific, definite, and concrete. The greatest
> writers . . . are effective largely because they deal in particulars and
> report the details that matter.

Specific, definite, concrete, particular details—these are the life of fiction. Details (as every good liar knows) are the stuff of persuasiveness.
Mary is sure that Ed forgot to go pay the gas bill last Tuesday, but Ed says,
"I know I went, because this old guy in a knit vest was in front of me in
the line, and went on and on about his twin granddaughters"—and it is
hard to refute a knit vest and twins even if the furnace doesn't work. John
Gardner in *The Art of Fiction* speaks of details as "proofs," rather like the
steps that together demonstrate a geometric theorem or evidence in a
court case. The novelist, he says, "gives us such detail about the streets,
stores, weather, politics, and concerns of Cleveland (or wherever the setting is) and such detail about the looks, gestures, and experiences of his
characters that we cannot help believing that the story he tells us must
be true."

A detail is "definite" and "concrete" when it appeals to the senses. It
should be seen, heard, smelled, tasted, or touched. The most superficial
survey of any bookshelf of published fiction will turn up dozens of examples. Here is a fairly obvious one.

> It was a narrow room, with a rather high ceiling, and crowded from
> floor to ceiling with goodies. There were rows and rows of hams
> and sausages of all shapes and colors—white, yellow, red and
> black; fat and lean and round and long—rows of canned preserves,
> cocoa and tea, bright translucent glass bottles of honey, marmalade
> and jam.
>
> I stood enchanted, straining my ears and breathing in the delightful
> atmosphere and the mixed fragrance of chocolate and smoked fish

and earthy truffles. . . . I spoke into the silence, saying: "Good day" in quite a loud voice; I can still remember how my strained, unnatural tones died away in the stillness. No one answered. And my mouth literally began to water like a spring. One quick, noiseless step and I was beside one of the laden tables. I made one rapturous grab into the nearest glass urn, filled as it chanced with chocolate creams, slipped a fistful into my coat pocket, then reached the door, and in the next second was safely round the corner.

—Thomas Mann, *Confessions of Felix Krull, Confidence Man*

The passage is a tour through the five senses. Mann lets us see: *narrow room, high ceiling, rows of hams and sausages, canned preserves, translucent glass bottles.* He lets us smell: *fragrance of chocolate and smoked fish and earthy truffles.* He lets us hear: *"Good day," unnatural tones died away in the stillness.* He lets us taste: *to water like a spring.* He lets us touch: *grab, slipped a fistful into my coat pocket.* The writing is alive because Mann lets us perceive the scene as we would live it, through our sense perceptions.

These sense images reverberate, suggesting ideas not stated. We are aware of a number of generalizations the author might have made but does not need to make; we will make them ourselves. Mann could have had his character "tell" us:

I was quite poor, and I was not used to seeing such a profusion of food, so that although I was very afraid there might be someone in the room and I might be caught stealing, I couldn't resist taking the risk.

Such a version would be flat, and no such telling is necessary, as all of these points are "shown." The character's relative poverty is implicit in the tumble of images of sight and smell; if he were used to such displays, his eyes and nose would not dart about as they do. His fear is apparent in the "strained, unnatural tones" of his loud call and its dying away in the stillness. His desire is in his watering mouth, his fear in the furtive speed of *quick, grab, slipped.*

The points to be made here are two, and they are both important. The first is that the writer must deal in sense detail. The second is that these must be details "that matter." As a writer of fiction you are at constant pains not simply to say what you mean, but to mean more than you say. Much of what you mean will be an abstraction or a judgment—*love requires trust, children can be cruel.* But if you write in abstractions or judgments, you are writing an essay, whereas if you let us use our senses and form our own interpretations, we will be involved as participants in a real way. Much of the pleasure

I'm drawn to images and seem to start with them. Or one. Something I imagine, a scene or detail, or even a photograph.
—Rachel Kushner

of reading comes from the egotistical sense that we are clever enough to understand. When the author explains to us or interprets for us, we suspect that he or she doesn't think us bright enough to do it for ourselves.

A detail can also *matter* if it suggests a change in character or a development in the plot. Chekhov famously said that if a pistol is placed on a mantel in the first act, it must go off in the last. In Stuart Dybek's story "We Didn't," the narrator and his girl have been making out on the beach but are suddenly caught short. "Headlights bounded toward us, spotlights crisscrossing, blue dome lights revolving as squad cars converged." Here the police cars and searchlights change the scene, represent a turning point in the story, and also act metaphorically as they throw a spotlight on the young couple's problems.

In this excerpt from Colson Whitehead's *The Underground Railroad*, the girl slave Cora has been tending a small garden plot that had belonged to her grandmother:

> Wisps of white moisture hovered over the grounds. There she saw it—the remains of what would have been her first cabbages. Heaped by the steps of Blake's cabin, the tangled vines already drying out. The ground had been turned and tamped to make a nice yard for the mutt's house, which sat in the center of her plot like a grand mansion in the heart of a plantation.

In this instance, a violation of her territory—both physical and metaphorical—brings a docile girl to find her fierce strength.

A detail is *concrete* if it appeals to one of the five senses; it is *significant* if it also conveys an idea or a judgment or both. *The windowsill was green* is concrete, because we can see it. *The windowsill was shedding flakes of fungus-green paint* is concrete and also significant because it conveys the idea that the paint is old and suggests the judgment that the color is ugly. The second version can also be seen more vividly.

Here is a passage from a young writer that fails through lack of appeal to the senses:

> Debbie was a very stubborn and completely independent person and was always doing things her way despite her parents' efforts to get her to conform. Her father was an executive in a dress manufacturing company and was able to afford his family all the luxuries and comforts of life. But Debbie was completely indifferent to her family's affluence.

This passage contains a number of judgments that we might or might not agree with, and the author has not convinced us that we should. What constitutes stubbornness? Independence? Indifference? Affluence? Worse, since the judgments are supported by generalizations, we have no sense of the individuality of the characters, which alone would bring them to life on the page. What things was Debbie always doing? What efforts did her parents make to get her to conform? What level of executive? What dress manufacturing company? What luxuries and comforts? We can fill in the blanks in a multitude of ways:

> Debbie would wear a tank top to a tea party if she pleased, with fluorescent earrings and ankle-strap sandals.
>
> "Oh, sweetheart," Mrs. Chiddister would stand in the doorway wringing her hands. "It's not *nice*."
>
> "Not who?" Debbie would say, and add a fringed belt.
>
> Mr. Chiddister was Style Director of the Boston distributor for Dior and had a high respect for what he called "elegant textures," which ranged from handwoven tweed to gold filigree, and which he willingly offered his daughter. Debbie preferred her laminated wrist bangles.

We have not passed a final judgment on the merits of these characters, but we now know a good deal more about them, and we have drawn certain interim conclusions that are our own, not forced on us by the author. Debbie is independent of her parents' values, rather careless of their feelings, energetic, and possibly a tart. Mrs. Chiddister is quite ineffectual. Mr. Chiddister is a snob, though perhaps Debbie's taste is so bad we'll end up on his side.

But maybe that isn't at all what the author had in mind. The point is that we weren't allowed to know what the author did have in mind. Perhaps it was more like this version:

> One day Debbie brought home a copy of Ulysses. Mrs. Strum called it "filth" and threw it across the sunporch. Debbie knelt on the parquet and retrieved her bookmark, which she replaced. "No, it's not," she said.
>
> "You're not so old I can't take a strap to you!" Mr. Strum reminded her.
>
> Mr. Strum was controlling stockholder of Readywear Conglomerates and was proud of treating his family on his expense account. The summer before, he had justified their company on a trip to Belgium, where they toured the American Cemetery and the torture chambers of Ghent Castle. Entirely ungrateful, Debbie had spent the rest of the trip curled up in the hotel with a shabby copy of some poet.

Here we gain a much clearer understanding of Debbie's stubbornness, independence, and indifference and her family's affluence, both their natures and the value we are to place on them. This time our judgment is heavily weighted in Debbie's favor—partly because people who read books have a sentimental sympathy with people who read books, but also because we hear hysteria in "filth" and "take a strap to you," whereas Debbie's resistance is quiet and strong. Mr. Strum's attitude toward his expense account suggests that he's corrupt, and his choice of "luxuries" is morbid. The passage does contain two overt judgments, the first being that Debbie was "entirely ungrateful." But by the time we get to this, we're aware that the judgment is Mr. Strum's and have concluded that Debbie has little enough to be grateful for. We understand not only what the author says but also that she means the opposite of what she says, and we feel doubly clever to get it; that is the pleasure of irony. Likewise, the judgment that the poet's book is "shabby" shows Mr. Strum's crassly materialist attitude toward what we know to be the finer things. At the very end of the passage, we are denied a detail that we might very well be given: *what* poet did Debbie curl up with? Again,

An image is a starting point for a novel. It's a goal to which you can go in your sleep ... all that matters is that these images move something inside of you.
—Karl Ove Knausgaard

by this time we understand that we are being given her father's view of the situation and that it's Mr. Strum (not Debbie, not the author, and certainly not us) who wouldn't notice the difference between John Keats and Stanley Kunitz.

One may object that both rewrites are longer than the original passage. Doesn't "adding" so much detail make for long writing? The answer is yes and no. Yes, in that detail requires words. No, because what well-chosen details tell us about the values, activities, lifestyles, attitudes, and personalities of the characters would take many more words to tell through generalizations. When you set out to realize your characters through detail, you can't convey a whole person, or a whole action, or everything that could be said about a single moment of a single day. You must select the significant, the details that convey the characteristics essential to our understanding.

Which details are truly significant, however, may emerge only as you continue to develop and revise your story, for, as Flannery O'Connor says, "the longer you look at one object, the more of the world you see in it." Certain details "tend to accumulate meaning from the action of the story itself," becoming "symbolic in the way they work," she notes. "While having their essential place in the literal level of the story, [details] operate in depth as well as on the surface, increasing the story in every direction."

No amount of concrete detail will move us, therefore, unless it also implicitly suggests meaning and value. The following passage fails, not because it lacks detail, but because those details lack significance:

Terry Landon, a handsome young man of twenty-two, was six foot four and broad-shouldered. He had medium-length thick blond hair and a natural tan, which set off the blue of his intense and friendly long-lashed eyes.

Here we have a good deal of generic sensory information, but we still know very little about Terry. There are so many broad-shouldered twenty-two-year-olds in the world, so many blonds, and so on. This sort of cataloging of characteristics suggests an all-points bulletin: *male Caucasian, medium height, dark hair, last seen wearing gray raincoat.* Such a description may help the police locate a suspect in a crowd, but the assumption is that the identity of the person is not known. As an author you want us to know the character individually and immediately.

The fact is that all of our ideas and judgments are formed through sense perceptions, and daily, moment by moment, we receive information that is not merely sensuous in this way. Four people at a cocktail party may *do* nothing but stand and nibble canapés and may *talk* nothing but politics and the latest films. But you feel perfectly certain that X is furious at Y, who is flirting with Z, who is wounding Q, who is trying to comfort X. You have only your senses to observe with. How do you reach these conclusions? Through what gestures, glances, tones, touches, choices of words?

It may be that this constant emphasis on judgment makes the author, and the reader, seem opinionated or self-righteous. "I want to present my characters objectively/neutrally. I'm not making any value judgments. I want the reader to make up his or her own mind." Yet human beings are constantly judging: *How was the film? He seemed friendly. What a boring class! Do you like it here? She's very thin. That's fascinating. I'm so clumsy. You're gorgeous tonight. Life is crazy, isn't it?*

When we are not passing such judgments, it's because we aren't much interested; we are indifferent. Although you may not want to sanctify or damn your characters, you do want us to care about them, and if you refuse to direct our judgment, you may be inviting our indifference. Usually, when you "don't want us to judge," you mean that you want our feelings to be mixed, paradoxical, complex. *She's horribly irritating, but it's not her fault. He's sexy, but there's something cold underlying it.* If this is what you mean, then you must direct our judgment in both or several directions, not in none. In *Olive Kitteridge*, novelist Elizabeth Strout has a central character who is erratic, volatile, and controlling with her family—yet with vulnerable young people, she is sensitive and tender. She's awful and we feel with her. We recognize her contradictions as quintessentially human (our own?) through the details of what she feels and how she sees.

Even a character who exists only as a type or function will come to life if presented through significant detail, as in this portrait of an aunt in Dorothy Allison's story "Don't Tell Me You Don't Know." Like many of the female relatives the adult narrator mentions, the aunt embodies a powerful, nurturing force that nonetheless fails to protect the narrator from childhood abuse.

> My family runs to heavy women, gravy-fed working women, the kind usually seen in pictures taken at mining disasters. Big women, all of my aunts move under their own power and stalk around telling everybody else what to do. But Aunt Alma was the prototype, the one I had loved most, starting back when she had given us free meals in the roadhouse she'd run for a while. . . . Once there, we'd be fed on chicken gravy and biscuits, and Mama would be fed from the well of her sister's love and outrage.

For a character who is a "prototype," we have a remarkably clear image of this woman. Notice how Allison moves us from generalization toward sharpness of image, gradually bringing the character into focus. First she has only a size and gender, then a certain abstract "power," then a distinct role as the one who "had given us free meals."

The point is not that you, as an author, must never express an idea, general quality, or judgment, nor must you give us *all* the details. Some parts of your narrative will inevitably be more effectively told than shown; some periods of action want to passed over with the speed of summary. Too much detail can disperse focus and feel like self-indulgence on the writer's part. Everyone has read a description that goes on and on, taking up space with this or that minutia when, really, we got it long ago. Sometimes the pace and the magic of fiction is a rapid sail through time and space.

But even in the creation of groups or types, or a quickly passed-over period, a little specificity will bring a scene alive. Here in the clipped, matter-of-fact prose of Yaa Gyasi's *Homegoing*, a group of Pratt City, Alabama, miners have gone on strike:

> It took six more months of striking for the bosses to give in. They would all be paid fifty cents more. The running boy was the only one to die in the struggle. The pay increase was a small victory, but one that they would all take. After the day the running boy died, the strikers helped clean up the mess the fight had made. They picked up their shovels, found the boy who'd been gunned down, and buried him in the potter's field.

This passage contains many generalizations and categories that are given no particular imagery: *six more months, bosses, give in, pay increase, victory, all, strikers, mess, fight.* The "running boy," however, is a vivid image recalled from an earlier scene in which this child was humiliated and in flight. It's important that the pay increase is precisely fifty cents, because that matters to the men. And "picked up their shovels" particularizes the action of accepting the settlement. Note also how much would be lost if the narrative ended on a vague note:

In all genres, I wait in ambush for the exact, perfect, telling detail, the thing that makes the scene or line come alive.
—Lauren Groff

"found the boy who'd been gunned down and buried him." That he is buried "in the potter's field" conveys both the compassion and the poverty of the miners' circumstance.

Here is a still more intense presentation of an experience through a combination of judgment and detail:

> My wife could take your skin off with one glance, she was that excruciating. She could call you to her with one finger. She could do long division in her head. Another thing she could do really well was sob, and I envied her this, assuming it left nothing to eat at her inside. It is easy to be wrong about a person you are used to.
> —Emily Fridlund, "Expecting"

31

You may notice that even in the Thomas Mann passage quoted on pages 23–24, there are many generalizations and judgments (*narrow, high, rows and rows, all shapes and colors, enchanted, delightful, strained, unnatural*), each juiced with detail.

The Imagery of Emotion

"People can feel what they have not experienced," said the actress Mildred Dunnock—and fiction's job is to make us feel. But to evoke those feelings, it is often necessary to portray sensory details that the reader may have experienced. Simply labeling a character's emotion as love or hatred will have little effect, for such abstraction operates on a vague, intellectual level, whereas emotion is the body's physical reaction to information the senses receive. The great Russian director Konstantin Stanislavski, originator of realistic "Method" acting, urged his students to abandon the grand emotive postures of the nineteenth-century stage in favor of emotions evoked by the actor's recollection of sensory details connected with a personal past trauma. By recalling such details as the tingling of fingertips, the smell of singed hair, and the tensing of calf muscles, an emotion such as anger might naturally be induced within the actor's body.

Good writers may "tell" about almost anything in fiction except the characters' feelings. . . . Fear, love, excitement, doubt, embarrassment, despair become real only when they take the form of events—action (or gesture), dialogue or physical reaction to setting. Detail is the lifeblood of fiction.
—John Gardner

Similarly, in written fiction, if the writer depicts the precise physical sensations experienced by a character, a particular emotion may be triggered by the reader's own sense memory. For example, toward the end of Joyce Carol Oates's story "Where Are You Going, Where Have You Been?" the protagonist is so terrified that "the kitchen looked like a place she had never seen before." She tries to phone for help but "her fingers groped down to the dial but were too weak to touch it." Her beating heart seems "just a pounding, living thing inside this body that wasn't hers either." Here the reader may reflexively identify through a personal memory of fear, or perhaps a nightmare, in which vision became blurred, fingers fumbled at urgent tasks, a pumping heart felt too big for its chest. To simply state that the main character is afraid sets her at a dispassionate distance, but to dramatize her fear through physical detail allows a reader to share the experience.

One reason to avoid labeling emotion is that emotion is seldom pure. Conflicting feelings often run together; we experience but rarely stop to analyze our passions as we're caught up in them. In his story "The Easy Way," Tom Perrotta describes the moment in which a lottery winner learns of a jealous friend's death: "I stood perfectly still and let the news expand inside of me, like a bubble in my chest that wouldn't rise or pop. I waited for anger or grief to fill the space it opened, but all I felt just then was an unsteadiness in my legs, a faulty connection with the ground." By tracing the physical reaction and staying true to the shock of the moment, Perrotta conveys the complex impact of this loss.

Finding the specific expression of an emotion is *hard*. It is one of the most difficult things that a writer is consistently called upon to do. Yet neurobiologists assure us that this is what emotion *is*: a sensory response within the body to sensory input from the outside world, often in the presence of a basic need—food, sex, fight-or-flight. Unfortunately we are completely untrained in specifying these bodily reactions, and there are far too few ways of saying them. The Hawaiians may have seventy words for "pink," but when the doctor asks us to describe a pain, it's *on a scale of one to ten, sharp or ache or throbbing?*

Nevertheless, it's worth sitting with the image of your character's particular emotion and trying to find exactly how and where it resides in the body. I once had a character homesick in Japan. I tried and tried to describe the way homesickness felt in her stomach. It was *heavy, hollow, upset*—all too vague. Then I realized that she had just bought something from a street vendor thinking it was some kind of sweet. I had her eat one, which turned out to be an uncooked roll that had "an alkaline taste" and "was slimy on the roof of my mouth." Unwilling to spit it out on the street, she swallows it and it "seemed to lodge in my diaphragm, heavy and unassailable by digestive juices."

Seek the exact as opposed to the extreme. "Get control of emotion by avoiding the *mention* of the emotion," urges John L'Heureux. "To avoid melodrama, aim for a restrained tone rather than an exaggerated one." Chimamanda Ngozi Adichie demonstrates the principle in this passage from *Half of a Yellow Sun*. The heroine Olanna has come to visit her relatives during the Biafran war, only to find them slaughtered. Rather than saying some such thing as "I was numb with shock," the narrative registers shock with extreme focus:

> *Style is a very simple matter; it is all rhythm. Once you get that, you can't use the wrong words. But on the other hand here am I sitting after half the morning, crammed with ideas and visions, and so on, and can't dislodge them, for lack of the right rhythm.*
> —*Virginia Woolf*

She opened the car door and climbed out. She paused for a moment because of how glaringly bright and hot it was, with flames billowing from the roof, with grit and ash floating in the air, before she began to run toward the house. She stopped when she saw the bodies. Uncle Mbaezi lay facedown in an ungainly twist, legs splayed. Something creamy-white oozed through the large gash on the back of his head. Aunty Ifeka lay on the veranda. The cuts on her naked body were smaller, dotting her arms and legs like slightly parted red lips.

Filtering

John Gardner, in *The Art of Fiction*, points out a third potential failure, in addition to the faults of insufficient detail and excessive abstraction:

the needless filtering of the image through some observing consciousness. The amateur writes: "Turning, she noticed two snakes fighting in among the rocks." Compare: "She turned. In among the rocks, two snakes were fighting . . ." Generally speaking—though no laws are absolute in fiction—vividness urges that almost every occurrence of such phrases as "she noticed" and "she saw" be suppressed in favor of direct presentation of the thing seen.

The filter is a common fault and often difficult to recognize—although once the principle is grasped, cutting away filters is an easy means to more vivid writing. As a fiction writer you will often be working through "some observing consciousness." Yet when you step back and ask readers to observe the observer—to look *at* rather than *through* the character— you start to tell-not-show and rip us briefly out of the scene. Here, for example, is a student passage quite competent except for the filtering:

> Mrs. Blair made her way to the chair by the window and sank gratefully into it. *She looked out the window and there*, across the street, *she saw* the ivory BMW parked in front of the fire plug once more. *It seemed to her, though, that* something was wrong with it. *She noticed that* it was listing slightly toward the back and side, and *then saw that* the back rim was resting almost on the asphalt.

Remove the filters from this paragraph and we are allowed to stay in Mrs. Blair's consciousness, watching with her eyes, sharing understanding as it unfolds for her:

> Mrs. Blair made her way to the chair by the window and sank gratefully into it. Across the street the ivory BMW was parked in front of the fire plug again. Something was wrong with it, though. It was listing toward the back and side, the back rim resting almost on the asphalt.

A similar filtering occurs when the writer begins a flashback and mistakenly supposes that the reader is not clever enough to follow along without a guiding transition:

> *Mrs. Blair thought back to* the time that she and Henry had owned an ivory car, though it had been a Chevy. *She remembered clearly that* it had a hood shaped like a sugar scoop, and chrome bumpers that stuck out a foot front and back. And there was that funny time, *she recalled*, when Henry had to change the flat tire on Alligator Alley, and she'd thought the alligators would come up out of the swamp.

Just as the present scene will be more present to the reader without a filter, so will we be taken more thoroughly back to the time of the memory without a filter:

> She and Henry had owned an ivory car once, though it had been a Chevy, with a hood shaped like a sugar scoop and chrome bumpers that stuck out a foot front and back. And there was that funny time Henry had to change the flat tire on Alligator Alley, and she'd thought the alligators would come up out of the swamp.

Observe that the pace of the reading is improved by the removal of the filters—at least partly, literally, because one or two lines of type have been removed.

....

THE ACTIVE VOICE

If your prose is to be vigorous as well as vivid, if your characters are to "come to life," you must make use of the active voice.

The active voice occurs when the subject of a sentence performs the action described by the verb of that sentence: *She spilled the milk.* When the passive voice is used, the object of the active verb becomes the subject of the passive verb: *The milk was spilled by her.* The subject is acted upon rather than acting, and the effect is to weaken the prose and to distance the reader from the action.

The passive voice does have an important place in fiction, precisely because it expresses a sense that the character is being acted upon. If a prison guard is kicking the hero, then *I was slammed into the wall; I was struck blindingly from behind and forced to the floor* appropriately carries the sense of his helplessness.

In general, however, you should seek to use the active voice in all prose and to use the passive only when the actor is unknown or insignificant or when you want to achieve special stylistic effects like the one above.

But there are other grammatical constructions that are *in effect* passive and can distance the reader from a sense of immediate experience. Verbs modified by *auxiliaries* are effectively passive because they suggest an indefinite time and are never as sharply focused as simple active verbs. (Further editing the example cited above, Gardner contrasts the phrase "two snakes were fighting" with the improved "two snakes fought," which pinpoints a specific moment, and then suggests substituting active verbs, as in "two snakes whipped and lashed.")

Linking verbs invite complements that tend to be generalized or judgmental: *Her hair looked beautiful. He was very happy. The room seemed expensively furnished. They became morose.* Let her hair bounce, tumble, cascade, or swing; we'll see its beauty. Let him laugh, leap, cry, or hug a tree; we'll experience his joy.

The following is a passage with very little action, nevertheless made vital by the use of active verbs:

> At Mixt she neither drinks nor eats. Each of the sisters furtively stares at her as she tranquilly sits in post-Communion meditation with her hands immersed in her habit. *Lectio* has been halted for the morning, so there is only the Great Silence and the tinks of cutlery, but handsigns are being traded as the sisters lard their hunks of bread or fold and ring their dinner napkins. When the prioress stands, all rise up with her for the blessing, and then Sister Aimee gives Mariette the handsigns. *You, infirmary.*
> —Ron Hansen, *Mariette in Ecstasy*

Here, though the convent meal is silent and action is minimal, a number of the verbs suggest suppressed power: *stares, sits, lard, fold, ring, stands, rise, gives.*

Compare the first passage about Debbie on page 26 with the second of the rewrites on page 27. In the generalized original we have *was stubborn, was doing things, was an executive, was able, was indifferent.* Apart from the compound verb *was doing,* all of these are linking verbs. In the rewrite the characters *brought, called, threw, knelt, retrieved, replaced, said, reminded, justified, toured, spent,* and *curled up.* What energetic people! The rewrite contains two linking verbs: Mr. Strum *was a stockholder* and *was proud;* these properly represent static states, a position and an attitude.

One beneficial side effect of active verbs is that they tend to call forth significant details. If you say "she was shocked," you are telling us; but if you are to show us that she was shocked through an action, you are likely to have to search for an image as well. "She clenched the arm of the chair so hard that her knuckles whitened." *Clenched* and *whitened* actively suggest shock, and at the same time we see her knuckles on the arm of the chair.

To be is the most common linking verb and also the most overused, but all of the linking verbs invite generalization and distance. To feel, to seem, to look, to appear, to experience, to express, to show, to demonstrate, to convey, to display—all suggest, in fiction, that the character is being acted upon or observed by someone rather than doing something. She felt happy/sad/ amused/mortified does not convince us. We want to see her and infer her emotion for ourselves. He very clearly conveyed his displeasure. It isn't clear to us. How did he convey it? To whom?

> *Good writing is music.... It should not be a destination but a journey. It must concentrate, via the inner ear or even the voice reading aloud, on sound, on the balance of syllables, long, short, hard, soft, arranged in a graceful order.*
> *—Rosellen Brown*

Linking verbs, like the passive voice, can appropriately convey a sense of passivity or helplessness when that is the desired effect. In the passage by Thomas Mann quoted earlier in this chapter, where Felix Krull is momentarily stunned by the sight of the food before him, linking verbs are used—It was a narrow room, there were rows and rows—while all the colors and shapes buffet his senses. Only as he gradually recovers can he stand, breathe, speak, and eventually grab.

I don't mean to suggest that as an author you should analyze your grammar as you go along. Most word choice is instinctive, and instinct is often the best guide. However, I do mean to suggest that you should be aware of the vigor and variety of available verbs, and that if a passage lacks energy, it may be because your instinct has let you down. How often are subjects portrayed in some condition or seen to be acted upon, when they could more forcefully do?

A note of caution about active verbs: Make sparing use of what John Ruskin called the "pathetic fallacy"—the attributing of human emotions to natural and man-made objects. Even a description of a static scene can be invigorated if the houses stand, the streets wander, and the trees bend. But if the houses frown, the streets stagger drunkenly, and the trees weep, we will feel more strain than energy in the writing.

PROSE RHYTHM

Novelists and short story writers are not under the same obligation as poets to reinforce sense with sound. In prose, on the whole, the rhythm is all right if it isn't clearly wrong. But it can be wrong if, for example, the cadence contradicts the meaning; on the other hand, rhythm can greatly enhance the meaning if it is sensitively used.

> The river moved slowly. It seemed sluggish. The surface lay flat. Birds circled lazily overhead. Jon's boat slipped forward.

In this extreme example, the short, clipped sentences and their parallel structures—subject, verb, modifier—work against the sense of slow, flowing movement. The rhythm could be effective if the character whose eyes we're using is not appreciating or sharing the calm; otherwise it needs recasting.

> The surface lay flat on the sluggish, slow-moving river, the birds circling lazily overhead as Jon's boat slipped forward.

There is nothing very striking about the rhythm of this version, but at least it moves forward without obstructing the flow of the river.

> The first impression I had as I stopped in the doorway of the immense City Room was of extreme rush and bustle, with the reporters moving rapidly back and forth in the long aisles in order to shove their copy at each other or making frantic gestures as they shouted into their many telephones.

This long and leisurely sentence cannot possibly provide a sense of rush and bustle. The phrases need to move as fast as the reporters; the verbiage must be pared down because it slows them down.

> I stopped in the doorway. The City Room was immense, reporters rushing down the aisles, shoving copy at each other, bustling back again, flinging gestures, shouting into telephones.

The poet Rolfe Humphries remarked that "*very* is the least very word in the language." It is frequently true that adverbs expressing emphasis or suddenness—*extremely, rapidly, suddenly, phenomenally, quickly, immediately, instantly, definitely, terribly, awfully*—slow the sentence down and dilute the force of the intended meaning. "'It's a very nice day,'" said Humphries, "is not as nice a day as 'It's a day!'" Likewise, "They stopped very abruptly" is not as abrupt as "They stopped."

Just as action and character can find an echo in prose rhythm, so the starts and stops of prose tempo can guide our experience of a character's emotions and attitudes. In the following passage from *Persuasion*, Jane Austen combines generalization, passive verbs, and a staccato speech pattern to produce a kind of breathless blindness in the heroine.

> A thousand feelings rushed on Anne, of which this was the most consoling, that it would soon be over. And it was soon over. In two minutes after Charles's preparation, the others appeared; they were in the drawing room. Her eye half met Captain Wentworth's, a bow, a courtesy passed; she heard his voice—he talked to Mary, said all that was right; said something to the Miss Musgroves, enough to mark an easy footing; the room seemed full—full of persons and voices—but a few minutes ended it.

Often a change in the prose rhythm will signal a discovery or change in mood; such a shift can also reinforce a contrast in characters, actions, and attitudes. In "The Things They Carried," Tim O'Brien demonstrates a range of rhythms with a rich variation of effects. Here is one:

> The things they carried were largely determined by necessity. Among the necessities or near-necessities were P-38 can openers, pocket knives, heat tabs, wristwatches, dog tags, mosquito repellent, chewing gum, candy, cigarettes, salt tablets, packets of Kool-Aid, lighters, matches, sewing kits, Military Payment Certificates, C rations, and two or three canteens of water. Together, these items weighed between 15 and 20 pounds.

In this passage the piling of items one on the other has the effect of loading the men down and at the same time suggests the rhythm of their marching as they "hump" their stuff. Similar lists through the story create a rhythmic thread, while variations and stoppages underlie shifts of emotion and sudden crises.

....

MECHANICS

Significant detail, the active voice, and prose rhythm are techniques for achieving the sensuous in fiction, means of helping the reader "sink into the dream" of the story, in John Gardner's phrase. Yet no technique is of much use if the reader's eye is wrenched back to the surface by misspellings or grammatical errors, for once the reader has been startled out of the story's "vivid and continuous dream," that reader may not return.

> *An idea has to have some dirt on its shoes, or it's just air.*
> *—Marvin Bell*

Spelling, grammar, paragraphing, and punctuation are a kind of magic; their purpose is to be invisible. If the sleight of hand works, we will not notice a comma or a quotation mark but will translate each instantly into a pause or an awareness of voice; we will not focus on the individual letters of a word but extract its sense whole. When the mechanics are incorrectly used, the trick is revealed and the magic fails; the reader's focus is shifted from the story to its surface. The reader is irritated at the author, and of all the emotions the reader is willing to experience, irritation at the author is not one.

There is no intrinsic virtue in standardized mechanics, and you can depart from them whenever you produce a result that adequately compensates for a distracting effect. But only then. Sloppy mechanics signal amateurism to an editor and suggest that the story itself may be flawed. Unlike the techniques of narrative, the rules of spelling, grammar, and punctuation can be coldly learned anywhere in the English-speaking world—and they should be learned by anyone who aspires to write.

....

SUGGESTED STORIES
"Fjords of Killarney"
Kevin Barry

"Widow Water"
   Frederick Busch
"Linoleum Rose"
   Sandra Cisneros
"Without Inspection"
   Edwidge Danticat
"Expecting"
   Emily Fridlund
"Teen Sniper"
   Adam Johnson
"Emergency"
   Denis Johnson
"Where Are You Going, Where Have You Been?"
   Joyce Carol Oates
"The Things They Carried"
   Tim O'Brien
"Everything That Rises Must Converge"
   Flannery O'Connor

WRITING PROMPTS

1. Write a paragraph using significant details and active verbs about a
   character who conveys one of the following:
   - just adorable
   - complete nerd
   - brains fried
   - local psycho
   - leaning in
   - who does he think he is?
2. Take a scene you have already written and "shrink for details."
   Imagine yourself from the vantage of something very small—no
   bigger than a button, an earlobe, a baked bean—and write a page
   using the details you see from that perspective.
3. Write a passage in which a character enters a place and experiences
   the scene primarily through the sense of smell.

4. Imagine a character in a difficult or frightening situation. Write a passage beginning with the character's action, then show us the scene through the character's eyes. Use no "filters."

5. Give a character some illness or injury. Describe the pain or discomfort with exact reference to where the body hurts; detail the nature of the pain. (It's hard!)

6. Write a short sketch describing a person or an experience combining generalizations or judgments with details. Make the details significant and concrete. Rewrite it making the details extreme. Rewrite it making the details outrageous. Which version works best? Is the last one funny?

7. Write about one of the following and suggest the rhythm of the subject in your prose: a machine, a piece of music, sex, a spaceship in orbit, a car in rush-hour traffic, an avalanche.

3: Building Character

CHARACTERIZATION, PART I

Human character is in the foreground of all fiction, however the humanity might be disguised. Attributing human characteristics to the natural world may be frowned on in science, but it is a literary necessity. Bugs Bunny isn't a rabbit; he's a plucky youth in ears. Peter Rabbit is a mischievous boy. Brer Rabbit is a sassy rebel. The romantic heroes of *Watership Down* are out of the Arthurian tradition, not out of the hutch.

Your fiction can be only as successful as the characters who move it and move within it. Whether they are drawn from life or are pure fantasy—and all fictional characters lie somewhere between the two—we must find them interesting, we must find them believable, and we must care what happens to them.

....

DIRECT METHODS OF CHARACTER PRESENTATION

There are six basic methods of character presentation. The four direct methods—*dialogue, appearance, action,* and *thought*—show us the characters as they speak, look, move, and feel. They will be discussed in this chapter, dialogue first and at length because it plays such an essential role in bringing characters to life and presents so many possibilities and difficulties to the writer. The indirect methods—*authorial interpretation* and *interpretation by another character*—will be discussed in chapter 4. Employing a variety of these methods can help you create full characters.

DIALOGUE

Speech characterizes in a way that is different from appearance, because speech represents an effort, mainly voluntary, to externalize the internal and to manifest not merely taste or preference but also deliberated thought. Like fiction itself, human dialogue attempts to marry logic to emotion.

Summary, Indirect, and Direct Dialogue

Speech can be conveyed in fiction with varying degrees of directness. It can be summarized as part of the narrative so that a good deal of conversation is condensed:

> Otto Stern encouraged little Józsi and János to follow Mihály's example while there was still time, but a family council resolved that the two boys should not yet leave the family home. Ferenc and Ignác, on the other hand, were hoping to travel to Vienna and with someone's influence ask for admission to the cadet school.
> —Miklós Vámos, *The Book of Fathers*

It can be reported in the third person as *indirect speech* so that it carries, without actual quotation, the feel of the exchange:

> Had he brought the coffee? She had been waiting all day long for coffee. They had forgot it when they ordered at the store the first day. Gosh, no, he hadn't. Lord, now he'd have to go back. Yes, he would if it killed him. He thought, though, he had everything else. She reminded him it was only because he didn't drink coffee himself. If he did he would remember it quick enough.
> —Katherine Anne Porter, "Rope"

But usually when the exchange contains the possibility of discovery or decision, and therefore of dramatic action, it will be presented in *direct quotation*:

> "But I thought you hardly knew her, Mr. Morning."
> He picked up a pencil and began to doodle on a notebook page. "Did I tell you that?"
> "Yes, you did."
> "It's true. I didn't know her well."
> "What is it you're after, then? Who was this person you're investigating?"
> "I would like to know that too."
> —Siri Hustvedt, "Mr. Morning"

These three methods of presenting speech can be used in combination to take advantage of the virtues of each:

> They differed on the issue of the holiday, and couldn't seem to find a common ground. (*Summary.*) She had an idea: why not some Caribbean island over Christmas? Well, but his mother expected them for turkey. (*Indirect.*)
> "Oh, lord, yes, I wouldn't want to go without a yuletide gizzard." (*Direct.*)

Summary and indirect speech are often useful to get us quickly to the core of the scene, or when, for example, one character has to inform another of events that we already know, or when the emotional point of a conversation is that it has become tedious.

> Whenever it became necessary to get him some new clothing there would be a quarrel, and after much wrangling the two of them would drive off to one of the young men's shops where he would be turned over to a clerk experienced in these situations, and finally, after all three of them were exhausted, the purchase was made. The argument in regard to the gray suit was typical.
> "I've already got a suit."
> "But that's a summer suit."
> —Evan S. Connell, *Mrs. Bridge*

But nothing is more frustrating to a reader than to be told that significant events are taking place in talk and to be denied the drama of the dialogue.

> They whispered to each other all night long, and as he told her all about his past, she began to realize that she was falling in love with him.

Such a summary—it's *telling*—is a stingy way of treating the reader, who wants the chance to fall in love, too.

Because direct dialogue has a dual nature—emotion within a logical structure—its purpose in fiction is never merely to convey information. Dialogue may do that (although information often is more naturally conveyed in narration), but it needs simultaneously to characterize, provide exposition, set the scene, advance the action, foreshadow, or remind. William Sloane, in *The Craft of Writing*, says:

> There is a tentative rule that pertains to all fiction dialogue. It must do more than one thing at a time or it is too inert for the purposes of fiction. This may sound harsh, but I consider it an essential discipline. Call it Sloane's law.

With dialogue as with significant detail, when you write you are constantly at pains to mean more than you say. If a significant detail must both call up a sense image and *mean*, then the character's words, which presumably mean something, should simultaneously suggest image, personality, or emotion.

Dialogue, therefore, is not simply transcribed speech, but distilled speech. The "filler" we hear and overhear in live conversation ("phatic speech," the opposite of "emphatic") is edited away, even as the weight of implication is increased. It takes careful editing to create natural-sounding dialogue. Monologue in the right place can be a powerful tool, and some characters may be eloquent, but natural-sounding dialogue is probably ungrammatical; it may be full of slang, jargon, repetition, and various sorts of awkwardness. Generally, that means keeping things brief and paying attention to the rhythm of the sentences, which will itself reveal character, as will the failure or refusal to speak. A character who speaks several consecutive sentences might come across as a windbag (which of course may be your intention) or the author's puppet. Often the first and last words, phrases, or sentences of a character's speech can be eliminated. The character's intentions and preoccupations will shine through because of the leaps they make in their dialogue, as well as the the things they can't bring themselves to say aloud. Even rote exchanges, however, can call up images. A character who says, "It is indeed a pleasure to meet you" carries his back at a different angle, dresses differently, from a character who says, "Hey, man, what's up?"

I wonder why I do want to write about it, because I despise talk, and the people who talk, who tell others about themselves, and the dreadful necessity that pushes them to such confessions. They must talk. They must expose themselves. It helps them, and more horribly, it helps others.
—M. F. K. Fisher

The three brief speeches that follow portray three fictional men, sharply differentiated from each other not only by the content of what they say but also by their diction (choice and use of words) and their syntax (the ordering of words in a sentence) and the rhythms of their speech. These largely unconscious choices convey attributes of class, period, ethnicity, and so forth, as well as political or moral attitudes. How much do you know about each? How does each look?

> "I had a female cousin one time—a Rockefeller, as it happened—" said the Senator, "and she confessed to me that she spent the fifteenth, sixteenth, and seventeenth years of her life saying nothing but, 'No, thank you.' Which is all very well for a girl of that age and station. But it would have been a damned unattractive trait in a male Rockefeller."
> —Kurt Vonnegut, *God Bless You, Mr. Rosewater*

Lieutenant Axel's reason for calling Anna back became clear on the first morning of training, when he hollered at the group of thirty-five volunteers, "The dress weighs two hundred pounds. The hat alone weighs fifty-six. The shoes together are thirty-five. Now,

before you start rolling your eyes about carrying all that weight, you should know that that *girl* standing over there—she's on the tall side, but she's no Sherman tank, like a lot of the females you see around here—she not only wore the dress without bellyaching, walked in the dress without bellyaching, but she also untied a bowline on a bight wearing three-fingered gloves. How many of you gents can even tie a bowline on a bight?"
—Jennifer Egan, *Manhattan Beach*

"You think you the only one ever felt this way?" he asked. "You think I never felt this way? You think she never felt this way? Every last one of them back there one time in they life wanted to give up. She want to give up now. You know that? You got any idea how sick she is? Soon after he go, she's going too. I won't give her another year. I want her to believe he'll be up there waiting for her. And you can help me do it. And you the only one."
—Ernest Gaines, *A Lesson before Dying*

There are forms of insanity that condemn people to hear voices against their will, but as writers we invite ourselves to hear voices without relinquishing our hold on reality or our right to control. The trick to writing good dialogue is hearing voice. The question is, what would this particular person say? The answer is entirely in language. The choice of language reveals content, character, and conflict, as well as type.

It's logical that if you must develop voices in order to develop dialogue, you'd do well to start with monologue and develop voices one by one. Use your journal to experiment with speech patterns that will characterize. Some people speak in telegraphically short sentences missing various parts of speech. Some speak in convoluted eloquence or in rhythms tedious with qualifying phrases. Some rush headlong without a pause for breath until they're breathless; others are measured or terse or begrudge even forming a sentence. Trust your "inner ear" and use your journal to practice catching voices. Freewriting is invaluable to dialogue writing because it is the manner of composition closest to speech. There is no time to mull or edit. Any qualifications, corrections, and disavowals must be made part of the process and the text.

So sit for a moment with your character in mind. See him or her clearly. Put yourself inside the character and feel whatever feelings rise. Pick a phrase that character might use and start writing. Keep going. Write past the place you feel comfortable. If another character intrudes, let the monologue become an exchange but stay in the first character's body and feelings. Pay no attention to whatever failure you may feel at catching the right voice, just keep going; a little longer; longer still. Put the pages away or save them in a folder, and go have a cup of coffee or take a nap. Come back and look it over. What can you salvage that really does sound like that person talking? If it's as much or as little as line or two, you win.

My characters have trouble communicating. They rarely say what they mean or argue for what they want.... In life, I wear my heart on my sleeve, but in fiction, I'm attracted to characters who have a tough time saying the things they wish they could say.
—David James Poissant

To increase your ability to "hear" dialogue, try carrying a small pocket notebook or using the "Notes" feature on your phone, and jotting vivid lines or exchanges of eavesdropped dialogue verbatim. At home, look back through your notebook for speech that interests you and freedraft a monologue in your writing journal. Don't look for words that seem right; just listen to the voice and let it flow. You'll begin to develop your own range of voices, whether you catch a particular voice or not; even "hearing" it go wrong may help develop your ear.

You can also limber up in your journal by setting yourself deliberate exercises in making dialogue—or monologue—do more than one thing at a time. In addition to revealing character, dialogue can set the scene.

> "We didn't know no one was here. We thought hit a summer camp all closed up. Curtains all closed up. Nothing here. No cars or gear nor nothing. Looks closed to me, don't hit to you, J. J.?"
> —Joy Williams, "Woods"

Dialogue can *set the mood*.

> "I have a lousy trip to Philadelphia, lousy flight back, I watch my
> own plane blow a tire on closed-circuit TV, I go to my office, I find
> Suzy in tears because Warren's camped in her one-room apartment.
> I come home and I find my wife hasn't gotten *dressed* in two days."
> —Joan Didion, *Book of Common Prayer*

Dialogue can *reveal the theme* because, as William Sloane says, the characters talk about what the story is about.

> "You're so confusing," he says. "I still want to know . . ."
> "No, you don't." She strokes his leg, stroking him silent.
> "Listen," he says. "Do you ever get these black holes in your
> mind? I don't mean in a dream. Sometimes I'm walking along
> or, just, I'm talking to someone, and all of a sudden I don't know
> anything. It's like my electricity shuts off. It's pitch-black in my
> brain. Like, if I take a step I'll fall into a pit."
> —Sharon Solwitz, *Once, In Lourdes*

In all of the preceding passages, the dialogue fulfills Sloane's rule: in addition to conveying content, it either moves the story forward or enriches
our understanding.

Dialogue is also one of the simplest ways to *reveal the past* (a fundamental playwriting device is to have
a character who knows something
tell a character who doesn't), and it
is one of the most effective, because
we get both the drama of the memory and the drama of the telling.

> *The generalizing writer is like
> the passionate drunk, stumbling
> into your house mumbling:
> I know I'm not being clear,
> exactly, but don't you kind of
> feel what I'm feeling?*
> **—George Saunders**

Here is a passage from Toni Morrison's *The Bluest Eye* in which the past
is evoked, the speaker characterized, the scene and mood set, and the
theme revealed, all at the same time and in less than a dozen lines.

> "The onliest time I be happy seem like was when I was in the picture
> show. Every time I got, I went. I'd go early, before the show started.

They'd cut off the lights, and everything be black. Then the screen
would light up, and I'd move right on in them pictures. White men
taking such good care of they women, and they all dressed up in
big clean houses with the bathtubs right in the same room with the
toilet. Them pictures gave me a lot of pleasure, but it made coming
home hard, and looking at Cholly hard. I don't know."

Be careful, however, that you don't succumb to the temptation to slip
exposition into dialogue by allowing the characters to discuss things
they both already know just for the reader's benefit.

"I've missed you so much, Margie! It's been over a month since we
ran into each other at the Farmer's Market. That was the day you
told me that your grandson Eddie got into Julliard!"

"Yes, Suzie, and wasn't that right before the tornado came
through town? We were so scared when that siren went off!
Remember how we hid underneath the rickety table with the
watermelons on it?"

This kind of dialogue is both ridiculous and tedious. If we really need
to know about the farmer's market and Eddie and the tornado, tell us
in exposition. Don't weigh your characters' dialogue down with tedious
information.

Dialogue as Action

If the telling of a memory *changes the relationship* between the teller and
the listener, then you have a scene of high drama, and the dialogue can
advance the action.

This is an important device, because dialogue is most valuable to fiction when it is itself a means of telling the story.

In the following passage the mother of a seriously ill toddler looks
anxiously to a radiologist for information:

"The surgeon will speak to you," says the Radiologist.

"Are you finding something?"

"The surgeon will speak to you," the Radiologist says again. "There
seems to be something there, but the surgeon will talk to you about it."

"My uncle once had something on his kidney," says the Mother. "So they removed the kidney and it turned out the something was benign."

The Radiologist smiles a broad, ominous smile. "That's always the way it is," he says. "You don't know exactly what it is until it's in the bucket."

"In the bucket," the Mother repeats.

"That's doctor talk," the Radiologist says.

"It's very appealing," says the Mother. "It's a very appealing way to talk."

—Lorrie Moore, "People Like That Are the Only People Here"

Here the radiologist's speech alters the mother's feeling toward him from hopeful to hostile in one short exchange. The level of fear for the child rises, and the dialogue itself has affected change.

Dialogue is action when it contains the possibility of change. A crucial (and sometimes difficult) distinction to make is between speech that is mere discussion or debate and speech that is drama or action. If in doubt, ask yourself: Can this conversation between characters really change anything? When two characters have made up their minds and know each other's positions on some political or philosophical matter, for instance, they may argue with splendid eloquence but there will be no discovery and nothing to decide, and therefore no opportunity for change. No matter how significant their topic, we are likely to find them wooden and uninteresting. The story's question *what happened next?* will suggest only *more talk:*

"This has been the traditional fishing spot of the river people for a thousand years, and we have a moral responsibility to aid them in preserving their way of life. If you put in these rigs, it may undermine the ecosystem and destroy the aquifer of the entire county!"

"Join the real world, Sybil. Free enterprise is based on this kind of technological progress, and without it we would endanger the economic base."

Ho-hum. In order to engage us emotionally in a disagreement, the characters must have an emotional stake in the outcome; we need to feel that, even if it's unlikely they will change their minds, they might change their lives.

"If you sink that drill tomorrow morning, I'll be gone by noon."
"Sybil, I have no choice."

Further, if you find your characters getting stuck in a repetitive conflict (yes-you-are, no-I'm-not), you can jump-start the action if you remember that people generally change their tactics—become charming, threatening, seductive, guilt-inducing, and so on—when they are not succeeding in getting what they badly want. And if *each* character in the scene wants something from the other (probably not the same thing), the momentum *I love slang. I love hipster patois, racial invective, alliteration, argot of all kinds.*
—James Ellroy
will build. It's much harder, though not impossible, to maintain dramatic energy when one of the characters simply wants to get off stage.

Text and Subtext
Often the most forceful dialogue can be achieved by *not* having the characters say what they mean. People in extreme emotional states—whether of fear, pain, anger, or love—are at their least articulate. There is more narrative tension in a love scene where the lovers make anxious small talk, terrified of revealing their feelings, than in one where they hop into bed. A character who is able to say, "I hate you!" hates less than one who bottles the fury and pretends to submit, unwilling to expose the truth.

Dialogue can fall flat if characters define their feelings too precisely and honestly, because often the purpose of human exchange is to conceal as well as to reveal—to impress, hurt, protect, seduce, or reject. Anton Chekhov believed that a line of dialogue should always leave the sense that more could have been said. Playwright David Mamet suggests that people may or may not say what they mean, but always say something designed to get what they want.

In this example from Alice Munro's "Before the Change," the daughter of a doctor who performed illegal abortions up until his recent death takes a phone call:

A woman on the phone wants to speak to the doctor.

"I'm sorry. He's dead."

"Dr. Strachan. Have I got the right doctor?"

"Yes but I'm sorry, he's dead."

"Is there anyone—does he by any chance have a partner I could talk to? Is there anybody else there?"

"No. No partner."

"Could you give me any other number I could call? Isn't there some other doctor that can—"

"No. I haven't any number. There isn't anybody that I know of."

"You must know what this is about. It's very crucial. There are very special circumstances—"

"I'm sorry."

It's clear here that neither woman is willing to mention abortion, and that the daughter will not (and probably could not) speak about her complicated feelings toward her father and his profession. The exchange is rich with irony in that both women, and also the reader, know the "special circumstance" they are guardedly referring to; only the daughter and the reader, however, are privy to the events surrounding the doctor's death and to the daughter's feelings.

Notice that this is not a very articulate exchange, but it does represent dramatic action because for both women the stakes are high; they are both emotionally involved but in ways that put them at cross-purposes.

The idea of "reading between the lines" is familiar to most people, for in life we tend to react more to what is implied in dialogue than to what is actually said. The linkage of text and subtext—that is, the surface, plot-related dialogue and its emotional undercurrent—was famously described by Ernest Hemingway with the analogy of an iceberg:

> There is seven-eighths of it under water for every part that shows. Anything you know you can eliminate and it only strengthens your iceberg. It is the part that doesn't show.

When an unspoken subject remains unspoken, tension continues to build in a story. Often the crisis of a story occurs when the unspoken tension comes to the surface and an explosion results. "If you're trying to build pressure, don't take the lid off the pot" too early, Jerome Stern suggests in his book *Making Shapely Fiction*. "Once people are really candid, once the unstated becomes stated, the tension is released." He advises you to let the pot boil until we "feel the dialogue boil over."

"No" Dialogue

The passage from Alice Munro also illustrates an essential element of conflict in dialogue: tension and drama are heightened when characters are constantly (in one form or another) saying "no" to each other. In the following exchange from Hilary Mantel's *Wolf Hall*, Henry VIII and his fiancée Anne Boleyn are accosted outside a shrine by a Benedictine nun.

> "I am advised by Heaven," she says, "by the saints with whom I converse, that the heretics around you must be put into a great fire, and if you do not light that fire, then you yourself will burn."
>
> "Which heretics? Where are they? I do not keep heretics about my person."
>
> "Here is one."
>
> Anne shrinks against the king; against the scarlet and gold of his jacket she melts like wax.
>
> "And if you enter into a form of marriage with this unworthy woman, you will not reign seven months."
>
> "Come, madam, seven months? Round it off, can you not? What sort of prophet says 'seven months'?"
>
> "That is what Heaven tells me."

These characters, whatever they say to each other, whether in the oracular fervor of the nun or Henry's sarcasm, are also saying "no:" *This is the word from Heaven. No, it isn't. You're wrong. No, I'm not.*

It is only a few lines of dialogue. But look how much more it does than one thing at a time! It reveals the fundamental personalities and attitudes of the two speakers. It contains the core of the historical quarrel between the crown and the church. It encapsulates a widespread condemnation of the impending marriage. The nun says exactly what she means while the monarch uses his hauteur to evade the point. Anne's failure to speak, meanwhile, her betrayal of her attitude only through her body (and the metaphor "melts like wax"), shows us her emotional response—though it will not be long before she bursts out, "Surely she is mad?" Finally, the mood creates a narrative tension as it raises the possibility, as a prophecy always does, that there may be some grim truth being told.

Notice, however, that the conflict does not get stuck in a rut. The characters find new ways to taunt and challenge each other as each probes for the other's vulnerable points.

In dialogue as in narrative, we tend to believe a character who speaks in concrete details and to be skeptical of one who generalizes or who delivers judgments unsupported by example. If one character says, "It's perfectly clear from all his actions that he adores me and would do anything for me," and another says, "I had my hands all covered with the clay slick, and he reached over to lift a lock of hair out of my eyes," which character do you believe is the more loved?

Similarly, in conflict dialogue, "details are the rocks characters throw at each other," says Stephen Fischer. Our memories for hurts and slights are sadly long, and an accusation that begins as a general blame—"You never think of my feelings"—is likely to be backed up with specific proof as the argument escalates—"You said you'd pick me up at seven New Year's Eve, but you left me waiting for an hour in the snow." "There's nothing generic in our lives," Fischer explains, "and the sparks given off in conflict may reveal all the facts we need to know about the characters."

Whereas in narrative you will demonstrate control if you state the facts and let the emotional value rise off of them, in dialogue you will convey information more naturally if the emphasis is on the speaker's feelings. "My brother is due to arrive mid-afternoon and is bringing his four children with him" reads as bald exposition; whereas "That idiot brother of mine thinks he can walk in in the middle of the afternoon and plunk his four kids in my lap!" or "I can't wait till my brother gets here at three! You'll see—those are the four sweetest kids this side of the planet"—will sound like talk and slip us the information sideways.

Examine your dialogue to see if it does more than one thing at a time. Do the sound and syntax characterize the speakers by region, education, attitude? Do the choice of words and their phrasing reveal that the character is stiff, outgoing, stifling anger, ignorant of the facts, perceptive, bigoted, afraid? Is the conflict advanced by "no" dialogue, in which the characters say no to each other in different ways? Is the drama heightened by the characters' inability or unwillingness to tell the whole truth?

Once you are comfortable with the voice of your character, it is well to acknowledge that everyone has many voices and that what that character says will be, within his or her verbal range, determined by the character *to whom* it is said. All of us have one sort of speech for the surgeon and another for the man who cuts the grass. Huck Finn, whose voice is idiosyncratically his own, says "Yes, sir" to the judge and "Maybe I am, maybe I ain't" to his degenerate dad.

Pacing

Economy in dialogue—distilling it, avoiding a rehash of what the reader already knows, making sure that it does more than one job at a time—are important parts of pacing. At the same time, it's important not to leave out the drama that unfolds in a spoken exchange.

One reason readers enjoy dialogue is that it's the most direct experience of the characters we get in fiction, a chance for them to express (or betray) themselves without authorial interference. Freewrite dialogue exchanges and let them take their course. You can trim later, or you might find only a few lines to salvage, but don't be too quick to assume your characters have had their say. You might think you know what the outcome of a conversation is going to be, but give your characters a chance to surprise you and avoid foisting your own agenda on them. Some of my most—truly—thrilling moments as a writer have been when my characters turned on me. I thought I was writing a bossy, insensitive foil to my heroine's superior understanding, when the first character turned on the second with exactly the comeuppance she deserved. A hardnosed cattle boss betrayed an aching love for his baby granddaughter. A couple who believed themselves "post-racial" fell into using the very taunts they despised.

Fiction is a way of imagining, and allowing your readers to imagine, others. The subtext will be revealed in the interchanges of those others, and it's important to be open to human capacity and contradiction, to remember that the character being abandoned is not a passive sounding board, or that the prison guard also has a grandmother and a burden of loss.

There are additional ways to pace yourself when writing dialogue. Timing, as it is in stand-up comedy, is crucial. Vary your sentences and the placement of your dialogue tags. Decide where you want the reader to pause, what you want to emphasize.

In this excerpt from "Hunters in the Snow," Tobias Wolff structures the paragraph so that the reader gets the full benefit of Frank's zinger:

> Frank had his fingers fanned out, tips against the bark of the stump where he'd laid his foot. His knuckles were hairy. He wore a heavy wedding band and on his right pinky was another gold ring with a flat face and "F" printed out in what looked like diamonds. He turned it this way and that. "Tub," he said, "you haven't seen your own balls in years."

Repetition is a useful way to vary pace and emphasize certain words and emotions. In your narration you'll try not to repeat yourself, but your characters' can reveal themselves with their inability to vary their vocabulary. It becomes clear that the wife in Raymond Carver's "Cathedral" worries that her guest, Robert, the blind man, will sense her husband's hostility. The husband, who is the narrator, is listening to their exchange.

> My wife covered her mouth, and then she yawned. She stretched. She said, "I think I'll go upstairs and put on my robe. I think I'll change into something else. Robert, you make yourself comfortable," she said.
>
> "I'm comfortable," the blind man said.
>
> "I want you to feel comfortable in this house," she said.
>
> "I am comfortable," the blind man said.

With each repetition the word *comfortable* takes on a slightly different meaning, anxious on her part, assertive on his.

Format and Style

The *format and style of dialogue*, like punctuation, has as its goal to be invisible, and though there may be occasions when departing from the rules is justified by some special effect, it's best to consider such occasions rare. Here are some basic guidelines:

What a character says aloud should be in quotation marks; thoughts should not. This helps clearly differentiate between the spoken and the internal, especially by acknowledging that speech is more deliberately formulated. If you feel that thoughts need to be set apart from narrative, use italics instead of quotation marks.

Begin the dialogue of each new speaker as a new paragraph. This helps orient the reader and keep clear who is speaking. If an action is described between the dialogue lines of two speakers, put that action in the paragraph of the speaker it describes:

> "I wish I'd taken that picture." Larry traced the horizon with his index finger.
>
> Janice snatched the portfolio away. "You've got chicken grease on your hands," she said, "and this is the only copy!"

Notice that the punctuation goes inside the quotation marks.

A dialogue tag tells us who has spoken—*John said, Mary said, Tim announced*. When a tag is used, it is connected to the dialogue line with a comma, even though the dialogue line may sound like a full sentence: *"I'm paying tonight," Mary said.*

Avoid overusing the name of the person being spoken to in dialogue—it doesn't sound conversational.

> "For God sake, Benji, my job's more important than our marathon Monopoly game."
>
> "Ah, Mom, you're always taking things the wrong way."
>
> "Benji, you know that's not true."
>
> "Yup, true, Mom, every time."

Like a luggage tag or nametag, a dialogue tag serves the purpose of identification, and *said* is usually adequate to the task. People also *ask* and *reply* and occasionally *add, recall, admit,* or *remind.* But sometimes an unsure writer will strain for emphatic synonyms: *She gasped, he whined, they chorused, John snarled, Mary spat.* This is unnecessary and obtrusive. While unintentional repetition usually makes for awkward style, the word *said* is as invisible as punctuation; when reading we're scarcely aware of it, whereas we are forced to be aware of *she wailed.* If it's clear who is speaking without any dialogue tag at all, don't use one. Usually an identification at the beginning of a dialogue passage and an occasional reminder are sufficient. If the speaker is inherently identified in the speech pattern, so much the better.

Similarly, tonal dialogue tags should be used sparingly: *he said with relish, she added limply.* Such phrases are blatant "telling," and the chances are that good dialogue will convey its own tone. *"Get off my case!" she said angrily.* We do not need to be told that she said this angrily. If she said it sweetly, then we would probably need to be told. If the dialogue does not give us a clue to the manner in

I start with character and narrative voice. I want to hear the language in my ears before I start writing the story.
—Shawn Wong

which something is said, an action will often do so better than an adverb. *"I'll have a word with Mr. Ritter about it," he said with finality* is weaker than *"I'll have a word with Mr. Ritter about it," he said, and picked up his hat.*

It helps to make the dialogue tag unobtrusive if it comes within the spoken line: *"Don't give it a second thought," he said. "I was just going anyway."* (A midline tag has the added benefit of helping readers hear a slight pause or change in the speaker's inflection.) A tag that comes at the beginning of the line may look too much like a play script: *He said, "Don't give it a second thought . . ."* whereas a tag that comes after too much speech becomes confusing or superfluous: *"Don't give it a second thought. I was going anyway, and I'll just take these and drop them at the copy shop on the way," he said.* If we don't know who is speaking long before this tag appears, it's too late to be of use and simply calls attention to itself.

Vernacular

Vernacular is a tempting, and sometimes excellent, means of characterizing, but it is difficult to do well and easy to overdo. Dialect, regionality, and childhood are best communicated by word choice and syntax. Misspellings should be kept to a minimum because they distract and slow the reader, and worse, they tend to make the character seem stupid. There is no point in spelling phonetically any word as it is ordinarily pronounced: Almost all of us say things like "fur" for *for*, "uv" for *of*, "wuz" for *was*, "an" for *and*, and "sez" for *says*. It's common to drop the *g* in words ending in *ing*. When you misspell these words in dialogue, you indicate that the speaker is ignorant enough to spell them that way when writing. Even if you want to indicate ignorance, you may alienate the reader by the means you choose to do so. John Updike put this point well when he complained of a Tom Wolfe character:

> [His] pronunciations are steadfastly spelled out—"sump'm" for "something," "far fat" for "fire fight"—in a way that a Faulkner character would be spared. For Faulkner, Southern life was life; for Wolfe it is a provincial curiosity.

It is largely to avoid the charge of reducing characters to "provincial curiosities" that most fiction writers now avoid misspellings.

It can be even trickier catching the voice of someone for whom English is a second (or fifth) language, because when someone starts to learn English, the grammatical mistakes they make tend to be based on the grammatical structure of the native language. Unless you know French or Ibu, you will make mistaken mistakes, and your dialogue is likely to sound as if it comes from a second-rate sitcom.

In vernacular or standard English, the bottom-line rule is that dialogue must be speakable. If it isn't speakable, it isn't dialogue.

> "Certainly I had had a fright I wouldn't soon forget," Reese would say later, "and as I slipped into bed fully dressed except for my shoes, which I flung God-knows-where, I wondered why I had subjected myself to a danger only a fool would fail to foresee for the dubious pleasure of spending one evening in the company of a somewhat less than brilliant coed."

Nobody would say this because it can't be said. It is not only convoluted beyond reason but stumbles over its alliteration ("only a fool would fail to foresee for") and takes more breath than the human lungs can hold.

DIALOGUE TIPS

1. Consider when the most effective dialogue will be direct, indirect, or summarized.
2. Have your characters speak in short exchanges rather than monologues—unless you have a good reason to do otherwise.
3. Is your dialogue doing more than one thing at a time? Is it revealing character, setting a mood, moving the action?
4. Let dialogue express what the speaker wants, and what the story is about.
5. Dialogue is more interesting when characters are saying "no" to each other.
6. Keep exposition out of the dialogue.
7. Let your characters sometimes conceal or avoid instead of saying exactly what they mean, or let them be for some reason incapable of saying it.
8. Let your characters contradict themselves. Give them room to change or to reveal surprising turns of emotion.
9. Use "said" as a dialogue tag whenever possible.
10. Use an action rather than an adverb or other modifier to show how a character is feeling.
11. Vernacular is better conveyed by word choice and syntax than by misspellings.

Read your dialogue aloud and make sure it is comfortable to the mouth, the breath, and the ear. False, flabby, do-nothing dialogue will reveal itself, as will places that drag or seem rushed. This is the best way possible to tell if it's all coming together.

....

APPEARANCE

In human beings, the eyes are the most highly developed means of perception, and we therefore receive more non-sensuous information by sight than by any other sense. Beauty is only skin deep, but people are embodied, and whatever beauty—or ugliness—there is in them must somehow surface for us to perceive it. Such surfacing involves speech and action as well as appearance, but it is appearance that prompts our first reaction to people, and everything they wear and own presents some aspect of their inner selves.

Concerned with seeing beyond mere appearances, writers are sometimes inclined to neglect this power of the visible. In fact, much of the tension and conflict in character proceeds from the truth that appearance is not reality. But in order to know this, we must see the appearance first. Features, shape, style, clothing, and objects can make statements of internal values that are political, religious, social, intellectual, and essential. The man in the Ultrasuede jacket is making a different statement from the one in the holey sweatshirt. The woman with the cigarette holder is telling us something different from the one with the palmed joint. Even a person who has forsaken our materialistic society, sworn off supermarkets, and gone to the country to grow organic potatoes has a special relationship with his or her hoe. However indifferent we may be to our looks, that indifference is the result of experiences with our bodies. A twenty-two-year-old Apollo who has been handsome since he was six is a very different person from the man who spent his childhood cocooned in fat and burst the chrysalis at age sixteen.

Following are two very brief portraits of women. Each is mainly characterized by such trivialities as fabric, furnishings, and cosmetics. It would nevertheless be impossible to mistake the essential nature of the one character for that of the other.

> How beautiful Helen is, how elegant, how timeless: how she charms Esther Songford and how she flirts with Edwin, laying a scarlet fingernail on his dusty lapel, mesmerizing.
>
> She comes in a chauffeured car. She is all cream and roses. Her stockings are purest silk; her underskirt, just briefly showing, is lined with lace.
>
> —Fay Weldon, *Female Friends*

> As soon as I entered the room, a pungent odor of phosphorus told me she'd taken rat poison. She lay groaning between the quilts.

The tatami by the bed was splashed with blood, her waved hair was matted like rope waste, and a bandage tied round her throat showed up unnaturally white. . . . The painted mouth in her waxen face created a ghastly effect, as though her lips were a gash open to the ears.

—Masuji Ibuse, "Tajinko Village"

Vividness and richness of character are created in these two passages, which use nothing more than appearance to characterize.

Note that sense impressions other than sight are still a part of the way a character "appears." A limp handshake or a soft cheek; an odor of Chanel, oregano, or decay—these too can characterize, much the way looks do, if the narrative allows the reader to touch, smell, or taste a character.

The sound and associations of a character's name, too, can give a clue to personality. In the two rewrites of the Debbie paragraph in chapter 2, the affluent Mr. Chiddister is automatically a more elegant sort than the affluent Mr. Strum, just as Huck Finn must have a different life from that of the Marquis of Lumbria. Although names with a blatant meaning—Joseph Surface, Billy Pilgrim, Martha Quest—tend to stylize a character and should be used sparingly, if at all, ordinary names can hint at traits you mean to heighten, and it is worth combing any list of names, including the telephone book, to find suggestive sounds. My own telephone book yields, at a glance this morning, Linda Holladay, Marvin Entzminger, and Melba Peebles, any one of which might set me to speculating on a character.

Sound also characterizes as a part of "appearance" insofar as sound represents timbre, tenor, or quality of noise and speech, the reediness or gruffness of a voice, the lift of laughter or stiffness of delivery.

How a character physically moves is yet another aspect of appearance. Dancer and writer Maggie Kast reminds us that, "images of smell, taste and touch can evoke deeper responses than sight and hearing, but what about the kinesthetic sense, the sensations of position, movement and tension originating in muscles and joints?" Here, in Padma Viswanathan's

The Toss of a Lemon, a humiliated girl runs from her house, her emotion created by taste and movement:

> She scoots back an equal distance on her bottom, then stumbles to her feet and backs away. . . . Janaki runs out into the green and embraces from behind the young papaya whose succour Vairum had taken earlier.
>
> The earth in the pockets between the tree's roots tempts her. With one hand still fast round the tree, Janaki flips into her mouth a lump of dirt the size of the thaingai maavu balls the children have for after-school snack. The soil is crunchy and damply acrid, and contains a couple of jasmine petals. Its dark comfort spreads in her mouth. She sighs and leans her forehead on the tree, both arms clasped around it, its parasol of leaves nodding above.

It is important to understand the difference between *movement* and *action*, however, for these terms are not synonymous. Physical movement—the way he crosses his legs, the way she charges down the hall—characterizes without necessarily moving the plot forward. Often movement is part of the setup of the scene, a way of establishing the situation before change-producing action begins. But it can also, as in the scene above, intensify and move the action forward.

....

ACTION

The significant characters of a fiction must be capable both of causing an action and of being changed by it.

We have seen that dialogue becomes action where it presents the possibility of change. If we accept that a story records a process of change, how is this change brought about? Basically, human beings face chance and choice, or discovery and decision—the first of each pair involuntary and the second voluntary. In terms of story, this means that a character driven by desire takes an action with an expected result, but something intervenes. Some force outside the character presents itself, in the form of information or accident or the behavior of others or the elements. The unknown becomes known, and then the discoverer must either take action or deliberately not take action, involving readers in the tension of the narrative query: and then what happens?

Here is a passage from Toni Morrison's "Recitatif" that demonstrates first movement, then discovery, then decision:

> I was trying to fill the coffeepots and get them all situated on the electric burners when I saw her. She was sitting in a booth smoking a cigarette with two guys smothered in head and facial hair. Her own hair was so big and wild I could hardly see her face. But the eyes. I would know them anywhere. She had on a powder-blue halter and shorts outfit and earrings the size of bracelets. Talk about lipstick and eyebrow pencil. She made the big girls look like nuns. I couldn't get off the counter until seven o'clock, but I kept watching the booth in case they got up to leave before that. My replacement was on time for a change, so I counted and stacked my receipts as fast as I could and signed off. I walked over to the booth. . . .

We all carry contradictions and trivialities within us. . . . In fact, I'd say the jagged edge of paradox and contradiction brings a character closer to the truth of what it is to be human.
—Dennis Bock

Here, "trying to fill the coffeepots and get them all situated" is movement that represents scene-setting and characterization. The significant action begins with the discovery, "I saw her." Notice that "she" is characterized directly by appearance whereas the narrator is mainly characterized by her movements, expressed in active verbs—watching, counting, stacking, signing off—until the moment when she acts on her decision. At the points of both the discovery and the decision we anticipate the possibility of change: what happens next?

In the next passage, from John Cheever's "The Cure," the initial movement is seemingly innocuous but then shifts abruptly toward suspense:

> I turned on a light in the living room and looked at Rachel's books. I chose one by an author named Lin Yutang and sat down on a sofa

under a lamp. Our living room is comfortable. The book seemed interesting. I was in a neighborhood where most of the front doors were unlocked, and on a street that is very quiet on a summer night. All the animals are domesticated, and the only night birds that I've ever heard are some owls way down by the railroad track. So it was very quiet. I heard the Barstows' dog bark, briefly, as if he had been waked by a nightmare, and then the barking stopped. Everything was quiet again. Then I heard, very close to me, a footstep and a cough.

I felt my flesh get hard—you know that feeling—but I didn't look up from my book, although I felt that I was being watched.

This scene is set with movement and one choice—that book—that offers no particular opportunity for change and no particular dramatic force. With "Then I heard," however, a discovery or realization of a different sort occurs; there is suddenly the possibility of real change and so, suddenly, real dramatic tension. In the second paragraph the narrator discovers a familiar and entirely involuntary reaction—"I felt my flesh get hard"—followed by the decision not to take what would be the instinctive action. In fiction as in life, restraint, the decision to do nothing, is fraught with possible tension.

In most cases, writers do not want their technique to be too conspicuous so they conceal the decision and discovery structure. In the next example, from Raymond Carver's "Neighbors," the pattern of change—Bill Miller's gradual intrusion into his neighbor's house—is based on a series of decisions that Carver does not explicitly state. The passage ends with a turning point, a moment of discovery.

When he returned to the kitchen the cat was scratching in her box. She looked at him steadily before she turned back to the litter. He opened all the cupboards and examined the canned goods, the cereals, the packaged foods, the cocktail and wine glasses, the china, the pots and pans. He opened the refrigerator. He sniffed some celery, took two bites of cheddar cheese, and chewed on an apple as he walked into the bedroom. The bed seemed enormous, with a fluffy white bedspread draped to the floor. He pulled out a nightstand drawer, found a half-empty package of cigarettes and stuffed them into his pocket. Then he stepped to the closet and was opening it when the knock sounded at the front door.

There is hardly grand larceny being committed here, but the actions build toward tension through two distinct techniques. The first is that they do actually build: At first Bill only "examines." The celery he only sniffs, whereas he takes two bites of the cheese, then a whole apple, then half a pack of cigarettes. He moves from the kitchen to the bedroom, which is a clearer invasion of privacy, and from cupboard to refrigerator to nightstand to closet, each a more intimate intrusion than the last.

The second technique is that the narrative subtly hints at Bill's own sense of stealth. It would be easy to imagine a vandal who performed the same actions with complete indifference. But Bill thinks the cat looks "steadily" at him, which is of no importance except that he feels it to be. His awareness of the enormous white bed hints at sexual guilt. When the knock at the front door sounds, we start, as he must, in a clear sense of getting caught.

Thus it turns out that the internal or mental moment of change is where the action lies. Much movement in a story is mere event, and this is why descriptions of actions, like stage directions in a dull play, sometimes add little or nothing. When the wife picks up a cup of coffee, that is mere event. If she finds that the lipstick on the cup is not her shade, that is a dramatic event, a discovery; it makes a difference. She makes a decision to fling it at the woman with the Cherry Ice mouth. Flinging it is an action, but the dramatic change occurs with the second character's realization (discovery) that she has been hit—and so on.

Every story is a pattern of change (events connected, as the author E. M. Forster observed, primarily by cause and effect) in which small and large changes are made through decision and discovery.

....

THOUGHT

Fiction has a flexibility denied to film and drama, where everything the spectator knows must be shown. In fiction you have the privilege of entering a character's mind, sharing at its source internal conflict, reflection, and the crucial processes of decision and discovery. Like speech, a character's thought can be offered in summary (*He hated the way she ate*), or as indirect thought (*Why did she hold her fork straight up like that?*), or directly, as if we are overhearing the character's own mind (*My God, she's going to drop the yolk!*). As with speech, the three methods can be alternated in the same paragraph to achieve at once immediacy and pace.

Methods of presenting a character's thought will be more fully discussed in chapter 7 on point of view. What's most important to characterization is that thought, like speech, reveals more than information. It can also set mood, reveal or betray desires, develop theme, and so forth. It can also move the action forward, because fictional people, like their live counterparts, don't think about what they already *know*. They think about what is happening to them, or what they fear will happen, what puzzles them, or what they remember that still holds an emotional charge. Even people who repeat themselves *ad infinitum*—"It's not the cold I mind, it's the wind . . ." do so not because they are mentally engaged with the meteorological fact, but because here, just now, the wind has kicked up again, or because here, now, is a person who might respond. For the most part, people in books encounter new situations and must work mentally toward understanding them; or they encounter old situations and must think them through anew.

In fact, the territory of a character's mind is most likely to be the center of the action. Aristotle says that a man "is his desire," that is, his character is defined by his ultimate purpose, good or bad. *Thought*, says Aristotle, is the process by which a person works backward in his mind from his goal to determine what action he can take toward that goal at a given moment.

It is not, for example, your ultimate desire to read this book. Very likely you don't even "want" to read it; you'd rather be sleeping or jogging or making love. But your ultimate goal is, say, to be a rich, respected, and famous writer. In order to attain this goal, you reason, you must know as much about the craft as you can learn. To do this, you would like to take a graduate degree at the Writer's Workshop in Iowa. To do that, you must take an undergraduate degree in _____, where you now find yourself, and must get an A in Ms. or Mr. _____'s creative writing course. To do that, you must produce a character sketch from one of the prompts at the end of this chapter by a week from Tuesday. To do so, you must sit here reading this chapter now instead of sleeping, jogging, or making love. Your ultimate motive has led you logically backward to a deliberate "moral" decision on the action you can take at this minor crossroad. In fact, it turns out that you want to be reading after all.

> *The characters come by and it's almost like you're walking down the street and someone catches your eye and you meet them again and then you become friends. It's a bit like that.*
> **—Arundhati Roy**

The relation that Aristotle perceives among desire, thought, and action seems to me a very useful one for an author, both in structuring plot and in creating character. What does this protagonist want to happen in the last paragraph of this story? What is the particular thought process by which this person works backward to determine what she or he will do now, in the situation that presents itself on page one?

> That afternoon I prepared certain phrases and responses to use on Rebecca. I was terribly concerned that she think well of me, that she understand I was not the provincial dolt I feared I appeared to be. . . . So I sat at my desk and practiced my death mask—face in perfect indifference, no muscles twitching, eyes blank, still, brow furrowed ever so slightly.
> —Ottessa Moshfegh, Eileen

The action, of course, may be the wrong one. Thought thwarts us, because it leads to a wrong choice, or because thought is full of conflicting desires and consistent inconsistencies, or because there is enormous human tension between suppressed thought and expressed thought:

When he shuts off the shower, the phone is ringing. A sense that it has been ringing for a long time—can a mechanical noise have a quality of desperation?—propels him naked and dripping into the living room. He picks up the phone and his caller, as he has suspected, is Mieko. . . . He is already annoyed after the first hello. Mieko's voice is sharp, high, very Japanese, although she speaks superb English. He says, "Hello, Mieko," and he sounds annoyed.

—Jane Smiley, "Long Distance"

In Joyce Carol Oates's "Where Are You Going, Where Have You Been?" the protagonist Connie wants to get away, every chance she can, from a family she despises. From the opening paragraphs, she devises a number of schemes and subterfuges to avoid their company. One such scheme leads her to respond to the advances of a schemer who is cleverer than herself. At the end of the story her success is probably permanent, at a cost she had not figured into her plan. Through the story she is richly characterized, inventing two personalities in order single-mindedly to pursue her freedom, finally caught between conflicting and paralyzing desires.

A person, a character, can't do much about what he or she wants; it just is (which is another way of saying that character is desire). What we can deliberately choose is our behavior, the action we take in a given situation. Achievement of our desire would be easy if the thought process between desire and act were not so faulty and so wayward, or if there were not such an abyss between the thoughts we think and those that we are willing and able to express.

. . . .

SUGGESTED STORIES
"My Man Bovanne"
    Toni Cade Bambara
"Tandolfo the Great"
    Richard Bausch
"Every Tongue Shall Confess"
    ZZ Packer

"Rock Springs"
    Richard Ford
"Yours"
    Mary Robinson
"Cat Person"
    Kristen Roupenian
"6. 'He leaves the office . . .'"
    David Szalay
"The Tambourine Lady"
    John Edgar Wideman
"Bullet in the Brain"
    Tobias Wolff
"Thank You"
    Alejandro Zambra

WRITING PROMPTS

1. Two characters have an escalating disagreement. One of them says exactly and fully what she or he means. The other is unable or unwilling to speak freely. Give us the thoughts of the second character so that we understand the non-response.

2. A flirtation. Two people are feeling each other out, each unsure of the other's feelings, unsure how far to go; unsure, unsure.

3. A character who speaks in street slang, or a foreign accent—or perhaps it's a child—encounters a person who considers him/herself an expert at whatever is under discussion. Let us know through gesture and dialogue what each thinks of the other.

4. Everyone's family has an outlier—a black sheep, an embarrassment, a sponger, a felon, a know-it-all. Let such a character hold forth at a family gathering. Who challenges her/him? How? Give the thoughts of the challenger if you choose.

5. Two characters in a room. One is trying to throw stuff away that the other wants to keep. Characterize by dialogue, appearance, the objects, and the action. Let us infer what they are thinking.

6. Write an exchange that begins with the words, "I'm sorry, but . . ." What comes after the "but"? What does the other character say in

response? Let them carry on for a while. And a while after that. Keep them talking.

7. Put two characters in a situation in which they are forced to be cordial. Characterize them through appearance (including gesture, tone, movement, smell?) so that we understand the emotion between them, positive or negative.

4: The Flesh Made Word

CHARACTERIZATION, PART II

INDIRECT METHODS OF CHARACTER PRESENTATION

The four methods of direct characterization are forms of "showing" that bring character alive on the page. But there may also be times that you wish to shape our knowledge of and reaction to your characters by "telling" us about them, judging and interpreting for the reader. In some formulations these categories, direct and indirect, are reversed (for after all, the argument runs, in interpreting the author speaks directly to the reader), but to my mind there is a direct parallel here with the distinction between direct and indirect dialogue: in one the reader takes in directly the character's speech, or thoughts, actions, and appearance; in the other, and in dialogue summary, the author steps in to interpret or summarize (indeed, indirect and summary dialogue can be considered forms of indirect character presentation.)

There are two methods of indirect characterization—indirect in the sense that the character is described in summary, abstract, or judgmental terms by either the author or another speaker. Both of these methods are forms of "telling," and both may shape our overall view.

Authorial Interpretation

The first indirect method of presenting a character is authorial interpretation—"telling" us the character's background, motives, values, virtues, and the like. The advantages of this indirect method are enormous, for its use leaves you as the author free to move in time and space; to know anything you choose to know, whether the character knows it or not; and, godlike, to tell us what we are to feel. It allows you to convey a great deal of information in a short time.

> The most excellent Marquis of Lumbria lived with his two daughters, Carolina, the elder, and Luisa; and his second wife, Doña Vicenta, a woman with a dull brain, who, when she was not sleeping, was complaining of everything, especially of the noise . . .
>
> The Marquis of Lumbria had no male children, and this was the most painful thorn in his existence. Shortly after having become a widower, he had married Doña Vicenta, his present wife, in order to have a son, but she had proved sterile.
>
> The Marquis' life was as monotonous and as quotidian, as unchanging and regular, as the murmur of the river below the cliff or as the liturgic services in the cathedral.
>
> —Miguel de Unamuno, "The Marquis of Lumbria"

The disadvantage of this indirect method is that it distances the reader, as all generalizations and abstractions tend to do. Indeed, in the passage above, it may well be part of Unamuno's purpose to convey the "monotonous" and "quotidian" quality of the Marquis's life by this terse and distanced rehearsal of facts, motives, and judgments. Nearly every author uses the indirect method, and you will find it useful when you want to cover the exposition quickly. However, direct presentation of the characters—showing them in action and allowing readers to draw their own conclusions—will more actively engage the reader.

The authorial introduction of a character need not be distanced, however, and may, on the contrary, give us precisely the specifics of character and situation that will begin to draw us in. Here is an example from Anthony Doerr's *All the Light We Cannot See* in which the narrative, beginning in a neutral tone at a factual distance, literally draws us closer and closer, as in camera movement toward a close-up:

> In a corner of the city, inside a tall narrow house at Number 4 rue Vauborel, on the sixth and highest floor, a sightless sixteen-year-old named Marie-Laure LeBlanc kneels over a low table covered entirely with a model. The model is a miniature of the city she kneels within, and contains scale replicas of the hundreds of houses and shops and hotels within its walls. There's the cathedral with its perforated spire, and the bulky old Château de Saint-Malo . . .

The narrative rests on and caresses this intricate model for a few more lines, after which it is not surprising that we see the blind girl "run[ning] her fingertips along the centimeter-wide parapet," whispering to it as she lets "her fingers walk down a little staircase." And we are already half in love with her.

Note that although the "author" may be summarizing a period or a life, that voice may be half in the mind of the narrated character, giving us the flavor as well as the facts of the person:

> He'd never been asked to wear a suit for a job interview. Never been told to bring along a copy of his résumé. He hadn't even owned a résumé until the previous week when he'd gone to the library on Thirty-Fourth and Madison and a volunteer career counselor had written one for him, detailed his work history to suggest he was a man of grand accomplishments: farmer responsible for tilling land and growing healthy crops; street cleaner responsible for making sure the town of Limbe looked beautiful and pristine . . .
> —Imbolo Mbue, *Behold the Dreamers*

Interpretation by Another Character

A character may also be presented through the opinions of other characters, which may be considered a second indirect method. When this method is employed, however, the second character must express his or her opinions in speech, action, or thought. In the process, the observing character is inevitably also characterized. Whether we accept the opinion depends on what we think of that character as he or she is thus directly characterized. In this scene from Jane Austen's *Mansfield Park*, for example, the busybody Mrs. Norris gives her opinion of the heroine:

> "There is a something about Fanny, I have often observed it before,— she likes to go her own way to work; she does not like to be dictated to; she takes her own independent walk whenever she can; she certainly has a little spirit of secrecy, and independence, and nonsense, about her, which I would advise her to get the better of."
>
> As a general reflection on Fanny, Sir Thomas thought nothing could be more unjust, though he had been so lately expressing the same sentiments himself, and he tried to turn the conversation, tried repeatedly before he could succeed.

Here Mrs. Norris's opinion is directly presented in her speech and Sir Thomas's in his thoughts, each of them being characterized in the process. It is left to the reader to decide (without much difficulty) whose view of Fanny is the more reliable.

In this passage from Stephen Graham Jones's *Ledfeather*, four different judgments are implied toward a woman's violence: those of "the old days," the woman herself, a pack of local boys, and the woman's son:

> In the old days, the boy's mom would have gotten a name for what she did: Shoots the Car Twice or Four Holes in the Glass or Doesn't Ever Learn or Can't Stop Fighting.
>
> Now, though, everybody just calls here by her usual name. But some of the kids still hold up imaginary rifles when she's around. Growing up, the boy won't understand this, will think at first, without telling anybody, or asking, that his mom is marked in some tribal way . . . that his mom's a chief of some kind, if the Blackfeet even let women do that. But they probably would, for her.

Notice that a conflict is economically set up between the boy and his tribe, the woman and the tribe, the boy's beliefs and the truth that he will soon know.

Be aware also that if we are dealing with a narrator—that is, a character-as-teller of her or his own story—the hybrid author-character is likely to make generalizations with which we may or may not agree, judgments with which we may sympathize or not. This phenomenon of the narrator will be discussed more fully in chapter 7 on point of view. Meanwhile, here is an example of a narrator-author who has large opinions to give, which may tell us more about him than about the scene he reacts to:

> Everybody looks better singing, especially fifteen-year-olds.
> The same dutiful adults turn up at these high school musicals. I'm early tonight. Claiming two front-row seats, I spread my sogged overcoat. . . .
> This freezing November evening, the rain-ponchos crinkling indoors looked doused, not attractive. Kids onstage grow annually more slim and gifted. In their fringe and songs, how lithe each one. Why does such zest make us, their adult sponsorship, look ever more bushed? Just once I'd like some glamour here among the grown-ups smelling tonight of wet wool.
> —Allan Gurganus, "Overture"

. . . .

CONFLICT BETWEEN METHODS OF PRESENTATION
The conflict that is the essence of character can be effectively achieved in fiction by producing a conflict between methods of presentation. It may come automatically, or be done quite consciously. A character can be directly revealed to us through *appearance, dialogue, action,* and *thought.* If you set one of these methods (most frequently *thought*) at odds with the others, then dramatic tension will be produced. Imagine, for example, a character who is impeccably and expensively dressed, who speaks eloquently, who acts decisively, and whose mind is revealed to us as full of order and determination. He is inevitably a flat character. But suppose he is impeccable, eloquent, decisive, yet his mind is a mess of wounds and panic. He is at once interesting.

Never present ideas except in terms of temperaments and characters.
—André Gide

79

Here is the opening passage of Saul Bellow's *Seize the Day*, in which appearance and action are blatantly at odds with thought:

> When it came to concealing his troubles, Tommy Wilhelm was not less capable than the next fellow. So at least he thought, and there was a certain amount of evidence to back him up. He had once been an actor—no, not quite, an extra—and he knew what acting should be. Also, he was smoking a cigar, and when a man is smoking a cigar, wearing a hat, he has an advantage: it is harder to find out how he feels. He came from the twenty-third floor down to the lobby on the mezzanine to collect his mail before breakfast, and he believed—he hoped—that he looked passably well: doing all right.

Tommy Wilhelm is externally composed but mentally anxious. By contrast, in the next passage, from Samuel Beckett's *Murphy*, the landlady, Miss Carridge, who has just discovered a suicide in one of her rooms, is anxious in speech and action but is mentally composed.

> She came speeding down the stairs one step at a time, her feet going so fast that she seemed on little caterpillar wheels, her forefinger sawing horribly at her craw for Celia's benefit. She slithered to a stop on the steps of the house and screeched for the police. She capered about in the street like a consternated ostrich, with strangled distracted rushes towards the York and Caledonian Roads in turn, embarrassingly equidistant from the tragedy, tossing up her arms, undoing the good work of the samples, screeching for police aid. Her mind was so collected that she saw clearly the impropriety of letting it appear so.

In this third example, from Zora Neale Hurston's "The Gilded Six-Bits," it is the very intensity of the internal that both prevents and dictates action:

> Missie May was sobbing. Wails of weeping without words. Joe stood, and after awhile he found out that he had something in his hand. And then he stood and felt without thinking and without seeing with his natural eyes. Missie May kept on crying and Joe

kept on feeling so much; and not knowing what to do with all his feelings, he put Slemmon' watch charm in his pants pocket and took a good laugh and went to bed.

I have said that thought is most frequently at odds with one or more of the other three methods of direct presentation—reflecting the difficulty we have expressing ourselves openly or accurately—but this is by no means always the case. A character may be successfully, calmly, even eloquently expressing fine opinions while betraying himself by pulling at his ear, or herself by crushing her skirt. Captain Queeg of Herman Wouk's *The Caine Mutiny* is a memorable example of this, maniacally clicking the steel balls in his hand as he defends his disciplinary code.

Often we are not privy to the thoughts of a character at all, so that the conflict must be expressed in a contradiction between the external methods of direct presentation, appearance, speech, and action. Character A may be speaking floods of friendly welcome but betraying his real feeling by backing steadily away. Character B, dressed in Valentino silk and Jimmy Choo sandals, may wail pityingly over the miseries of the poor. Notice that the notion of "betraying oneself" is important here: We're more likely to believe the evidence unintentionally given than deliberate expression.

A classic example of such self-betrayal is found in Leo Tolstoy's *The Death of Ivan Ilyich*, where the widow confronts her husband's colleague at the funeral:

> Noticing that the table was endangered by his cigarette ash, she immediately passed him an ashtray, saying as she did so: "I consider it an affectation to say that my grief prevents my attending to practical affairs. On the contrary, if anything can—I won't say console me, but—distract me, it is seeing to everything concerning him." She again took out her handkerchief as if preparing to cry, but suddenly, as if mastering her feeling, she shook herself and began to speak calmly. "But there is something I want to talk to you about."

It is no surprise either to the colleague or to us that Praskovya Federovna wants to talk about money.

Finally, character conflict can be expressed by creating a tension between direct and indirect methods of presentation, and this is a source of much irony. The author presents us with a judgment of the character and then lets him or her speak, appear, act, or think in contradiction to this judgment.

> Sixty years had not dulled his response; his physical reactions, like his moral ones were guided by his will and strong character, and these could be seen plainly in his features. He had a long tube-like face with a long rounded open jaw and a long depressed nose.
> —Flannery O'Connor, "The Artificial Nigger"

What we see here in the details of Mr. Head's features are not will and strong character but grimly unlikable qualities. "Tube-like" is an ugly image, an "open jaw" suggests stupidity, and "depressed" connotes more than shape, while the repetition of "long" stretches the face grotesquely.

Though critics often praise literature for exhibiting characteristics of the individual, the typical, and the universal all at the same time, I don't think this is of much use to the practicing writer. For though you may labor to create an individual character, and you may make that character a credible example of type, I don't think you can set out to be "universal."

It is true, I believe, that if literature has any social justification or use it is that readers can identify the common humanity in, and can therefore identify with, characters vastly different from themselves in century, geography, gender, culture, and beliefs; and that this enhances the scope of the reader's sympathy. Yet, paradoxically, if you aim for the universal, you're likely to achieve the pompous, whereas if you aim for the individual, you're more apt to create a character in whom a reader can see aspects of himself or herself.

Even though my initial drafts might look like a chaotic mess on the page, even though those drafts might end up being three times as long as the final drafts will be, the process of exploring my characters' lives fully helps me to understand what the story is really about.
—Andrew Porter

Imagine this scene: The child chases a ball into the street. The tires screech, the bumper thuds, the blood geysers into the air, the pulp of the small body lies inert on the asphalt. How would a bystander react? (Is it universal?) How would a passing doctor react? (Is it typical?) How would Dr. Henry Lowes, coming home from the maternity ward of his own hospital, where his wife just had her fourth miscarriage, react? (Is it individual?) Each question narrows the range of convincing reaction, and as a writer you want to convince in each range. If you succeed in the third, you are likely to have succeeded in the other two.

My advice, then, is to labor in the range of the particular. If you aim for a universal character you may end up with a vague or dull or windy one. If you set out to write a typical character you're likely to produce a caricature, because people are typical only in the generalized qualities that lump them together. *Typical* is the most provincial adjective in a writer's vocabulary, signaling that you're writing only for those who share your assumptions. A "typical" schoolgirl in Dar es Salaam is a very different type from one in San Francisco. Furthermore, every person is typical of many things successively or simultaneously. She may be in turn a typical schoolgirl, bride, divorcée, and feminist. He may be at one and the same time a typical New Yorker, math professor, doting father, and adulterer. It is in the confrontation and convolution of types that much of our individuality is produced.

Writing in generalities and typicalities is akin to bigotry—we see only what's alike about people, not what's unique. When effective, a description of type blames the character for the failure to individualize, and if an author sets out deliberately to produce types rather than individuals, then that author invariably wants to condemn or ridicule those types. Mark Helprin, in "The Schreuderspitze," takes the ridicule of type to comic extreme:

In Munich are many men who look like weasels. Whether by genetic accident, meticulous crossbreeding, an early and puzzling migration, coincidence, or a reason that we do not know, they exist in great numbers. Remarkably, they accentuate this unfortunate tendency by wearing mustaches, Alpine hats, and tweed. A man who resembles a rodent should never wear tweed.

This is not to say that all characters must be fully drawn or "round." Flat characters—who exist only to exhibit a function or a single characteristic—can be useful and necessary. Eric Bentley suggests in *The Life of the Drama* that if a messenger's function in a play is to deliver his message, it would be tedious to stop and learn about his psychology. The same is true in fiction: in Margaret Atwood's "Happy Endings," the character of James, "who has a motorcycle and a fabulous record collection," exists for no purpose other than to make Mary's adulterous lover John jealous, and we do not want to hear about his adventures "away on his motorcycle, being free." Nevertheless, onstage even a flat character has a face and a costume, and in fiction detail can give even a flat character a few angles and contours. The motorcycle and record collection swiftly give us an image of James, and are as much as we need to know. The servant classes in the novels of Henry James are notoriously absent as individuals because they exist only in their functions (that excellent creature had already assembled the baggage, etc.), whereas Charles Dickens, who peoples his novels with dozens of flat characters, brings even these alive in detail:

> And Mrs. Miff, the wheezy little pew opener—a mighty dry old lady, sparely dressed, with not an inch of fullness anywhere about her—is also here.
> —*Dombey and Son*

To borrow a notion from George Orwell's *Animal Farm*, all good characters are created round, but some are created rounder than others.

....

CREDIBILITY

Though you aim at individuality and not typicality in characters, your characters will exhibit typicality in the sense of "appropriateness." A Texan Baptist behaves differently from an Italian nun; a rural schoolboy behaves differently from a professor emeritus at Harvard. If you are to succeed in creating an individual character, particular and alive, you will have to know what is appropriate to that sort of person and to let us know as much as we need to know to feel the appropriateness of the behavior.

For instance, we need to know early on, preferably in the first paragraph, the character's gender identification, age, and race or ethnicity. We need to know something of this character's class, period, and region. A profession (or the clear lack of one) and a marital status help, too. *Almost any reader can identify with almost any character; what no reader can identify with is confusion.* When some or several of the fundamentals of type are withheld from us—when we don't know whether we're dealing with a man or a woman, an adult or a child—the process of identifying cannot begin, and the story is slow to move us.

None of this information need come as information; it can be implied by appearance, tone, action, or detail. In the next example, from *The Poisonwood Bible*, Barbara Kingsolver plunges the character of Leah Price and her family into a new life for which they are ill-prepared, practically and politically. Although they are focused on their destination, by the end of the first two paragraphs, we know a lot about the family and the culture its members carry with them.

> We came from Bethlehem, Georgia, bearing Betty Crocker cake mixes into the jungle. My sisters and I were all counting on having one birthday apiece during our twelve-month mission. "And heaven knows," our mother predicted, "they won't have Betty Crocker in the Congo."
>
> "Where we are headed, there will be no buyers and sellers at all," my father corrected. His tone implied that Mother failed to grasp our mission, and that her concern with Betty Crocker confederated her with the coin-jingling sinners who vexed Jesus till he pitched a fit and threw them out of the church. "Where we are headed," he said, to make things perfectly clear, "not so much as a Piggly Wiggly." Evidently Father saw this as a point in the Congo's favor. I got the most spectacular chills, just from trying to imagine.

We know that the family is Southern, not only because their town of origin is named, but also from expressions such as "vexed" and "pitched a fit"; we know something about their class because they shop at the Piggly Wiggly. Not only do we know that they are missionaries, but we hear the father's sermonizing voice in his repetition of the phrase "where we are headed," preaching that is echoed in the implication that the mother is "confederated" with "the coin-jingling sinners." We hear hints also of the harsh pleasure the father will take in the family's hardship. The Betty Crocker mixes tell us that the women are trying to hang on to a little bit of home comfort, yet at the same time they are taking all-American 1950s culture to a place where it is irrelevant and ultimately destructive—indeed, the cake mixes are quickly ruined by jungle humidity. And although we don't know the exact age of the narrator, she seems to be a teenager old enough to hear the subtext of her father's reprovals and to relish the false sophistication of phrases like "the most spectacular chills." In a very short space, Kingsolver has sketched the family, their dangerous ignorance, and the father's divisive, single-minded determination.

The following passage is an even more striking example of implied information:

> Every time the same story. Your Barbie is roommates with my
> Barbie, and my Barbie's boyfriend comes over and your Barbie steals
> him, okay? Kiss kiss kiss. Then the two Barbies fight. You dumbbell!
> He's mine. Oh no he's not, you stinky! Only Ken's invisible, right?
> Because we don't have money for a stupid-looking boy doll when
> we'd both rather ask for a new Barbie outfit next Christmas. We
> have to make do with your mean-eyed Barbie and my bubblehead
> Barbie and our one outfit apiece not including the sock dress.
> —Sandra Cisneros, "Barbie-Q"

Here there is no description whatever of the characters, and no direct reference to them except for the designations *you* and *I*. What do we nevertheless know about their gender, their age, their financial status, the period in which they live, their personalities, their attitudes, their relationship, the narrator's emotions?

Students of writing are sometimes daunted by the need to give so much information immediately. The thing to remember is that credibility consists in the combination of appropriateness and specificity. The trick is to find telling details that will convey the information while our attention remains on the desire or emotion of the character. Nobody wants to read a story that begins, "She was a twenty-eight-year-old suburban American woman, relatively affluent, who was extremely distressed when her husband, Peter, left her." But most of that, and much more besides, could be contained in a few details:

> After Peter left with the VCR, the microwave, and the key to the garage, she went down to the kitchen and ate three jars of peanut butter without tasting a single spoonful.

Unlike even those closest to us in real life—our spouses, our lovers, our kin, whom we can never know completely— fictional people retain only as much privacy and secrecy as those who create them decide to let them keep.
—Douglas Bauer

I don't mean to imply that it is necessarily easy to signal the essentials of type immediately. It would be truer to say that it is necessary and hard. The opening paragraph of a story is its second strongest statement (the final paragraph is the strongest) and sets the tone for all that follows. If the right words don't come to you as a gift, you may have to sit sifting and discarding the inadequate ones for a long time before you achieve both clarity and interest.

....

PURPOSE

Your character's purpose—that is, the desire that impels her or him to action—will determine our degree of identification and sympathy, on the one hand, or judgment, on the other.

Aristotle, in The Poetics, says that "there will be an element of character if what a person says or does reveals a certain moral purpose; and a good element of character, if the purpose so revealed is good." It might seem that the antiheroes, brutes, hoods, whores, perverts, and bums who people modern literature do very little in the way of revealing good moral purpose. The history of Western literature shows a movement downward and inward: downward through society from royalty to gentry to the middle classes to the lower classes to the dropouts; inward from heroic action to social drama to individual consciousness to the subconscious to the unconscious. What has remained consistent is that, for the time spent in an author's world, we stand with the protagonist or protagonists, we "see their point of view," and the fiction succeeds largely because we are willing to grant them a goodness that we would not grant them in life. While you read, you expand your mental scope by identifying with, temporarily "becoming," a character, borrowing a different mind. Fiction, as critic Laurence Gonzales says of rock music, "lets you wander around in someone else's hell for a while and see how similar it is to your own."

The older we get . . . As life becomes more and more limiting, there is something wonderful about being able to get inside the skin of people unlike yourself.
—Lee Smith

Obviously we don't identify with all characters, and those whose purpose is revealed as ambiguous or evil will invite varying degrees of judgment. In Elizabeth Strout's novel *My Name Is Lucy Barton*, the protagonist of that name is admitted to hospital.

> I was pushed into a room and someone put a small tube in my arm and another small tube down my throat. "Hold still," they said. I couldn't even nod.
>
> After a long time—but what I mean by that, I don't know in real time or terms—I was pushed into the CAT scan circle and there were some clicks and then it went dead. "Shit," said a voice behind me. For another long time I lay there. "The machine's broken," the voice said, "but we need this scan or the doctor will kill us." I lay there a long time, and I was very cold. I learned that hospitals are often cold. I was shivering, but no one noticed; I'm sure they would have brought me a blanket. They only wanted the machine to work, and I understood that.

Here without delivering any overt judgment the author leads us to be exasperated at the insensitivity of the nurses, then to understand that they are also treated insensitively, then to ask ourselves if Lucy's magnanimity isn't just a little over the top.

COMPLEXITY

If the characters of your story are credible through being appropriate and individual, and if they invite identification or judgment through a sense of their purpose, they also need to be complex. They need to exhibit enough conflict and contradiction that we can recognize them as belonging to the contradictory human race, and they should exhibit a range of possibility, so that a shift of power in the plot can also produce a shift of purpose or morality. That is, they need to be capable of change.

Conflict is at the core of character, as it is of plot. If plot begins with trouble, then character begins with a person in trouble, and trouble most dramatically occurs because we all have traits, tendencies, and desires that are at war, not simply with the world and other people, but with other traits, tendencies, and desires of our own. All of us probably know a woman of the strong, striding, independent sort, attractive only to men who like a strong and striding woman. And when she falls in love? She becomes a clinging sentimentalist. All of us know a father who is generous, patient, and dependable. And when the children cross the line? He smashes crockery and wields a strap. All of us are gentle, violent; logical, schmaltzy; tough, squeamish; lusty, prudish; sloppy, meticulous; energetic, apathetic; manic, depressive. Perhaps you don't fit that particular list of contradictions, but you are sufficiently in conflict with yourself that as an author you have characters enough in your own psyche to people the work of a lifetime; you need only identify, heighten, and dramatize these conflicts within character, which Aristotle called "consistent inconsistencies."

If you think of the great characters of literature, you can see how inner contradiction—consistent inconsistency—brings each to a crucial dilemma. Hamlet is a strong and decisive man who procrastinates. Dorothea Brooke of *Middlemarch* is an idealistic and intellectual young woman, and a total fool in matters of the heart. Ernest Hemingway's Francis Macomber wants to test his manhood against a lion and cannot face the test. In the opening moment of crisis from *Mom Kills Self and Kids*,

Alan Saperstein reveals with great economy the consistent inconsistency of his protagonist, a man who hadn't much time for his family until their absence makes clear how dependent he has been on them.

> When I arrived home from work I found my wife had killed our two sons and taken her own life.
>
> I uncovered a blast of foul, black steam from the pot on the stove and said, "Hi, hon, what's for dinner?" But she did not laugh. She did not bounce to her feet and pirouette into the kitchen to greet me. My little one didn't race into my legs and ask what I brought him. The seven-year-old didn't automatically beg me to play a game knowing my answer would be a tired, "Maybe later."

In "The Self as Source," Cheryl Moskowitz proposes a fiction technique that relies specifically on identifying conflicting parts of the writer's personality. She points to Robert Louis Stevenson's *The Strange Case of Dr. Jekyll and Mr. Hyde* as a fairly blatant model for such fiction:

> I thus drew steadily nearer to that truth . . . that man is not truly one, but two. I say two, because the state of my own knowledge does not pass beyond that point. . . . I hazard the guess that man will ultimately be known for a mere polity of multifarious, incongruous and independent denizens.

It is, of course, impossible to know to what degree Shakespeare, Eliot, Hemingway, or Saperstein consciously used their own inner contradictions to build and dramatize their characters. An author works not only from his or her own personality but also from observation and imagination, and I fully believe that you are working at full stretch only when all three are involved. The question of autobiography is a complicated one, and as a writer you frequently won't know yourself how much you have experienced, how much you have observed, and how much you have invented. Actress Mildred Dunnock, as we heard in chapter 2, once observed that drama is possible "because people can feel what they haven't experienced," an observation that surely extends to the writing and reading of fiction. If you push yourself to write at the outer edge of your emotional experience—what you can imagine yourself doing, even if you might not risk such actions in life—then all of your writing is autobiographical in the sense that it has passed through your mind.

....

CHANGE

In a story, as opposed to a sketch or anecdote, people and situations significantly *change*. The easiest way to check the plot of your story is to ask, *Does my character change from opening to end? Do I give the sense that his or her life will never be quite the same again?* Or as novelist Charles Baxter more eloquently puts it, "You just ask yourself, 'What is visible now at the end of this story that wasn't visible when the story started?' Sometimes the characters can't see what's come up to the surface, but the reader can."

Often the notion of change is misunderstood by new writers to mean change that is abrupt and absolute, from Scrooge to do-gooder—but this rarely happens in life or in convincing fiction. Rather, change can be as subtle as a step in a new direction, a slight shift in belief, or a willingness to question a rigid view or recognize previously unseen value in a person or situation. Something is visible that was not visible before. One of the vicarious pleasures fiction offers is the chance to experience the workings of change within a character's consciousness.

John L'Heureux offers a psychological framework for viewing change: "A story is about a single moment in a character's life when a definitive choice is made, after which nothing is the same." The decision the main character makes at this pivotal moment regards—and determines—his or her essential *integrity*. L'Heureux emphasizes this concept, integrity in its primal sense of "wholeness," since at the moment of choice the character elects to live either more in harmony or more at odds with his or her best self. The decision made in that moment affects the character's relationship with the self forever.

"What we do determines what we become," Nancy Huddleston Packer affirms. "The consequences of the story come from the character who determines events. Our decisions make us who we are forever afterward."

....

REINVENTING CHARACTER

There are others ways to make a character fresh and forceful in your mind before you start writing. Here are a couple of them:

If the character is based on you or on someone you know, drastically alter the model in some external way: change blond hair to dark or thin to thick; imagine the character as different in gender or radically alter the setting in which the character must act. Part of the trouble with writing directly from experience is that you know too much about it—what "they" did, how you felt. Under such circumstances it's hard to know whether everything in your mind is getting onto the page. An external alteration forces you to re-see, and so to see more clearly, and so to convey more clearly what you see.

We are not unitary selves . . . we are very polymorphous. To make characters in a book interesting and alive they have to be like that—if they are only one thing they are dead.
—Salman Rushdie

On the other hand, if the character is created primarily out of your observations or invention and is unlike yourself, try to find an internal area that you have in common with the character. If you are a blond, slender young woman and the character is a fat, balding man, do you nevertheless have in common a love of French *haute cuisine*? Are you haunted by the same sort of dream? Do you share a fear of public performance or a susceptibility to fine weather?

I can illustrate these techniques only from my own writing, because I am the only author whose self I can identify with any certainty in fictional characters. In one novel, I wanted to open with a scene in which the heroine buries a dog in her backyard. I had recently buried a dog in my backyard. I wanted to capture the look and feel of red Georgia earth at sunrise, the tangle of roots, and the smell of decay. But I knew that I was likely to make the experience too much my own, too little my character's. So I set about making her not-me. I have straight dark hair and an ordinary figure, and I tend to live in jeans. I made Shaara Soole big boned, lanky, melon-breasted, her best feature was a head of rusty barbed-wire hair that she tried to control with a wardrobe of scarves and headband things. Like most costume designers, she dressed with more originality than taste, usually on the Oriental or Polynesian side, sometimes with voluminous loops of thong and matte metal over an ordinary shirt. This was somewhat eccentric in Hubbard, Georgia, but Shaara was oblivious to her eccentricity, being so concerned to keep her essential foolishness in check.

Having thus separated Shaara from myself, I was able to bury the dog with her arms and through her eyes rather than my own. Then a few pages later I was faced with the quite different problem of introducing her ex-husband, Boyd Soole. I had voluminous notes on this character, and I knew that he was almost totally unlike me. A man, to begin with, and a huge man, a theater director with a natural air of power and authority and very little interest in domestic affairs. I sat at my desk for several days, unable to make him move convincingly. My desk oppressed me, and I felt trapped and uncomfortable, my work thwarted, it seemed, by the very chair and typewriter. Then it occurred to me that Boyd was *also* sitting at a desk trying to work.

> The dresser at the Campus Side was some four inches too narrow and three inches too low. If he set his feet on the floor his knees would sit free of the drawer but would be awkwardly constricted left and right. If he crossed his legs, he could hook his right foot comfortably outside the left of the kneehole but would bruise his thigh at the dresser. If he shifted back he was placed at an awkward distance from his script. And in this position he could not work.

This passage did not instantly allow me to live inside Boyd Soole's skin, nor did it solve all my problems with his characterization. But it did let me get on with the story, and it gave me a flash of sympathy for him that later grew much more profound than I had foreseen.

Often, identifying what you have in common with the feelings of your character will also clarify what about her or him is important to the story—why, in fact, you chose to write about such a person at all. Even if the character is presented as a villain, you have something in common, and I don't mean something forgivable. If he or she is intolerably vain, watch your own private gestures in front of the mirror and borrow them. If he or she is cruel, remember how you enjoyed hooking the worm.

I have a hard time imagining that we would still be staging or reading a Chekhov whose characters were always more busy, cheerful and resourceful than we are. . . . Because for me it's usually when a character begins to be thorny that he or she turns interesting.
—Rosellen Brown

There is no absolute requirement that a writer behave honestly in life; there is absolutely no such requirement. Great writers have been public hams, domestic dictators, emotional con artists, and Nazis. What is required for fine writing is honesty on the page—not how the characters *should* react at the funeral, the surprise party, in bed, but how they *would*. In order to develop such honesty of observation on the page, you must begin with a willing honesty of observation (though mercifully not of behavior) in yourself.

....

CREATING A GROUP OR CROWD

Sometimes it is necessary to introduce several or many people in the same scene. This needn't present a problem, because the principle is pretty much the same in every case, and is the same as in film: pan, then close-up. In other words, give us a sense of the larger scene first, then a few details to characterize individuals. If you begin by concentrating too long on one character, we will tend to see that person as being alone.

Herm peered through the windshield and eased his foot up off the gas. Damn, he thought, it's not going to let up. The yellow lights made slick pools along the shoulder. He fiddled with the dial, but all he could get was blabber-radio and somebody selling vinyl siding. His back ached. His eyes itched. A hundred and forty miles to go.

At this point, if you introduce a wife, two children, and a dog to the scene, we will have to make rapid and uncomfortable adjustments in our mental picture. Better to begin with the whole carful and then narrow it down to Herm:

> Herm peered through the windshield and glanced over at Inga, who was snoring lightly against the window. The kids hadn't made a sound for about half an hour either, and only Cheza was wheezing dogbreath now and then on the back of his neck. He eased his foot up off the gas. Damn, he thought . . .

If the action involves several characters who therefore need to be seen right away, introduce them as a group and then give us a few characterizing details:

> All the same there were four guns on him before he'd focused enough to count. "Peace," he said again. There were three old ones, one of them barely bigger than a midget, and the young one was fat. One of the old ones had on a uniform jacket much too big for him, hanging open on his slack chest. The young one spun a string of their language at him.

If the need is to create a crowd, it is still important, having established that there is a crowd, to give us a few details. We will believe more thoroughly in large numbers of people if you offer us an image. Here, for example, in a passage from Underworld, Don LeLillo introduces two parts of a crowd, the boys who are waiting to sneak into the ballpark and the last legitimate arrivals:

> They have found one another by means of slidy looks that detect the fellow foolhard and here they stand, black kids and white kids up from the subways or off the local Harlem streets, bandidos, fifteen in all, and according to topical legends maybe four will get through for every one that's caught.

They are waiting nervously for the ticket holders to clear
the turnstiles, the last loose cluster of fans, the stragglers and
loiterers. They watch the late-arriving taxis from downtown and the
brilliantined men stepping dapper to the windows, policy bankers
and supper club swells and Broadway hotshots, high aura'd, picking
lint off their mohair sleeves.

Notice in the first paragraph how deftly unexpected or slangy language—
slidy looks, foolhard, bandidos, topical legends—shows the particularity of
this familiar batch of boys; and in
the second how details—*cluster of*
fans, brilliantined, dapper, supper club
swells, Broadway hotshots—make us
see a crowd of men personally un-
identified. Note also that DeLillo saves the very most focused image—
picking lint off their mohair sleeves—for last, a little click of the narrative
lock on that paragraph.

> **The bore is meeting people who
> say the usual things.
> —Virginia Woolf**

Note the still more erudite character of the crowd in this scene: "It is
relatively calm in the lobby of Pitié-Salpêtrière," where the philosopher
Roland Barthes lies in a coma. Here the coming-in-for-the-closeup technique is similar:

Friends, admirers, acquaintances, and the merely curious line up to
sit at the great man's bedside; they fill the hospital foyer, conversing
in undertones, a cigarette or a sandwich or a newspaper in hand, or
a book by Guy Debord or a Milan Kundera novel.
—Laurent Binet, *The Seventh Function of Language*

Again, notice how the details grow increasingly specific, how they move
us closer to understanding the kind of person who is likely to be found
in this crowd—from undertones to cigarettes, newspapers, and sand-
wiches to high-minded reading matter for a precise taste.

If the crowd is introduced by a narrating character, it will inevitably characterize the narrator as much as the crowd. The excerpt from
Allan Gurganus's "Overture" on page 79 is a good example of this
technique.

THE CHARACTER JOURNAL

Whether indirect, direct, or, most commonly, both direct and indirect methods are used, a full and rich fictional character will need to be both credible and complex, to show purpose (and that purpose will reveal something about his or her morality), and in the course of the story to undergo some change, perhaps small but nonetheless significant. In exploring these elements of character, your journal can be an invaluable help.

As a writer you may have the lucky, facile sort of imagination to which characters spring full-blown, complete with gestures, histories, and passions. Or it may be that you need to explore at length, to draw your characters out gradually and coax them into being. That can be lucky too.

For either kind of writer, but especially the latter, the journal lets you coax and explore without committing yourself to anything or anyone. It allows you to know everything about your character, whether you use it or not. Before you put a character in a story, know how well that character sleeps, what he eats for lunch, what she buys and how the bills get paid. Know how your character would prefer to spend evenings and weekends and why such plans get thwarted, what memories the character has of pets and parents, cities, snow, or school. You may end up using none of this information, but knowing it may teach you how your bookperson taps a pencil or twists a lock of hair, and when and why. When you know these things, you will have taken a step past invention toward the moment of imagination in which you become your character, live in his or her skin, and produce an action that, for the reader, rings universally true.

Use the journal to note your observations of people. Try writing down your impressions of the library assistant who annoys you or the loner at the bar who intrigues you. Try to capture a gesture or the messages that physical features and clothing send. Invent a reason for that harshness or that loneliness; invent a past. Then try taking the character out of that context and setting her or him in another. Get your character in trouble, and you may be on your way to a short story.

CHARACTER: A SUMMARY

It may be helpful to summarize the practical advice on character in this and the previous chapter.

1. Be aware of the four methods of direct character presentation— appearance, speech, action, and thought—and of the indirect methods, authorial interpretation and presentation by another character.
2. Reveal the character's conflicts by presenting attributes in at least one of these methods that contrast with attributes you present in the others.
3. Know all the influences that go into the making of your character's type: age, gender, race, nationality, marital status, region, education, religion, profession.
4. Focus sharply on how the character looks, on what she or he wears and owns, and on how she or he moves. Let us focus on it, too.
5. Examine the character's speech to make sure it does more than convey information. Does it characterize, accomplish exposition, and reveal emotion, intent, or change? Does it advance the conflict through "no" dialogue? Speak it aloud: does it "say"?
6. Use your journal to explore and build ideas for characters. Know the details of your character's life: what he or she does during every part of the day, thinks about, remembers, wants, likes and dislikes, eats, says, means.
7. Know what your character wants, both generally out of life, and specifically in the context of the story. Keeping that desire in mind, "think backward" with the character to decide what he or she would do in any situation presented.
8. Identify, heighten, and dramatize consistent inconsistencies. What does your character want that is at odds with whatever else she wants? What patterns of thought and behavior work against his primary goal?
9. If the character is based on a real model, whether yourself or someone else, make a dramatic external alteration.

10. If the character is unlike or alien to you, identify a mental or emotional point of contact.

11. Build action by making your characters discover and decide. Make sure that what happens is action and not mere event or movement, that is, that it contains the possibility for human change.

....

SUGGESTED STORIES

"Girls at War"
  Chinua Achebe
"Aren't You Happy for Me"
  Richard Bausch
"Saint Marie"
  Louise Erdrich
"Girl"
  Jamaica Kincaid
"Kindness"
  Yiyun Li
"Orbiting"
  Bharati Mukherjee
"St. Lucy's Home for Girls Raised by Wolves"
  Karen Russell
"Love and Hydrogen"
  Jim Shepard
"A Different Road"
  Elizabeth Strout
"The Flowers"
  Alice Walker

WRITING PROMPTS

1. One character is trying to teach another how to do something specific (practical, domestic, mechanical, or technological). The teacher is not much of a teacher, and the pupil is not much of a learner. Present one of them through authorial interpretation and the other through dialogue.

2. Write a scene in which a man (or boy) questions a woman (or girl) about her mother. Characterize all three.

3. Write a scene using the four direct elements of presentation: appearance, action, speech and thought. Put one element in conflict with the other three.

4. Write a character sketch describing the character in authorial interpretation, both general and judgmental, and also in specific details. Let the details contradict the generalizations. (*Larry was the friendliest kid on the block. He had a collection of brass knucks he would let you see for fifty cents, and he would let you cock his BB gun for him as long as you were willing to hold the target.*) What does this character say? To whom? What action ensues?

5. Have your character accept a ride from someone he or she doesn't know well. Using indirect authorial voice, let us know all about the car—make, model, color, condition, and so forth. Using direct presentation, let us know who these people are, what they say, and what happens. You as author may tell us the outcome.

6. As author, create a crowd. Then pick two characters from it (or in it), show them directly, and let us know from their dialogue how differently each sees the event or experience. When you move back to the crowd, move back to the authorial voice. Make this switch several times.

5: Long Ago and Far Away
FICTIONAL SETTING

Our relation to place, time, and weather, like our relation to clothes and other objects, is charged with emotion more or less subtle, more or less profound. It is filled with judgment mellow or harsh. And it alters according to what happens to us. In some rooms you are always trapped; you enter them with grim purpose and escape them as soon as you can. Others invite you to settle in, to nestle or carouse. Some landscapes lift your spirits; others depress you. Cold weather gives you energy and bounce, or else it clogs your head and makes you huddle, struggling. You describe yourself as a night person or a morning person. The house you loved as a child now makes you, precisely because you were once happy there, think of loss and death.

All such emotion can be used, heightened, or invented to dramatic effect in fiction. Just as significant detail calls up a sense impression and also an abstraction, so the setting of a story imparts both information and emotion. Likewise, just as the rhythm of your prose must work with and not against your intention, so your use of narrative place and time must work with and not against your ultimate meaning. Like dialogue, setting must do more than one thing at a time, from revealing emotion to illuminating character to suggesting the story's symbolic underpinnings.

Character itself is a product of place and culture. We need to know in what atmosphere a character operates in order to understand the significance of the action. Scarlett O'Hara of Margaret Mitchell's *Gone with the Wind* operates as she does because she grew up in heat, damp, and luxury, surrounded by slaves whose loyalty she counts on without examining their lives. Sethe of Toni Morrison's *Beloved* behaves as she does because she grew up enslaved in the same heat and damp, in perpetual terror of the master who comes for her and her babies after she reaches freedom. Fiction writer Michael Martone says that a truly effective evocation of fictional setting might resemble those New Deal post office murals from the 1930s and early '40s. Any one of the figures in the murals has his or her own story while at the same time being embedded in the larger story of the whole painting. As we observe the figures, we may see the social interactions between them but at the same time are aware of the layers of history and social forces evidenced in their buildings, their inventions, appliances, transportation, agriculture, and efforts to tame and control nature.

"These murals attempt," says Martone, "by the design of hundreds of details, to convey the simultaneous presence of the historic and social life of the greater community with the personal specific struggle of a protagonist. Purely as a practical matter, placing stories in such fertile media will make it easier for things to happen, for characters to do things."

....

ATMOSPHERE: TIME, PLACE, AND MOOD
Your fiction must have an atmosphere because without it your characters will be unable to breathe.

Part of the atmosphere of a story is its setting, including the locale, period, weather, and time of day. Part of the atmosphere is its *tone*, an attitude taken by the narrative voice that can be described in terms of a mood, emotion, or quality—sinister, satirical, formal, solemn, wry. The two facets of atmosphere, setting and tone, are often inextricably mixed in the ultimate effect: a sinister atmosphere might be achieved partly by syntax, rhythm, and word choice, partly by night, mist, and a desolate landscape. You can orient your reader in place and time with straight information, (*On the southern bank of the Bayou Teche in the summer of '69 . . .*), and that may be the best beginning for your purposes, but as with the revelation of character you may more effectively reveal setting through concrete detail (*The bugs hung over the black water in clusters of a steady hum . . .*). Here the information is indirect and we may have to wait for

My books all begin the same way . . . usually just a strong sense of time and place. A real sense of atmosphere—that's always my entry point.
—Jennifer Egan

some of it, but the experience is direct, dropping us immediately into the scene and revealing an attitude that implies a character's relation to the scene.

The very language in which setting is expressed will carry significant clues to the ultimate meaning of a piece. Here, in the novel *All the Pretty Horses* by Cormac McCarthy, a sonorous narrative voice suggests the wisdom of the ages:

> They said that a man leaves much when he leaves his own country. They said that it was no accident of circumstance that a man be born in a certain country and not some other and they said that the weathers and seasons that form a land form also the inner fortunes of men in their generations.

By contrast, the heroine of my novel *Cutting Stone*, suffering over the fact that she must leave her own country, makes the same observation as a personal, more modest discovery:

> She thought: *Over time a landscape takes its shape, and then over time it takes its shape in you. I'm the shape of this place.*

In practice, because words carry accumulated connotations, it's almost inevitable that the mood will also be suggested by place and time. The standard opening of a fairy tale connotes a remote and magical setting and sets up an expectation of what might happen here. Any individual details will alter and add to that expectation. What, for example, would you expect from the following beginnings of fairy tales?

Once upon a time in a kingdom by the sea . . .

Once upon a time in a humble cottage beside a cabbage patch . . .

Once upon a time in the deepest, darkest forest . . .

The connotations of "kingdom" and "sea," "humble cottage" and "cabbage patch," or "deepest, darkest forest" instantly let us know what kind of story we're in for. You can take advantage of, and heighten, such atmosphere by choosing words whose connotations make vivid the evocation of time and place. Here are three contemporary authors at work on settings in North Korea, Africa, and London. What words and phrases evoke what expectations of what might happen here? Which of these places is the most dangerous?

> And then in the year Juche 85, the floods came. Three weeks of
> rain, yet the loudspeakers said nothing of terraces collapsing, earth
> dams giving, villages cascading into one another. The Army was
> busy trying to save the Sungli 58 factory from the rising water, so
> the Long Tomorrows boys were given ropes and long-handled gaffs
> to try to snare people from the Chongjin River before they were
> washed into the harbor.
> —Adam Johnson, *The Orphan Master's Son*

> They breezed through the checkpoints and soon were on the open
> road, circling the pale city from above. Dolly noticed vendors by the
> road. Often they were children, who held up handfuls of fruit or
> cardboard signs as the jeeps approached.
>   It was a relief when they left the city behind and began driving
> through empty land that looked like desert, antelopes and cows
> nibbling the stingy plant life.
> —Jennifer Egan, *A Visit from the Goon Squad*

> The complexities of London's electricity network were such that a
> few motes of nighttime brightness remained in Saeed and Nadia's
> locality, at properties on the edges, near where barricades and
> checkpoints were manned by armed government forces, and in
> scattered pockets that were for some reason difficult to disconnect,

and in the odd building here and there where an enterprising migrant had rigged together a connection to a still-active high-voltage line, risking and in some cases succumbing to electrocution.
  —Mohsin Hamid, Exit West

Harmony and Conflict Between Character and Setting
If character is the foreground of fiction, setting is the background, and as in a painting's composition, the foreground may be in harmony or in conflict with the background. If we think of the famous impression-ist painting Sunday Afternoon on the Grande Jatte by Georges Seurat, for example, we think of the harmony of women with light-scattering para-sols strolling in a summer landscape under light-scattering trees. By con-trast, the Spanish painter Francisco Cortijo has a portrait of a girl on her Communion day, Primera comunión. She sits curled and ruffled, in a lace mantilla, on an ornately carved Mediterranean throne against a backdrop of stark, harshly lit, poverty-stricken shacks.

I do think character emerges from place. So much emerges from place, actually. A writer can mine much from a given locale: narrative voice, metaphors large and small, characters, conflict, and more.
—Andrew Scott

Mood within a setting will most often represent an emotional response of the protagonist whose view we share. In fiction, period, place, mood, character, and action impinge on each other constantly, each reinforcing, qualifying, contradicting, and creating the other.

> The apartment Helena rented in Salvador had high ceilings, marble floors, vast windows. It always looked cool, even when the blaze of the Brazilian summer crept inside in the late afternoon. If she leaned from her balcony, she could see the former convent that curved around her street cul-de-sac; she could see over the red tile roofs of the building across the way to where the harbor opened into ocean.
>   —Lauren Groff, "Salvador"

Here period, time of day, and place work with details to create an atmosphere of light and calm in what the protagonist sees: *high ceilings, vast windows, across the way, opened into ocean.* In Don DeLillo's *Underworld,* a more ambivalent mind observes the day:

> The old nun rose at dawn, feeling her pain in every joint. She'd been rising at dawn since her days as postulant, kneeling on hardwood floors to pray. First she raised the shade. That's creation out there, little green apples and infectious disease.

Two things to notice: first, that character, setting, and mood occur simultaneously in these rich and efficient passages and, second, that setting can be manipulated to mean either the expected or the unexpected. In the next passage, from "Chronopolis," J. G. Ballard depicts a third character looking out his window and creates a cheerful prison:

> Luckily, his cell faced south and sunlight traversed it for most of the day. He divided its arc into ten equal segments, the effective daylight hours, marking the intervals with a wedge of mortar prised from the window ledge. Each segment he further subdivided into twelve smaller units.

By contrast with the prison's paradox, in this picture of war, the hardships of soldiers may match our expectations, but they too are given emotional weight and depth through the use of detail:

> The rain fed fungus that grew in the men's boots and socks, and their socks rotted, and their feet turned white and soft so that the skin could be scraped off with a fingernail, and Stink Harris woke up screaming one night with a leech on his tongue. When it was not raining, a low mist moved across the paddies, blending the elements into a single gray element, and the war was cold and pasty and rotten.
> —Tim O'Brien, *Going After Cacciato*

Where disharmony between setting and the character's mood occurs, there is already "narrative content," or the makings of a story. The nun's pain and her ambivalence toward creation, and the soldiers' grim condition, already introduce conflict. But as readers we might also reasonably expect that a prison is not going to be a reasonably structured space, and we are not surprised when, in the light and pleasant room of the Groff story, a man soon appears staring up at the protagonist from the street.

Notice that in all of these passages, harmony, familiarity, and ease or their opposites are not measured in terms of either the reader's or the writer's comfort with such places, but are an attitude of the character whose viewpoint we share. It is also possible to set up a disconnect between the character's view and the reader's, signaling a whole or partial judgment on that character. In my novel *Cutting Stone*, for example, which is set in Arizona in 1914, we know that Eleanor Poindexter is an Irish Catholic socialite from Baltimore, exiled in a dusty little desert town. Seeking the solace of her church, she ventures to the Mexican quarter:

> The brown cubes were patched with corrugated metal, cratewood, rags. From one of them a woman's voice kept up its scolding. A rooster with bald thighs scratched at the threshold of the first hut she passed. Across the street a male child, not yet steady on its feet and wearing nothing but an undershirt with a hole at center belly, hung on the cloth door and regarded her without interest. It all seemed remotely familiar—as if, had she been asked what one could expect to find on the central street of a desert shantytown, she might with a little effort have come up with a molting rooster and a baby in a ragged undershirt.

Here Eleanor, in a setting alien to her, finds the "familiar" in her own prejudices, and there is consequently a distance created between her and the reader. As you might expect, the novel concerns her transformation, until she comes to choose a life among the Mexicans.

In a similar vein, reader anticipation can be aroused by an unspecified narrator's insistent single attitude toward setting; in this case the reader, being a contrary sort of person, is likely to anticipate a change or paradox. Here is the opening paragraph of E. M. Forster's *A Passage to India*:

> Except for the Malabar Caves—and they are twenty miles off— the city of Chandrapore presents nothing extraordinary. Edged

rather than washed by the River Ganges, it trails for a couple of miles along the bank, scarcely distinguishable from the rubbish it deposits so freely. . . . The streets are mean, the temples ineffective, and though a few fine houses exist they are hidden away in gardens or down alleys whose filth deters all but the invited guest.

The narrative continues in this way, an unrelenting portrait of the dreariness of Chandrapore—*made of mud, mud moving, abased, monotonous, rotting, swelling, shrinking, low but indestructible form of life.* The images are so one-sided, so fanatical a condemnation, that we are led to expect (accurately again) that in the pages that follow somehow mystery and beauty will break forth. Likewise, but in the opposite way, the opening pages of Virginia Woolf's *Mrs. Dalloway* burst with affirmation, the beauty of London and spring, love of life and love of life again! We suspect (accurately once more) that death and hatred lurk.

Any well-known city is a challenge to use as a setting. . . . I write about the sweet, dark heart of this place and about the sorts of things and people who are living their lives well beyond the view of the tourist.
—Barb Johnson

Realistic setting may be constructed from memory or research, but an intensely imagined fantasy world makes new and different boundaries for the mind. *Long ago and far away, a dream, hell, heaven, a garbage shaft, Middle Earth, Hogwarts Boarding School,* and *the subconscious* have all been the settings of effective fiction. Even Utopian fiction, set *Nowhere* (with a capital N, or spelled backward, as in Samuel Butler's *Erehwon*), happens in a nowhere with distinct physical characteristics. *Outer space* is an exciting setting precisely because its physical boundary is the edge of our known world. Obviously this does not absolve the writer of the necessity of giving outer space its own characteristics, atmosphere, and logic. If anything, these must be more intensely realized within the fiction, since we have less to borrow from in our own experience.

The westering sun shining on his face woke Shevek as the dirigible, clearing the last high pass of the Ne Theras, turned due south. . . .

He pressed his face to the dusty window, and sure enough, down there between two low rusty ridges was a great walled field, the Port. He gazed eagerly, trying to see if there was a spaceship on the pad. Despicable as Urras was, still it was another world; he wanted to see a ship from another world, a voyager across the dry and terrible abyss, a thing made by alien hands. But there was no ship in the Port.

 —Ursula Le Guin, *The Dispossessed*

We may be in outer space, unfamiliar even to the protagonist, but we are on a planet that shares certain aspects with our own—a "westering" sun, a mountain pass, a wall, a field, ridges—and we feel the character's expectations as very like our own in a new environment. And "sure enough," we've gone someplace specific and real. It is that specific reality that allows us to get lost in the story.

Symbolic Place

Since the rosy-fingered dawn illuminated the battlefield of Homer's *Iliad* (and no doubt well before that), poets and writers have used the context of history, night, storm, stars, sea, city, and plain to give their stories a sense of reaching out toward the universe.

 Sometimes the universe resonates with an answer. In his plays Shakespeare consistently drew parallels between the conflicts of heavenly bodies and the conflicts of nations and characters. In "The Life You Save May Be Your Own," Flannery O'Connor uses the elements in a consciously Shakespearean way, letting the setting reflect and affect the theme. In this classic story the protagonist con man, Mr. Shiftlet, first woos and then abandons a disabled country girl and, stealing her car, drives on in weather that "grows hot and sultry." Shiftlet prays that the Lord will "break forth and wash the slime from this earth." The behavior of the elements, in ironic juxtaposition to the title, shows that the life Shiftlet damns may be his own.

After a few minutes there was a guffawing peal of thunder from behind and fantastic raindrops, like tin-can tops, crashed over the rear of Mr. Shiftlet's car.

Yet the reader is never aware of this symbolic intrusion. The setting throughout remains natural and convincing, until the heavens are ready to make their guffawing comment.

I acknowledge this symbolic possibility in the interests of inclusion. Symbolic setting is a difficult and advanced technique, fine for Shakespeare and O'Connor, but not something I would advise for a beginning writer. Still, one great advantage of being a writer is that you may create the world. Places, time, and the elements have the emotional effect you give them in language. Charles Baxter, in *Burning Down the House*, admonishes the writer toward the finest ideal of the process:

> The object and things surrounding the fictional characters have the same status and energy as the characters themselves. Setting in the way that I want to define it—is not just a place where the action happens. (Nor is the Earth just a prized location where our lives happen to happen.)

....

SOME ASPECTS OF NARRATIVE TIME

Literature is, by virtue of its nature and subject matter, tied to time in a way that the other arts are not. A painting traditionally represents a frozen instant of time, and the viewing time is a matter of the viewer's choice; no external standard must be satisfied in order to say that you have seen the painting. Music takes a certain time to hear, and the timing of the various parts is of utmost importance; but the time scheme is generally self-enclosed and makes no reference to time in the world outside itself. A book, too, takes time to read, but the reader chooses his or her rate and may put it down and take it up at will.

But in the narrative itself, the vital temporal relationship is to content time, the period covered in the story. It is possible to write a story that takes about twenty minutes to read and covers about twenty minutes of action (Jean-Paul Sartre performed experiments in this *durational realism*), but no one has suggested such a relationship as a fictional requirement. Sometimes the period is telescoped, sometimes stretched. The history of the world up to now can be covered in a sentence, or four seconds of crisis may take a chapter. It's even possible to do both at once. William Golding's entire novel *Pincher Marin* takes place between the time the drowning protagonist begins to take off his boots and the moment he dies with his boots still on. But when asked by a student, "How long does it really take?" Golding replied, "Eternity."

Summary and Scene

Summary and scene are methods of treating time in fiction. A summary covers a relatively long period of time in relatively short compass; a scene deals at length with a relatively short period of time.

Summary is a useful and often necessary device: to give information, fill in a character's background, let us understand a motive, alter pace, create a transition, leap moments or years. Here is an example of a summary that covers fifty years and gives us all the background and history of the situation we need to know in three sentences:

> For fifty years now, nag, nag, nag and harp, harp, harp. No matter what my sister did, it wasn't good enough for my mother, or for my father either. She moved to England to get away, and married an Englishman, and when he died, she married another Englishman, but that wasn't enough.
> —Lydia Davis, "My Sister and the Queen of England"

It is the next line that introduces the particular scene we are to be concerned with: "Then she was awarded the Order of the British Empire."

Summary can be called the mortar of the story, but scenes are the building blocks. Scene, which involves an action, is the crucial means of allowing your readers to experience the story with the characters; and though summary may be a useful narrative tool, scene is *always* necessary to fiction, for it allows the reader to see, hear, and sense the drama moment to moment. Jerome Stern, in *Making Shapely Fiction*, observes that, like a child in a tantrum, when you want everyone's full attention, you "make a scene," using the writer's full complement of "dialogue, physical reactions, gestures, smells, sounds, and thoughts."

It is quite possible to write a story in a single scene, without any summary at all. It is not possible to write a successful story entirely in summary. One of the common errors of beginning fiction writers is to summarize event rather than realize them as moments.

In the following paragraphs from Margaret Atwood's *Lady Oracle*, the narrator has been walking home from her Brownie troop with older girls who tease and terrify her with threats of a bad man.

> The snow finally changed to slush and then to water, which trickled down the hill of the bridge in two rivulets, one on either side of the path; the path itself turned to mud. The bridge was damp, it smelled rotten, the willow branches turned yellow, the skipping ropes came out. It was light again in the afternoons, and on one of them, when for a change Elizabeth hadn't run off but was merely discussing the possibility with the others, a real man actually appeared.
>
> He was standing at the far side of the bridge, a little off the path, holding a bunch of daffodils in front of him. He was a nice-looking man, neither old nor young, wearing a good tweed coat, not at all shabby or disreputable. He didn't have a hat on, his taffy-colored hair was receding and the sunlight gleamed on his high forehead.

The first paragraph of this quotation covers the way things were over a period of a few months and then makes a transition to one of the afternoons; the second paragraph specifies a particular moment. Notice that although the summary sets us at a distance from the action, sense details remain necessary to its life: *snow, path, bridge, willow branches, skipping ropes.* These become more sharply focused as we concentrate on a particular moment. More importantly, the scene is introduced when the moment of confrontation occurs. That the threatened bad man does appear and that he is surprisingly innocuous promises a

The myth of exoticism is busted immediately when you go to Calcutta, India, and ask someone there to tell you what's exotic, and they'll say, "Iowa!" Every place that's not yours is exotic.
—*Bob Shacochis*

turn of events and a change in the relationship among the girls. We need to see the moment when this change occurs.

Throughout *Lady Oracle*, which is by no means unusual in this respect, the pattern recurs: a summary leading up to, and followed by, a scene that represents a turning point.

> My own job was fairly simple. I stood at the back of the archery range, wearing a red leather apron, and rented out the arrows. When the barrels of arrows were almost used up, I'd go down to the straw targets. . . .
>
> The difficulty was that we couldn't make sure all the arrows had actually been shot before we went to clear the targets. Rob would shout, "Bows DOWN, please, arrows OFF the string," but occasionally someone would let an arrow go, on purpose or by accident. This was how I got shot. We'd pulled the arrows and the men were carrying the barrels back to the line; I was replacing a target face, and I'd just bent over.

The summaries in these passages are of the two most common types. The summary in the first passage is *sequential*; it relates events in a sequence but compresses them: *snow finally changed to slush and then to water, willow branches turned yellow, skipping ropes came out*—the transition from winter to spring is made in a paragraph. The summary in the second excerpt is *circumstantial*; it describes the general circumstances during a period of time: this is what usually or frequently happened. The narrator *stood at the back of the range*, then *went to clear the targets*, and *Rob would shout*. Again, when the narrator arrives at an event that changes her circumstance (*I got shot*), she focuses on a particular moment: *I was replacing a target face, and I'd just bent over.*

To clarify the difference between summary and scene, compare the ideas of sequence, circumstance, and scene to the process of your own memory, which also drastically condenses. You might think of your own past as a movement through time: *I was born in Arizona and lived there with my parents until I was eighteen; then I spent three years in New York before going on to England.* Or you might remember the way things were during a period of that time: *In New York we used to go down to Broadway for a midnight snack, and Judy would always dare us to some nonsense or other before we got back to the dorm.* But when you think of the events that signally altered your life, your memory will present you with a scene: *Then one afternoon Professor Bovie stopped me in the hall after class and wagged his glasses at me. "Have you thought about studying in England?"*

The function of summary, both sequential and circumstantial, is precisely to heighten scene. It may be used both before and within scene to suggest a relation to the past, to intensify mood, to delay while augmenting our anticipation of what will happen next. It will still be in the scene that we experience the drama—discovery, decision, potential for change—that engages our attention. This example from Rosellen Brown's *Before and After*, in which a father disturbed by reports of a young girl's murder is checking out his son's car in a dark garage, does all three.

> The snow was lavender where the light came down on it, like the weird illumination you see in planetariums that changes every color and makes white electric blue. Jacob and I loved to go to the science museum in Boston—not that long ago he had been at that age when the noisy saga of whirling planets and inexplicable anti-gravitational feats, narrated by a man with a deep official-facts voice, was thrilling. He was easily, unstintingly thrilled, or used to be.

Notice how Brown uses brief summaries both of the way things used to be (circumstantial) and the way things have changed over time (sequential), as well as images of time, weather, and even the whirling cosmos, to rouse our ear toward the "instant" in which major change occurs:

> At the last instant I thought I'd have a look at the trunk. I was beginning to feel relief wash over me like that moon-white air outside—a mystery, still, where he might be, but nothing suspicious. The trunk snapped open and rose with the slow deliberation of a drawbridge, and then I thought I'd fall over for lack of breath. Because I knew I was looking at blood.

Examining your own mind for the three kinds of memory—sequential, circumstantial, and scene—will help make evident the necessity of scene in fiction. The moments that altered your life you remember at length and in detail. Your memory tells you a story, and it is great storyteller.

White Space

It was the tradition of the Victorian novel to be divided into chapters with no internal breaks in the narrative, and that habit carried into the twentieth century. This meant that if a character or characters needed to go from here to there in order to get from one scene to another, whether across the country or up the stairs, from night to morning or from childhood to adulthood, the reader needed to be taken with them. Nothing is clumsier than to end one paragraph with the family piling into the car and begin the next with "Three hours later they arrived in . . ." In such a case the trick is to create the intervening space or time quickly, with an image or two, an indication of mood, a sense of the miles or years involved. Here is E. M. Forster in *A Passage to India* demonstrating the technique on the way to a crucial scene:

> They meant to climb to the rocking-stone on the summit, but it was too far, and they contented themselves with the big group of caves. *En route* for these, they encountered several isolated caves, which the guide persuaded them to visit, but really there was nothing to see; they lit a match, admired its reflection in the polish, tested the echo and came out again. Aziz was "pretty sure they should come on some interesting old carvings soon," but only meant he wished there were some carvings.

Forster is a master of making the trip itself meaningful, but many of us are not, and some transitions read as if they are there for their own sake and merely drag the story along. I used to sweat and suffer when I came to write a passage that needed simultaneously to condense and stretch the time in such a way.

But now familiarity with film has accustomed us so thoroughly to the "cut to" that this effort is no longer needed. Early moving pictures would grant us a gradual transition from scene to scene: a slow fade-out, a black screen, a "swipe" or "cameo" shot. Now, and for the better part of a century, the film scene shifts abruptly, and we understand that a change of light or setting takes us instantly to the next day, the next locale. Fiction has adopted the *white space* as the narrative equivalent of the cut-to, and as readers we understand that a visual break in the lines of prose means that we begin fresh, the next city over, the next morning, in somebody's else's point of view.

Here, in Aravind Adiga's *Selection Day*, the scene does all three and shifts mood besides—moves several hours in time, from a cricket field to a rich man's apartment, from the viewpoint of a minor character to that of the protagonist, and from violence to shame, with the simple cut-to of white space:

> Deennawaz was about to turn around to ask again for water, when he felt something hit him at the top of his neck, pounding him like a sledgehammer, compressing the length of his backbone, until the tip of his spine almost pierced through skin.
> The cricket stopped when the players heard the scream.

> Instructing his father to stand still for a moment, Manju signed the guard's register for both of them. The elevator waited behind a collapsible lattice gate. There was no elevator boy inside: just a cold wooden stool. Getting in, Manju held the lattice gate open for his father.

Sometimes, of course, the transition itself is part of the story and contains its own necessary scene. But if not, if you find yourself bored with the task of getting the characters from here to there or then to now, you will probably bore your reader too. Instead, try leaping across the white space.

Flashback

Flashback is one of the most magical of fiction's contrivances, easier and more effective in this medium than in any other, because the reader's mind is a swifter mechanism for getting to the past than anything that has been devised for stage or even film. All you must do is give the reader a smooth passage into the past, and the force of the story will be time-warped to whenever and wherever you want it.

Nevertheless, many beginning writers overuse flashbacks. This happens because flashback can be a useful way to provide what has come to be known as *backstory*—information on a character's childhood or motivation or the history of events—and is often seen as the easiest or only way. It isn't. Dialogue, brief summary, a reference or detail can often tell us all we need to know, and when that would suffice, a flashback becomes cumbersome, taking us from the present where the story and our interest lie. These intrusive passages tend to come early in the story, before we are caught up in the action.

Backstory should only be employed to advance the front story.
—William H. Coles

You as the writer may need to know a great deal about your main characters' backgrounds, experiences, disappointments, or traumas, but it may take only the lightest of sketching to tell us readers what *we* need to know. After so much television, so many movies, books, and news items, we are so narrative-literate that we don't need all the explanatory transitions. We get it in a flash. Two and a half sentences and we know what kind of marital trouble these two are in, whether these two others will kiss, how long it will take for the sinner to be punished or the hero tested.

If you are tempted to use flashback to fill in the whole past, try using your journal to explore background. Write down everything you can think of, fast. Then take a hard look at it to decide just how little of it you can use, how much of it the reader can infer, how you can sharpen an image to imply a past incident or condense a grief into a line of dialogue. Trust the reader's experience of life to understand events from attitude, gesture, tone. And keep the present of the story moving.

When flashback is used effectively, to *reveal something from the past at the right time*, it does not so much take us from as contribute to the central action of the story: as readers we suspend the forward motion of the narrative in our minds while our understanding of it deepens.

If you find you need an excursion into the past to reveal why a character reacts as she does, or how totally he is misunderstood by those around him, or some other point of emotional significance, then there are several ways to get the reader to cooperate.

Provide some sort of transition. A connection between what's happening in the present and what happened in the past will help transport the reader, just as it does the character.

Avoid blatant transitions such as "Henry thought back to the time . . ." or "I drifted back in memory . . ." Assume the reader's intelligence and ability to follow your leap.

> The kid in the high-tops lifted off on the tips of his toes and slam-dunked it in.
> Joe'd done that once, in the lot off Seymour Street, when he was still four inches shorter than Ruppert and had already started getting zits.

A graceful transition to the past allows you to summarize necessary background quickly. In this example from Elizabeth Strout's "Windmills," the protagonist, Patty, ranges in her mind from her father's death to the distressing events of the day to a whole telegraphed précis of family relationships:

> The sun had set, and by the time Patty was halfway home—past the windmills—the full moon was starting to rise. The night her father died the moon was full, and in Patty's mind every time the moon became full she felt that her father was watching her. She wiggled her fingers from the steering wheel as a hello to him. Love you, Daddy. . . .
>
> At home, the lights she'd left on made her house appear cozy; it was one of many things she had learned about living alone, leaving lights on. And yet as she put her pocketbook down, moved through the living room, the ghastliness descended; her day had been a bad one. Lila Lane had shaken her profoundly, and what if the girl reported her, told the principle that Patty had called her a piece of filth? She could do that, Lila Lane. She was up to doing that. Patty's sister had been no help, there was no point calling her other sister, who lived in L.A. and never had time to talk, and her mother—oh, her mother.

Here a long past memory of the father and a more immediate memory of the day prepare us for events of the story that are already in motion.

It takes the merest brushstroke to signal the family dynamic of the four women, as opposed to Patty's loving memory of her father.

If you are writing in the past tense, begin the flashback in the past perfect (*she had driven, he'd worked*) and use the construction "had + (verb)" two or three times more. Then switch to the simple past (*she raced, he crept*); the reader will be with you. If you are writing in the present tense, you may want to keep the whole flashback in the past tense.

Try to avoid a flashback within a flashback. If you find yourself tempted by this awkward shape, it probably means you're trying to make flashback carry too much of the story.

When the flashback ends, be very clear that you are catching up to the present again. Repeat an action or image that the reader will remember belongs to the basic time period of the story (*she wiggled her fingers, Patty's sister had been no help*). It may take very little to jog the reader's memory, even if the flashback was on the long side. If in the present time of the story the character is eating dinner in a fancy restaurant, for instance, you could bring us back into the present by mentioning the food he chews, the sound of silverware, the look on the face of the person across the table. Often simply beginning the paragraph with "Now . . ." will accomplish the reorientation.

Slow Motion

Flashback and *cut-to* are terms borrowed from film, and I want to borrow one more—*slow motion*—to point out a correlation between narrative time and significant detail.

When people experience moments of great intensity, their senses become especially alert and they register, literally, more than usual. In extreme crisis people have the odd sensation that time is slowing down, and they see, hear, smell, and remember ordinary sensations with extraordinary clarity. This psychological fact can work artistically in reverse: you can create the intensity by using detail with special focus and precision. The phenomenon is so universal that it has become a standard film technique to register a physical blow, a gunshot, sexual passion, or extreme fear in slow motion. The technique works forcefully in fiction.

Recall the quotation from Rosellen Brown, where the trunk "snapped open and rose with the slow deliberation of a drawbridge."

Ian McEwan, in *A Child in Time*, demonstrates the technique:

He was preparing to overtake when something happened—he did not quite see what—in the region of the lorry's wheels, a hiatus, a cloud of dust, and then something black and long snaked through a hundred feet towards him. It slapped the windscreen, clung there a moment and was whisked away before he had time to understand what it was. And then—or did this happen in the same moment?—the rear of the lorry made a complicated set of movements, a bouncing and swaying, and slewed in a wide spray of sparks, bright even in sunshine. Something curved and metallic flew off to one side. So far Stephen had had time to move his foot towards the brake, time to notice a padlock swinging on a loose flange, and "Wash me please" scrawled in grime. There was a whinnying of scraped metal and new sparks, dense enough to form a white flame which seemed to propel the rear of the lorry into the air.

> *I believe if you get the landscape right, the characters will step out of it, and they'll be in the right place. The story will come from the landscape.*
> *—Annie Proulx*

Anyone who has faced some sort of accident can identify with the experience of sensuous slowdown McEwan records. But the slow-motion technique works also with experiences most of us have not had and to which we must submit in imagination:

Blood was spurting from an artery in my left leg. I could not see it, and I do not recall how I knew it . . . for a short time I was alone with Patrick. I told myself I was in good hands, but I did not do this with words; I surrendered myself. I focused only on breathing. I slowed my breathing, and tried to remain absolutely in the present, in each moment. . . . That waiting to die or stay alive was like getting an injection as a child, when you first learned not to think, but to gather yourself into the present, to breathe slowly, to relax your muscles, even your arm as the nurse swabbed it with alcohol, to feel the cool alcohol, to smell it, to feel your feet on the floor and see the color of the wall, and nothing else as your slow breathing opened you up to the incredible length and breadth and depth of one second.

—Andre Dubus, "Breathing"

The technique will work as well when the intensity or trauma of the moment is not physical but emotional:

They were in the deep sleep of midnight when Pauline came quietly into her son's room and saw that there were two in his bed. She turned on the light. The room was cold and stuffy; warm in the core of it was the smell of a body she had known since she gave birth to him, unmistakable to her as the scent that leads a bitch to her puppy, and it was mingled with the scents of sexuality caressed from the female nectary. The cat was a rolled fur glove in an angle made by Sasha's bent knees. The two in the bed opened their eyes; they focussed out of sleep and saw Pauline. She was looking at them, at their naked shoulders above the covers.

—Nadine Gordimer, *A Sport of Nature*

Central to this technique are the alert but matter-of-fact acceptance of the event and the observation of small, sometimes apparently random, details. The characters do not say, "Oh my God, we're going to die!" or "What an outrage!" Instead they record a padlock swinging, the cool feel of an alcohol swab, a cat rolled into the angle of bent knees.

Beginning writers often skimp on the elements of setting and time, probably out of dreary memories of long descriptions they have read. Certainly, we have yawned over passages in which authors indulge themselves in plum-colored homilies on the beauties of nature or the wealth of decor. But when atmosphere is well created, we do not experience it as description; we simply experience it. Just as dialogue that only offers information is too inert for the purposes of fiction, so too is description that only describes. The full realization of place and period, the revelation of a character through his house or of emotion through the weather, the advancement of plot through changes in season and history, are among the pleasures of both writer and reader. Once you become adept at the skill of manipulating atmosphere, you will find that the necessity of setting your story in some particular place at some specific time is a liberating opportunity.

....

SUGGESTED STORIES
"A Serious Talk"
  Raymond Carver
"The Bella Lingua"
  John Cheever
"Mrs. Dutta Writes a Letter"
  Chitra Banerjee Divakaruni
"Battle Royal"
  Ralph Ellison
"Car Crash While Hitchhiking"
  Denis Johnson
"The Interpreter of Maladies"
  Jhumpa Lahiri
"Real Women Have Bodies"
  Carmen Maria Machado
"A Very Old Man with Enormous Wings"
  Gabriel García Márquez
"You're Ugly Too"
  Lorrie Moore
"The Masked Marvel's Last Toehold"
  Richard Selzer

WRITING PROMPTS
1. Consider the ideas of home, homesickness, foreignness, alienation. Place a character in a scene where these ideas are evoked by place, time, and weather.

2. Two characters are in conflict over a setting. One wants to stay, the other wants to go. The more interesting the setting you choose, the more interesting the scene will be. Let the disagreement escalate. Resolve it. Who wins? How? Why?

3. Write a scene with a flashback in which the information about the past is *crucial* to understanding the present.

4. Place a character in a territory that has been stripped of its usual characteristics: a beach without water, a forest without trees, a city without buildings (whatever landscape you please). What does your character do there?

5. The far past or the far future. Write a scene in which the members of a group disagree. How are conflicts differently resolved in this time period from how they would be in our familiar society?

6. Write a scene from the perspective of an adult or old person looking back on her/his childhood or youth. Let the difference in the older person's current setting color the recollection.

7. Imagine an accident of any seriousness—a cut finger or a car crash, a broken vase or a house fire, and write it in several versions: a one-sentence summary, a paragraph, a scene, slow motion. Think of it in film terms, the camera moving from panoramic shot to middle shot, zooming in ever nearer till it ends it extreme close-up.

6: The Tower and the Net

PLOT AND STRUCTURE

It seems likely that the earliest storytellers—in the tent or the harem, around the campfire or on the Viking ship—told stories out of an impulse to tell stories. They made themselves popular by distracting their listeners from a dull or dangerous evening with heroic exploits and a skill at creating suspense: What happened next? And after that? And then what happened?

Natural storytellers are still around, and a few of them are very rich. Some are on the best-seller list; more are in television and film; some are in comic books and video games. But it's probable that your impulse to write has little to do with the desire or the skill to work out a plot. On the contrary, you want to write because you are a sensitive observer. You have something to say that does not answer the question *What happened next?* You share with most—and the best—contemporary fiction writers a sense of the injustice, the absurdity, and the beauty of the world, and you want to register your protest, your laughter, your affirmation.

Yet readers still want to wonder what happened next, and unless you make them wonder, they will not turn the page. You must master plot, because no matter how profound or illuminating your vision of the world may be, you cannot convey it to those who do not read you.

When editors take the trouble to write a rejection letter to a young author (and they do so only when they think the author talented), the gist most frequently is: "This piece is sensitive (perceptive, vivid, original, brilliant, funny, moving), but it is not a *story*."

How do you know when you have written a story? And if you're not a natural-born wandering minstrel, can you go about learning to write one?

It's interesting that we react with such different attitudes to the words "formula" and "form" as they apply to a story. A *formula story* is hackwork: to write one, you check out what's on the rack at the supermarket checkout, read half a dozen romances, fantasies, or space stories, make a list of what kinds of characters and situations the editors buy, shuffle nearly identical characters around in slightly altered situations, and sit back to hope for a check. Whereas *form* is a term of the highest artistic approbation, even reverence, with overtones of *order, harmony, model, archetype*.

And "story" is a "form" of literature. Like a face, it has necessary features in a necessary harmony. We're aware of the infinite variety of human faces, aware of their unique individuality, which is so powerful that once you know a face you can recognize it twenty years after you last saw it despite the changes it has undergone. We're aware that minute alterations in the features can express grief, anger, or joy. If you place side by side two photographs of, say, Gal Gadot and Geronimo, you are instantly aware of the fundamental differences of age, race, sex, class, and century; yet these two faces are more like each other than either is like a foot or a fern, both of which have their own distinctive forms. Every face has two eyes, a nose between them, a mouth below, a forehead, two cheeks, two ears, and a jaw. If a face is missing one of these features, you may say, "I love this face in spite of its lacking a nose," but you must acknowledge the *in spite of*. You can't simply say, "This is a wonderful face."

The same is true of a story. You might say, "I love this piece even though there's no crisis action in it." You can't simply say, "This is a wonderful *story*."

....

CONFLICT, CRISIS, AND RESOLUTION

One useful way of describing the necessary features of story form is to speak of *conflict, crisis,* and *resolution*.

Conflict is, as we've seen, a fundamental element of fiction. Playwright and director Elia Kazan describes it simply as "two dogs fighting over a bone." William Faulkner reminds us that in addition to a conflict of wills, fiction shows "the heart in conflict with itself"; that is, conflict seethes both within and between characters. In life, "conflict" often carries negative connotations, yet in fiction, be it comic or tragic, dramatic conflict is fundamental, because in literature only trouble is interesting.

> *I like the definition of tension from physics:* **two equal forces pulling in opposite directions.** ***Tension between forces: Expression versus repression. Motion versus status. Not knowing versus knowing.***
> **—Debra Monroe**

Only trouble is interesting. This is not so in life. Life offers periods of comfortable communication, peaceful pleasure, and productive work, all of which are extremely interesting to those involved. But passages about such times by themselves make for dull reading; they can be used as lulls in an otherwise tense situation, as a resolution, even as a hint that something awful is about to happen. They cannot be used as a whole plot.

Suppose, for example, you go on a picnic. You find a beautiful deserted meadow with a lake nearby. The weather is splendid and so is the company. The food's delicious, the water's fine, and the insects have taken the day off. Afterward, someone asks you how your picnic was. "Terrific," you reply, "really perfect." No story.

Now suppose the next week you go back for a rerun. You set your picnic blanket on an anthill. You all race for the lake to get cold water on the bites, and one of your friends goes too far out on the plastic raft, which deflates. He can't swim and you have to save him. On the way in you gash your foot on a broken bottle. When you get back to the picnic, the ants have taken over the cake and a possum has demolished the chicken. Just then the sky opens up. When you gather your things to race for the car, you notice an irritated bull has broken through the fence. The others run for it, but because of your bleeding heel the best you can do is hobble. You have two choices: try to outrun him or stand perfectly still and hope he's interested only in a moving target. At this point, you don't know if your friends can be counted on for help, even the nerd whose life you saved. Nor do you know if it's true that a bull is attracted by the smell of blood.

A year later, assuming you're around to tell about it, you are still saying, "Let me tell you what happened last year." And your listeners are saying, "What a story!"

As Charles Baxter, in *Burning Down the House*, more vividly puts it:

> Say what you will about it, Hell is story-friendly. If you want a compelling story, put your protagonist among the damned. The mechanisms of hell are nicely attuned to the mechanisms of narrative. Not so the pleasures of Paradise. Paradise is not a story. It's about what happens when the stories are over.

If it takes trouble to make a picnic into a story, this is equally true of the great themes of life: birth, love, sex, work, and death. Here is a very interesting love story to live: Jan and Jon meet in college. Both are beautiful, intelligent, talented, popular, and well adjusted. They're of the same race, class, religion, and political persuasion. They are sexually compatible. Their parents become fast friends. They marry on graduating, and both get rewarding work in the same city. They have three children, all of whom are healthy, happy, beautiful, intelligent, and popular; the children love and respect their parents to a degree that is the envy of everyone. All the children succeed in work and marriage. Jan and Jon die peacefully, of natural causes, at the same moment, at the age of eighty-two, and are buried in the same grave.

No doubt this love story is very satisfying to Jan and Jon, but you can't make a novel of it. Great love stories involve intense passion and a monumental impediment to that passion's fulfillment. So: they love each other passionately, but their parents are sworn enemies (*Romeo and Juliet*). Or: they love each other passionately, but he's black and a foreigner, and he has an enemy who wants to punish him (*Othello*). Or: they love each other passionately, but she's married (*Anna Karenina*). Or: he loves her passionately, but she falls in love with him only when she has worn out his passion ("Frankly, my dear, I don't give a damn").

In each of these plots, there is both intense desire and great danger in the pursuit of that desire; generally speaking, this shape holds true for all plots. It can be called 3-D: *drama* equals *desire* plus *danger*. One common fault of talented young writers is to create a main character who is essentially passive. This is understandable; as a writer you are an observer of human nature and activity, and so you identify easily with a character who observes, reflects, and suffers. But such a character's passivity transmits itself to the page, and the story also becomes passive. Charles Baxter laments that "in writing workshops, this kind of story is often the rule rather than the exception." He calls it "the fiction of finger-pointing":

> In such fiction, the plot involves a search for someone or something to blame as a cause of the protagonist's unhappiness. That's the whole story. When blame has been assigned, the story is over.

In such flawed stories, the central character (and by implication, the story's author) seems to take no responsibility for what she or he wants to have happen. This is quite different from Aristotle's rather startling claim that a man *is* his desire, or Robert Olen Butler's definition of fiction as "the art of human yearning."

In order to engage our attention and sympathy, the protagonist of fiction must *want*, and want intensely. The thing that the character wants need not be violent or spectacular; it is the intensity of the wanting that introduces an element of danger. She may want, like the protagonist in David Madden's *The Suicide's Wife*, no more than to get her driver's license, but if so, she must feel that her identity and her future depend on her getting a driver's license, while a corrupt highway patrolman tries to manipulate her. He may want, like Samuel Beckett's Murphy, only to tie himself to his rocking chair and rock, but if so, he will also want a woman who nags him to get up and get a job. She may want, like the heroine of Margaret Atwood's *Bodily Harm*, only to get away from it all for a rest, but if so, she must need rest for her survival, while tourists and terrorists involve her in machinations that begin in discomfort and end in mortal danger.

It's important to realize that the great dangers in life and in literature are not necessarily the most spectacular. Another mistake frequently made by young writers is to think that they can best introduce drama into their stories by way of murderers, chase scenes, crashes, and vampires, the external stock dangers of pulp and TV. In fact, all of us know that the most profound impediments to our desire usually lie close to home, in our own bodies, personalities, friends, lovers, and families. More people will suffer a parent's neglect than a stranger's violence; fewer will die from a gunshot than a heart attack; more passion is destroyed at the breakfast table than in a time warp.

A frequently used critical tool divides possible conflicts into several basic categories: man against man, man against nature, man against society, man against machine, man against God, man against himself. Most stories fall into these categories, and in a literature class they can provide a useful way of discussing and comparing works. But the emphasis on categories can be misleading to new writers, insofar as it suggests that literary conflicts take place in these abstract, cosmic dimensions. A writer needs a specific story to tell, and if you sit down to pit "man" against "nature," you will have less of a story than if you pit seventeen-year-old James Tucker of Weehawken, New Jersey, against a two-and-a-half-foot bigmouth bass in the backwoods of Toomsuba, Mississippi. (The value of specificity is a point to which we return again and again.)

Once conflict is established and developed in a story, the conflict must come to a crisis—the final turning point—and a resolution. Order is a major value that literature offers us, and order implies that the subject has been brought to closure. In life this never quite happens, but whether or not the lives of fictional characters end, the story does, and we are left with a satisfying sense of completion.

What follows are several ways—they are all essentially metaphors—of seeing this pattern of *conflict-crisis-resolution* in order to make the shape and its variations clearer, and particularly to indicate what a crisis action is.

The Arc of the Story

Novelist John L'Heureux says that a story is about a single moment in a character's life that culminates in a defining choice, after which nothing will be the same again. Plotting is a matter of finding the decision points that lead to this final choice and choosing the best scenes through which to dramatize them.

The editor and teacher Mel McKee states flatly that "a story is a war. It is sustained and immediate combat." He offers four imperatives for the writing of this "war" story:

(1) get your fighters fighting, (2) have something—the stake—worth their fighting over, (3) have the fight dive into a series of battles with the last battle in the series the biggest and most dangerous of all, (4) have a walking away from the fight.

The stake over which wars are fought is usually a territory, and it's important that the "territory" in a story be as tangible and specific as the Gaza Strip. As in wars among nations, this territory can represent all sorts of serious abstractions—self-determination, domination, freedom, dignity, identity—but the action consists of soldiers fighting yard by yard over a particular piece of grass or sand.

And just as a minor "police action" may gradually escalate into a holocaust, story form follows its most natural order when each "complication" is bigger than the last. It begins with a ground skirmish, which does not decide the war. Then one side brings in spies, the other, guerrillas; these actions do not decide the war. So one side brings in the air force, and the other answers with antiaircraft. One side launches missiles, which are answered with rockets. One side has poison gas, and the other has a hand on the nuclear button. Metaphorically, this is what happens in a story. As long as one antagonist can recoup enough power to counterattack, the conflict goes on. But, at some point in the story, one of the antagonists will produce a weapon from which the other cannot recover. *The crisis action is the last battle and makes the outcome inevitable;* there can no longer be any doubt who wins the particular territory—though there can be much doubt about moral victory. When this has happened the conflict ends with a significant and permanent *change*—which is the definition, in fiction, of a resolution.

Notice that although a plot involves desire and a corresponding danger, it does not necessarily end happily if the desire is achieved, nor unhappily if it is not. The more morally complex the story, the less straightforward the idea of winning and losing becomes. Hamlet's desire is to kill King Claudius, and for most of the play he is prevented from doing so—by other characters, by intrigues, and by his own mental state. When he finally succeeds, it is at the cost of every significant life in the play, including his own. Although the hero "wins" his particular "territory," the play is a tragedy. In William Carlos Williams's story "The Use of Force," the war is fought over the territory of a little girl's mouth, as the protagonist doctor battles to open it in order to check for diphtheria. The fight begins narrowing to that territory from the first paragraph. He fights with charm, a tongue depressor, a heavy spoon, and finally all his fury to save the "savage brat," ending in success—and personal shame. In Margaret Atwood's novel *Bodily Harm*, on the other hand, the heroine ends up in a political prison. Yet the discovery of her own strength and commitment is such that we know she has achieved salvation. *What does my character win by losing his struggle, or lose by winning?* John L'Heureux suggests the writer ask.

> *When you have a structure, it's so much easier for the imagination to flourish.*
> *—Ann Patchett*

Patterns of Power

In his writing classes, novelist Michael Shaara used to describe a story as a power struggle between equal forces. It is imperative, he argued, that each antagonist have sufficient power that the reader is left in doubt about the outcome. We may be wholly in sympathy with one character and even reasonably confident that she or he will triumph. But the antagonist must represent a real and potent danger, and the pattern of the story's complications will be achieved by *shifting the power back and forth from one antagonist to the other.* Finally, an action will occur that will shift the power irreversibly in one direction.

"Power" takes many forms—physical strength, charm, knowledge, moral power, wealth, ownership, rank, and so on. Most obvious is the power of brute force, as wielded by a dictator or a gang. Moral complication arises from the fact that nobody considers him/herself unjustified. Here is the mobster Max Blue in Leslie Marmon Silko's novel *Almanac of the Dead*:

Max thinks of himself as an executive producer of one-night-only performances, dramas played out in the warm California night breezes, in a phone booth in downtown Long Beach. All Max had done was dial a phone number and listen while the pigeon repeats, "Hello? Hello? Hello? Hello?" until .22-pistol shots snap *pop!pop!* and Max hangs up.

Remember that "power" takes many forms, some of which have the external appearance of weakness. Anyone who has ever been tied to the demands of an invalid can understand this: sickness can be great strength. Weakness, need, passivity, an ostensible desire not to be any trouble to anybody—all these can be used as manipulative tools to prevent the protagonist from achieving his or her desire. Martyrdom is immensely powerful, whether we sympathize with it or not; a dying man absorbs all our energies.

The power of weakness has generated the central conflict in many stories and in such plays as *Uncle Vanya* and *The Glass Menagerie*. Here is a passage in which it is swiftly and deftly sketched:

> This sepulchral atmosphere owed a lot to the presence of Mrs. Taylor herself. She was a tall, stooped woman with deep-set eyes. She sat in her living room all day long and chain-smoked cigarettes and stared out the picture window with an air of unutterable sadness, as if she knew things beyond mortal bearing. Sometimes she would call Taylor over and wrap her long arms around him, then close her eyes and hoarsely whisper, "Terence! Terence!" Eyes still closed, she would turn her head and resolutely push him away.
> —Tobias Wolff, *This Boy's Life*

Connection and Disconnection

Some students, as well as critics, object to the description of narrative as a war or power struggle. Seeing the world in terms of conflict and crisis, enemies and warring factions, not only constricts the possibilities of literature, they argue, but also promulgates an aggressive and antagonistic view of our own lives.

Speaking of the "gladiatorial view of fiction," Ursula Le Guin writes:

People are cross-grained, aggressive, and full of trouble, the storytellers tell us; people fight themselves and one another, and their stories are full of their struggles. But to say that that is the story is to use one aspect of existence, conflict, to include and submerge other aspects, which it does not include and does not comprehend.

Romeo and Juliet is a story of the conflict between two families, and its plot involves the conflict of two individuals within those families. Is that all it involves? Isn't *Romeo and Juliet* about something else, and isn't it the something else that makes the otherwise trivial tale of a feud into a tragedy?

I'm indebted to dramatist Claudia Johnson for this further—and, it seems to me, crucial—insight about that "something else": whereas the dynamic of the power struggle has long been acknowledged, narrative is also driven by a pattern of connection and disconnection between characters that is the main source of its emotional effect. Over the course of a story, and within the smaller scale of a scene, characters make and break emotional bonds of trust, love, understanding, or compassion with one another. A connection may be as obvious as a kiss or as subtle as a glimpse; a connection may be broken with an action as obvious as a slap or as subtle as an arched eyebrow.

In *Romeo and Juliet*, for example, the Montague and Capulet families are fiercely disconnected, but in spite of that the young lovers manage to connect. Throughout the play they meet and part, disconnect from their families in order to connect with each other, finally parting from life in order to be with each other eternally. Their ultimate departure in death reconnects the feuding families.

Johnson puts it this way:

Underlying any good story, fictitious or true—is a deeper pattern of change, a pattern of connection and disconnection. The conflict and the surface events are like waves, but underneath is an emotional tide, the ebb and flow of human connection.

While the pattern of either conflict or connection may dominate in a given work, a story which is only about the conflict will be shallow. There must be some deepening of our understanding of the characters, which is achieved not just through conflicts between good and bad, but through conflicts of one good versus another: does a man join up to serve his country, or stay home to help protect and raise his children? The writer strives to bring art to a level where a story is not just about the inevitable trouble, and not just about the conflict of good and bad, but also about the conflict of loyalty with loyalty, honesty with honesty, love with love.

You only see *the structure in a badly structured story, and call it formula.*
—Stephen Fischer

Human wills clash; human belonging is necessary. In discussing human behavior, psychologists speak in terms of "tower" and "network" patterns, the need to climb (which implies conflict) and the need for community, the need to win out over others and the need to belong to others—and these two forces also drive fiction. Like conflict and its complications, connection and its complications can produce a pattern of change, and both inform the process of change recorded in scene and story.

Story Form as a Check Mark

The nineteenth-century German critic Gustav Freytag analyzed plot in terms of a pyramid of five actions: an exposition, followed by a complication (or *nouement*, "knotting up," of the situation), leading to a crisis, which is followed by a "falling action" or anticlimax, resulting in a resolution (or *dénouement*, "unknotting").

In the compact short story form, the falling action is likely to be brief or nonexistent, and often the crisis action itself implies the resolution, which is not necessarily stated but exists as an idea established in the reader's mind.

So for our purposes it is probably more useful to think of story shape not as a pyramid with sides of equal length but as an inverted check mark. If we take the familiar tale of Cinderella and diagram its power

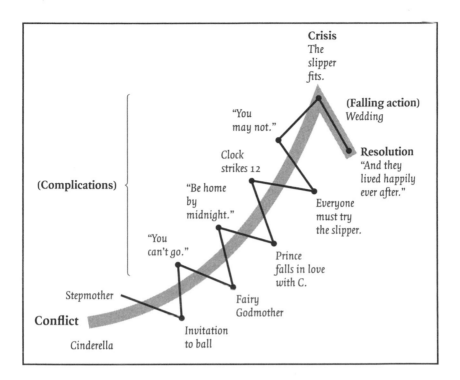

struggle using this model, we can see how the various elements reveal themselves even in this simple children's story.

At the opening of the tale we're given the basic conflict: Cinderella's mother has died, and her father has married a brutal woman with two waspish daughters. Cinderella is made to do all the dirtiest and most menial work, and she weeps among the cinders. The Stepmother has on her side the strength of ugliness and evil (two very powerful qualities, in literature as in life). With her daughters she also has the strength of numbers, and she has parental authority. Cinderella has only beauty and goodness, but (in literature and life) these are also very powerful.

At the beginning of the struggle, the power is clearly on the Step-mother's side. But the first event (action, battle) of the story is that an invitation arrives from the Prince, which explicitly states that all the ladies of the land are invited to a ball. Cinderella's desire, we should note, is not to triumph over her Stepmother (though she eventually will, much to our satisfaction); such a desire would diminish her goodness. She simply wants to be relieved of her mistreatment. She wants equality, and the Prince's invitation, which specifically gives her a right equal to the Stepmother's and Stepdaughters' rights, shifts the power to her.

The Stepmother takes the power back by blunt force: you may not go; you must get us ready to go. Cinderella does so, and the three leave for the ball.

Then what happens? The Fairy Godmother appears. It is *very* powerful to have magic on your side. The Fairy Godmother offers Cinderella a gown, glass slippers, and a coach with horses and footmen, giving her more force than she has yet had.

But the magic is not all-potent. It has a qualification that portends bad luck. It will last only until midnight (unlike the Stepmother's authority), so Cinderella must leave the ball before the clock strikes twelve or risk exposure and defeat.

What happens next? She goes to the ball and the Prince falls in love with her—and love is an even more powerful weapon than magic in a literary war. In some versions of the tale, the Stepmother and Stepsisters marvel at the beauty of a Princess they don't recognize, pointing to the irony of Cinderella's new power.

And then? The magic quits. The clock strikes twelve, and Cinderella runs down the steps in her rags to her rats and pumpkin, losing a slipper, bereft of her power in every way.

And after that? The Prince sends out a messenger with the glass slipper and a dictum that every female in the land is to try on the slipper—a dramatic repetition of the invitation to the ball. Cinderella is again given her rights by royal decree.

What happens then? In most good retellings, the Stepmother also repeats her assumption of brute authority by hiding Cinderella away, while our expectation of triumph is tantalizingly delayed with grotesque comedy: one sister cuts off a toe, the other a heel, trying to fit into the heroine's slipper.

After that, Cinderella tries on the slipper and it fits. *This is the crisis action.* Magic, love, and royalty join to recognize the heroine's true self;

evil, numbers, and authority are powerless against them. At this point, the power struggle has been decided; the outcome is inevitable. When the slipper fits, no further action can occur that will deprive Cinderella of her desire. Nothing will be the same again: the change in the lives of all concerned is significant and permanent.

The tale has a brief "falling action" or "walking away from the fight": the Prince sweeps Cinderella up on his white horse and gallops away to their wedding. The story comes to closure with the classic resolution of all comedy: they lived happily ever after.

Every dramatic story is a quest of some kind. No matter how complex the quest may be, it traditionally boils down to one character trying to achieve one overriding, all-important goal. . . . The quest succeeds or fails as a result of everything that happened along the way.
—Will Dunne

If we also look at "Cinderella" in terms of connection/disconnection, we see a pattern as clear as that represented by the power struggle. The first painful disconnection is that Cinderella's mother has died; her father has married (connected with) a woman who spurns (disconnects from) her; the Prince's invitation offers connection; the Stepmother's cruelty alienates again. The Fairy Godmother connects as a magical friend, but the disappearance of the coach and gown disconnect Cinderella temporarily from that grand and glorious fairy-tale union, marriage to the Prince. If we consult the emotions that this tale engenders—pity, anger, hope, fear, romance, anticipation, disappointment, triumph—we see that both the struggle between antagonist/protagonist and the pattern of alienation/connectedness is necessary to ensure, not only that there is an action, but also that we care about its outcome. The traditional happy ending is the grand connection, marriage; the traditional tragic outcome is the final disconnection, death.

Cinderella, and all fairy tales, typically begin with "telling," straightforwardly setting up the situation. But a skilled writer can imply a complex of relationships involving a complex of connections and disconnections in a few sentences. Here, in Peggy Shinner's "Tax Time," relationships between narrator, father, stepmother, and mother reminiscent of

Cinderella are sketched through the visual device of a tax accountant's fingernails:

> I notice Steve's fingers. They're wound around the pencil as he scribbles some figure from the computer. They're short and stubby, like my father's, and impeccably groomed. Does he get his nails done? Is that a vanity he allows himself? My father had a manicure once when he was seeing Rose, and at the time I saw it as jumping ship. He was, by slapping on some nail polish, trying to abandon his class for Rose's—Rose, a woman who subscribed to the symphony, and tried to break his use of double negatives. He was also dandying himself up, something I wondered if he'd ever done for my mother when she was alive.

In the *Poetics*, the first extant work of Western literary criticism, Aristotle referred to the crisis action of a tragedy as a *peripeteia*, or reversal of the protagonist's fortunes. Critics and editors agree that a reversal of some sort is necessary to all story structure, comic as well as tragic. Although the protagonist need not lose power, land, or life, he or she must in some significant way be changed or moved by the action. Aristotle specified that this reversal came about because of *hamartia*, which has for centuries been translated as a "tragic flaw" in the protagonist's character, usually assumed to be, or defined as, pride. But more recent critics have defined and translated *hamartia* much more narrowly as a "mistake in identity" with the reversal coming about in a "recognition."

It is true that recognition scenes have played a disproportionately large role in the crisis actions of plots both comic and tragic, and that these scenes frequently stretch credibility. In real life, you are unlikely to mistake the face of your mother, son, uncle, or even friend, and yet such mistakes have provided the turning point of many traditional plots. If, however, the notion of "recognition" is extended to more abstract and subtle realms, it becomes a powerful metaphor for moments of "realization." In other words, the "recognition scene" in literature may stand for that moment in life when we "recognize" that the man we have considered good is evil, the event we have considered insignificant is crucial, the woman we have thought out of touch with reality is a genius, the object we have thought desirable is poison. There is in this symbolic way a recognition in "Cinderella." We knew that she was essentially a princess, but until the Prince recognizes her as one, our knowledge must be frustrated.

James Joyce developed a similar idea when he spoke of, and recorded both in his notebooks and in his stories, moments of what he called *epiphany*. As Joyce saw it, epiphany is a crisis action in the mind, a moment when a person, an event, or a thing is seen in a light so new that it is as if it has never been seen before. At this recognition, the mental landscape of the viewer is permanently changed.

In many of the finest modern short stories and novels, the true territory of struggle is the main character's mind, and so the real crisis action must occur there. Yet it is important to grasp that Joyce chose the word *epiphany* to represent this moment of reversal, and that the word means "a *manifestation* of a supernatural being"—specifically, in Christian doctrine, the manifestation of Christ to the gentiles. By extension, then, in a short story any mental reversal that takes place in the crisis of a story must be *manifested*; it must be triggered or shown by an action. The slipper must fit. It would not do if the Stepmother just happened to change her mind and give up the struggle; it would not do if the Prince just happened to notice that Cinderella looked like his love. The moment of recognition must be manifested in an action.

This point, that the crisis must be manifested or externalized in an action, is absolutely central, although sometimes difficult to grasp when the struggle of the story takes place in a character's mind. In Tim O'Brien's story "The Things They Carried," for example, a young lieutenant's desperate determination to change himself into a hardened leader is manifested in the action of burning photographs, letters from the girl he loved, and finally a village.

In a revenge story, it is easy to see how the conflict must come to crisis. The common revenge plot, from *Hamlet* to *Black Panther*, takes this form: someone important to a major character (self, father, sister, lover, friend) is killed, and for some reason the authorities who ought to administer justice can't or won't avenge the death. The hero or his antagonist must do so, then, and the crisis action is manifested in the flight of the arrow, the blast of the gun, the swallowing of the poison, whatever.

But suppose the story is about a struggle between two brothers on a fishing trip, and the change that takes place is that the protagonist, believing for most of the action that he holds his older brother in contempt, discovers at the end of the story that they are deeply bound by love and family history. Clearly this change is an epiphany, a mental reversal. A writer insufficiently aware of the nature of crisis action might signal the change in a paragraph that begins "Suddenly Larry remembered their father and realized that Jeff was very much like him." Well, unless that memory and that realization are manifested in an action, the reader is unable to share them, and therefore cannot be moved with the character.

> *Conflict is no more monolithic than love is. . . . The variations are infinite; the point is that they may both be gentle, intelligent people, without easy access to automatic weapons, but between desire and fulfillment of that desire springs conflict.*
> *—Cary Groner*

> Jeff reached for the old net and neatly bagged the trout, swinging round to offer it with a triumphant, "Got it! We got it, didn't we?" The trout flipped and struggled, giving off a smell of weed and water and fecund mud. Jeff's knuckles were lined with grime. The knuckles and the rich river smell filled him with a memory of their first fishing trip together, the sight of their father's hands on the same scarred net.

Here the epiphany, a memory leading to a realization, is triggered by an action and sensory details that the reader can share; the reader now has a good chance of also being able to share the epiphany.

Yet much great fiction, and the preponderance of serious modern fiction, echoes life in its suggestion that there are no clear or permanent solutions, that the conflicts of character, relationship, and the cosmos cannot be permanently resolved. Most such stories end, in Vladimir

Nabokov's words, "with no definite full-stop, but with the natural motion of life." None could end "they lived happily ever after" or even "they lived unhappily ever after."

Yet the story form demands a resolution. Is there such a thing as a no-resolution resolution? Yes, and it has a very specific form. Go back to the metaphor "a story is a war." After the skirmish, after the guerrillas, after the air strike, after the poison gas and the nuclear holocaust, imagine that the two surviving combatants, one on each side, emerge from their fallout shelters. They crawl, then stumble to the fence that marks the border. Each possessively grasps the barbed wire with a bloodied fist. The "resolution" of this battle is that neither side will ever give up and no one will ever win; *there will never be a resolution.* This is a distinct reversal (the recognition takes place in the reader's mind) of the opening scene, in which it seemed eminently worthwhile to open a ground skirmish. In the statement of the conflict was an inherent possibility that one side or the other could win. Inherent in the resolution is a statement that no one can ever win. That is a distinct reversal and a powerful change.

This kind of story may offer readers an epiphany that the main character neglects to see. Such characters are often on the verge of change, yet lack the maturity or courage to take that difficult leap to recognition. In "Pharmacy," the opening story of Elizabeth Strout's collection *Olive Kitteridge*, for example, the protagonist is as nice a fellow as you could hope to meet: cordial, calm, self-effacing, happy in his job as a pharmacist, yet incapable of self-examination or self-knowledge. A neglectful husband and father, he is bewildered by his wife's outbursts and his son's sullenness; and, incapable of recognizing his own sexual impulses, he ends the story as it began, suggesting that he and his wife invite over a couple, of whom he is attracted to the woman. His wife will cook for them, of course. This unstated knowledge on the reader's part, together with the closing dialogue—"We need to have them over soon"—clicks home the point that he cannot and will never change.

It can be, and has been, argued that in times of social suffering or cultural despair, the no-resolution resolution is the go-to form of the literary story, and especially of the short story.

....

STORY AND PLOT

So far, I have used the words "story" and "plot" interchangeably. The equation of the two terms is so common that they are often comfortably understood as synonyms. When an editor says, "This is not a story," the implication is not that it lacks characters, theme, setting, or even incident, but that it has no plot.

Yet there is a distinction between the two terms, a distinction that, although simple in itself, gives rise to manifold subtleties in the craft of narrative and that also represents a vital decision you as a writer must make: Where should your narrative begin?

The simple distinction: A *story* is a series of events recorded in their chronological order. A *plot* is a series of events deliberately arranged so as to reveal their dramatic, thematic, and emotional significance. A story gives us only "what happened next," whereas plot's concern is what, how, and why, with scenes ordered to highlight the workings of cause and effect.

Here, for example, is a fairly standard story: A sober, industrious, and rather dull young man meets the woman of his dreams. She is beautiful, brilliant, passionate, and compassionate; more wonderful still, she loves him. They plan to marry, and on the eve of their wedding his friends give him a stag party, in the course of which they tease him, ply him with liquor, and drag him off to a whorehouse for a last fling. There he stumbles into a cubicle . . . to find himself facing his bride-to-be.

Where does this story become interesting? Where does the plot begin?

You may start, if you like, with the young man's *Mayflower* ancestry. But if you do, we'll struggle to figure out what the story is about, and we're likely to close the book about the middle of the nineteenth century. You may begin with the first time he meets the extraordinary woman, but even then you must cover at least weeks, probably months, in a few pages; and that means you must summarize, skip, and generalize, and you'll have a hard time both maintaining your credibility and holding our attention. Begin at the stag party? Better. If you do so, you will somehow have to let us know all that has gone before, either through dialogue or through the young man's memory, but you have only one evening of action to cover, and we'll get to the conflict quickly. Suppose you begin instead the next morning, when the man awakes with a hangover, in bed in a brothel with his bride on his wedding day. Is that, perhaps, the best of all? An immediate conflict that must lead to a quick and striking crisis?

E. M. Forster distinguishes between plot and story by describing story as

> the chopped-off length of the tapeworm of time . . . a narrative of events arranged in their time sequence. A plot is also a narrative of events, the emphasis falling on causality. "The king died, and then the queen died," is a story. "The king died, and then the queen died of grief," is a plot. The time-sequence is preserved, but the sense of causality overshadows it. Or again: "The queen died, no one knew why, until it was discovered that it was through grief at the death of the king." This is a plot with a mystery in it, a form capable of high development. It suspends the time sequence, it moves as far away from the story as its limitations will allow. Consider the death of the queen. If it is in a story we say, "and then?" If it is in a plot we ask, "why?"

The human desire to know *why* is as powerful as the desire to know what happened next, and it is a desire of a higher order. Once we have the facts, we inevitably look for the links between them, and only when we find such links are we satisfied that we "understand." Rote memorization in a science class bores almost everyone. Grasp and a sense of discovery begin only when we perceive *why* "a body in motion tends to remain in motion" and what an immense effect this actuality has on the phenomena of our lives.

The same is true of the events of a story. Random incidents neither move nor illuminate; we want to know why one thing leads to another and to feel the inevitability of cause and effect, even if one of the causes is chance.

Here is a series of uninteresting events chronologically arranged.

Ariadne had a bad dream.
She woke up tired and cross.

She ate breakfast
She headed for class.
She saw Leroy.
She fell on the steps and broke her ankle.
Leroy offered to take notes for her.
She went to a hospital.

This series of events does not constitute a plot, and if you wish to fashion it into a plot, you can do so only by letting us know the meaningful relations among the events. We first assume that Ariadne woke in a temper because of her bad dream, and that Leroy offered to take notes for her because she'd broken her ankle. But why did she fall? Perhaps because she saw Leroy? Does that suggest that her bad dream was about him? Was she, then, thinking about his dream-rejection as she broke her egg irritably on the edge of the frying pan? What is the effect of his offer? Is it a triumph or just another polite form of rejection when, really, he could have missed class once to drive her to the x-ray lab? The emotional and dramatic significance of these ordinary events emerges in the relation of cause to effect, and where such relation can be shown, a possible plot comes into existence. Notice also that in this brief attempt to form the events into a plot, I have introduced both conflict and a pattern of connection/disconnection.

Ariadne's is a story you might very well choose to tell chronologically: it needs to cover only an hour or two, and that much can be handled in the compressed form of the short story. But such a choice of plot is not inevitable even in this short compass. Might it be more gripping to begin with the wince of pain as she stumbles? Leroy comes to help her up and the yolk yellow of his T-shirt fills her field of vision. In the shock of pain she is immediately back in her dream . . .

When "nothing happens" in a story, it is because we fail to sense the causal relation between what happens first and what happens next. When something does "happen," it is because the resolution of a short story or a novel describes a change in the character's life, an effect of the events that have gone before. This is why Aristotle insisted with such apparent simplicity on "a beginning, a middle, and an end."

A story is capable of many meanings, and it is first of all in the choice of structure—which portion of the story forms the plot—that you offer us the gratifying sense that we "understand."

....

THE SHORT STORY AND THE NOVEL

Many editors and writers insist that the short story and the novel are vastly different creatures. It is my belief, however, that, like the distinction between story and plot, the distinction between the two forms is very simple, and that many and profound possibilities of difference proceed from that simple source: a short story is short, and a novel is long.

Because of this, a short story can waste no words. It usually features the perspective of one or a very few characters. It may recount only one central action and one major change in the life of the central character or characters. It can afford no digression that does not directly affect the action. A short story strives to create what Edgar Allan Poe called "the single effect"—a single emotional impact that imparts a flash of understanding, though both impact and understanding may be complex. The virtue of a short story is its density, for it raises a single "what if" question, while a novel may raise many. If it is tight, sharp, economic, well-knit, and charged, then it is a good short story because it has exploited a central attribute of the form—that it is short.

All of these qualities remain praiseworthy in a novel, but a novel may also be comprehensive, vast, and panoramic. It may have power not because of its economy but because of its scope, breadth, and sweep—the virtues of a medium that is long. A novel may range through many consciousnesses, cover many years or generations, and travel the world. It may deal with a central line of action and one or several subplots. Many characters may change, many and various effects may constitute our final understanding. Many digressions may be tolerated and will not destroy the balance of the whole as long as they lead finally to some nuance of that understanding.

Occasionally in workshops, a new writer struggling to craft the shape of conflict-crisis-resolution may wonder if a story's lack of one of these elements means the work "must be a novel." Tempting as this hope may

145

be, it usually only sidesteps the inevitable challenge of plotting, for not only must a novel have a large-scale plot structure, but individual chapters or episodes frequently are shaped around a pattern of conflict-crisis-incremental change that impels the novel onward.

Further, while no literary form is superior to another, few novelists achieve publication without first having crafted any number of short stories. The greater the limitation of space, the greater the necessity for pace, sharpness, and density. Short stories ask the writer to rise to the challenges of shaping, "showing," and making significance again and again, experiences that may save that writer countless hours and pages when the time to tackle a novel comes along.

The form of the novel is an expanded story form. It asks for a conflict, a crisis, and a resolution, and no technique described in this book is irrelevant to its effectiveness.

Nor is the short story to be considered slight in a culture as rushed and at the same time sophisticated as our own. The twenty-first-century attention span may be curtailed, but it is trained in implication and inference. There is a consequent resurgence of interest in the short story form that is manifest in podcasts, blogs, and online magazines, and also in adaptations of fiction, both short and episodic, for the small screen. Live storytelling has found

You are going to love some of your characters, because they are you or some facet of you, and you are going to hate some of your characters for the same reason. But no matter what, you are probably going to have to let bad things happen to some of the characters you love or you won't have much of a story.
—Anne Lamott

new blood and regular attendees on campuses and among the theaters of the larger cities. As early as the "radios" of Jerome Stern and others in the 1970s and '80s, radio broadcasting began reopening to the form and now finds a full audience in such productions as This American Life. There may be a feedback loop from writing programs to publishing to writers, such that more story collections are published than heretofore and the "novel in stories" has become an admired framework. There are also increasing numbers of writers, like Raymond Carver and Alice Munro before them, who find the short story most in tune with their gifts and do not find it necessary to move to the longer form.

....

TYPES OF FICTION

While it's true that all stories need characters, a plot, a setting, and a particular point of view, it's also true that different types of fiction emphasize some of these elements more than others—and conceive of them in their own particular ways.

Readers of *genre fiction* have very specific expectations when it comes to plot, characters, setting, and theme, and each genre has its own conventions and rules. *Literary fiction* differs from genre fiction fundamentally in the fact that the former is character-driven, the latter plot-driven. There is a strong tendency in genre fiction—though not a binding rule—to imply that life is fair and to let the hero or heroine, after great struggle, win out in the end; and a complementary tendency in literary fiction to posit that life is not fair, that triumph is partial and happiness tentative, that human existence is full of ambiguities, and that the hero and heroine are subject to mortality. Literary fiction also strives to reveal its meaning through the creation of unexpected or unusual characters, through patterns of action and turns of event that will surprise the reader, and through illuminating use of language.

Readers of the *romance* genre, which has its roots in the fiction of the Bronte sisters, will expect a plucky-but-down-on-her-luck heroine, a handsome and mysterious hero with some dark secret (usually a woman) in his background, a large house, a woods (through which the heroine will at some point flee in scanty clothing), and an eventual happy ending with the heroine in the hero's arms.

Other genres have likewise developed from kinds of fiction that were once mainstream and represented major social problems or concerns. Early romance dealt with the serious question of how a woman was to satisfy the need for both stability and love in married life, how to be both independent and secure in a society with rigid sexual rules. The *detective* story evolved alongside widespread and intense interest in science, and an optimistic expectation that violence and mystery could be

147

rationally explained. The *western* dealt with the ambivalence large numbers of westward-traveling Euro-Americans felt about the civilizing of the wilderness, the desire to rid the west of its brutality, and the fear that "taming" it would also destroy its promise of solitude.

Science fiction, the most recently developed and still developing genre, similarly deals with ambivalence about technology, the near-miraculous accomplishments of the human race through science, and the dangers to human feeling, soul, and environment. The surge in popularity of *fantasy fiction* can probably be attributed to nostalgia for a time unfettered by technological accomplishment and threat, since much fantasy employs a medieval setting and solves problems through magic, whereas science fiction is generally set in the future and solves problems through intelligence and technology. It is relevant that science fiction usually deals with some problem that can be seen to have a counterpart in contemporary culture (space travel, interplanetary intrigue, artificial intelligence, mechanical replacement of body parts, genetic manipulation), whereas the plots of fantasies tend to deal with obsolete or archaic traumas (wicked overlords, demon interlopers, and so forth).

Similarly, the renewed popularity of the *vampire* genre probably reflects a concern with bullying and the rejection of the Other, and of horror with either those problems or, in the case of the "walking dead," with the possibility of human annihilation.

In any case, the many other genres, including but not confined to *adventure, spy,* and *thriller,* each have their own set of conventions regarding character, language, and events. Note again that the very naming of these kinds of fiction implies a narrowing, and an appeal to a particular range of interest.

Young adult, or YA fiction, and its *middle-grade* subset, are not really genres but a marketing tool of publishers capitalizing on the success of series like Cressida Cowell's *How to Train Your Dragon* and J. K. Rowling's *Harry Potter*—and hoping to foster the reading habit in technologically inclined generations. YA books have always been written but not called that: *Huckleberry Finn* by Mark Twain, *Alice in Wonderland* by Lewis Carroll, *A Wrinkle in Time* by Madeleine L'Engle, *The Chronicles of Narnia* by C. S. Lewis, to name but a few classics.

Many teachers of fiction writing do not accept manuscripts in genre, believing that, whereas writing literary fiction can teach you how to write good genre fiction, writing genre fiction does not teach you how to write good literary fiction—does not, in effect, teach you "how to write," by which I mean how to be original and meaningful in words.

Others take a different stance, telling students who want to write stories containing vampires or Vulcans to go ahead, bearing in mind that they are not immune from reader expectations about what makes a good story—character development, credible plot, vivid setting and details, nuanced theme, and so forth.

Realism—the attempt to render an authentic picture of life, in such a way that the reader identifies with one or more characters—is a fair starting point for the pursuit of literary fiction. The writer's attempt at verisimilitude is comparable to the scientific method of observation and verification. Realism is also a convention, and not the only way to begin to write, but like the drawing of still life in the study of painting, it can impart skills that will be useful in more sophisticated efforts whether they are realistic or not.

In any case, the tendency of recent literature is to move away from rigid categories, toward a loosening or crossing of story types—so-called genre-busting or genre-bending, in which genre fiction presses at the bounds of literary fiction. Many writers are eager to experiment with pieces that blur the distinctions, approaching genre fiction with literary ambition and intent. There are literary spy novels from John Le Carré and literary fairy tales from Angela Carter and Robert Coover. There is literary science fiction from Philip K. Dick, Ursula K. Le Guin, Doris Lessing, Margaret Atwood, Lauren Beukes, James Smythe, and Aliette de Bodard. Dan Chaon writes literary horror stories; Kate Atkinson and Michael Chabon, detective fiction (Chabon even a Sherlock Holmes novel); Justin Cronin, vampire stories. It's worth taking a look, as an example of such genre-bending, at Tobias Wolff's "Bullet in the Brain," which adopts the setup of a bank heist tale and then bends it into a story about loss and language. There are also myriad examples of *hybrid fiction*, where fiction incorporates other media or genres—photography, poetry, drama, memoir. Adam Thorpe's novel *Ulverton* ends in a screen play. Jennifer Egan's novel *A Visit from the Goon Squad* contains a chapter in Power Point. *Hypertext fiction* is a genre of literary fiction that is interactive and nonlinear.

Magic realism uses the techniques and devices of realism—verisimilitude, ordinary lives and settings, familiar psychology—and introduces events of an impossible or fantastic nature, never leaving the tone and techniques of realism. Whereas fantasy attempts to bedazzle its readers with the amazing quality of the magic, magic realism works in the opposite direction, to convince the reader that the extraordinary occurs in the context and the guise of the ordinary. Gabriel García Márquez is considered the master of magic realism and his *100 Years of Solitude* its apotheosis. In Donald Barthelme's novel *The Dead Father*, children travel with the literal burden of the not-dead-enough dead father. Karen Russell's *St. Lucy's Home for Girls Raised by Wolves* matter-of-factly brings these wolf-parented girls to a boarding school. In Brenna Gomez's "Corzo," a seventh-grade girl calmly though bloodily reaches in and removes her father's heart.

Experimental fiction is difficult to define, because by definition the experimental is the thing that nobody expects or predicts. There are, however, a number of kinds of experiment that have come to be recognized as subsets of literary fiction. *Metafiction*, for example, takes as its subject matter the writing of fiction, calls attention to its own techniques, and insists that what is happening is that a story is being written and read. Often, the writing of the story is taken as a metaphor for some other human struggle or endeavor, as in the stories of John Barth.

Minimalism (also called *miniaturism*) refers to a flat, spare, and subdued style of writing, characterized by an accumulation of (sometimes apparently random) detail that gives an impression of benumbed emotion. The point of view tends to be objective or near-objective, the events reported without interpretation and accumulating toward a tense, disturbing—and inconclusive—conclusion. Raymond Carver is the primary example of a minimalist writer.

The *short-short story* is a story under 2,000 words. *Microfiction* and *flash fiction* are terms used for stories under 250 words. Such pieces, according to Nancy Huddleston Packer, "push to the limits the basic elements of all short stories—compression, suggestion, and change . . . these stories are so compressed, they explode." Microfiction is also sometimes called hybrid fiction because it is often difficult to tell, in this short compass, the distinction between a story and a poem. Many hundreds of authors write in this form; Lydia Davis is among the best known.

....

SUGGESTED STORIES
"Happy Endings"
   Margaret Atwood
"Silver Water"
   Amy Bloom
"We Didn't"
   Stuart Dybek
"Corzo"
   Brenna Gomez
"How Far She Went"
   Mary Hood
"Everything That Rises Must Converge"
   Flannery O'Connor
"Binocular Vision"
   Edith Pearlman
"The Second Tree from the Corner"
   E. B. White
"The Use of Force"
   William Carlos Williams
"Bullet in the Brain"
   Tobias Wolff

WRITING PROMPTS
1. Write a scene placing two characters in this fundamental conflict: one wants something that the other does not want to give. Let the conflict escalate. Who uses what tactics to get her/his way? Who wins?
2. A slightly more complicated variation on the same theme: one has half of something that is no good without the other half; each wants the other's half. Do they connect or disconnect?

3. Write a scene between two characters in conflict over a trivial object or issue. Let us know that the real tension is about something more significant (e.g., not control of the remote, but about control and being remote).

4. Place a character in conflict with some aspect of nature; it may be as small as a mosquito or as big as an avalanche. Balance the forces so that the reader doesn't know who will "win" until the crisis action.

5. Write a story, no longer than three pages, in which the protagonist does *not* get what she or he wants, but which nevertheless ends happily.

6. Pick a scene or setup of genre fiction (fantasy kingdom, western bar, discovery of the body, or other familiar story form) and write a scene in which the real action is in the character's mind.

7. Write a short story on a postcard. Send it. Notice that if you're going to manage a conflict, crisis, and resolution in this microfiction space, you'll have to introduce conflict immediately.

7: Call Me Ishmael

POINT OF VIEW

Point of view is the most complex element of fiction. We can label and analyze it in a number of different ways, but however we describe it, point of view ultimately concerns the relationship among writer, characters, and reader.

The first thing to do is to set aside the common use of the phrase "point of view" as synonymous with "opinion," as in *It's my point of view that they all ought to be shot.* Begin instead with the more literal synonym "vantage point." *Who* is standing *where* to watch the scene?

Since we are dealing with words on a page, these questions might be better translated as: *Who speaks? To whom? In what form? At what distance from the action?*

....

WHO SPEAKS?
The primary point-of-view decision, which you as author must make before you can set down the first sentence of the story, is *person*. This is

the simplest and crudest subdivision that must be made in deciding who speaks. The story can be told

in the third person (she walked out into the harsh sunlight),
in the second person (you walked out into the harsh sunlight), or
in the first person (I walked out into the harsh sunlight).

From the reader's perspective, third- and second-person stories are told by an author, first-person stories by the character acting as "I."

Third Person
Third person, in which the author is telling the story, can be subdivided again according to the degree of knowledge the author assumes.

Omniscience
The *omniscient author* has total knowledge and tells us directly what we are supposed to think. As omniscient author you are God. You can

1. objectively report the action of the story;
2. go into the mind of any character;
3. interpret for us that character's appearance, speech, actions, and thoughts, even if the character cannot do so;
4. move freely in time or space to give us a panoramic, telescopic, microscopic, or historical view, telling us what has happened elsewhere or in the past or what will happen in the future; and
5. provide general reflections, judgments, and truths.

In all of these aspects, we will accept what the omniscient author tells us. If you tell us that Ruth is a good woman, that Jeremy doesn't really understand his own motives, that the moon is going to explode in four hours, and that everybody will be better off for it, we will believe you. Here is a paragraph that blatantly exhibits all five of these areas of knowledge:

(1) Joe glared at the screaming baby. (2) Frightened by his scowl, the baby gulped and screamed louder. I hate that thing, Joe thought. (3) But it was not really hatred that he felt. (4) Only two years ago he himself had screamed like that. (5) Children can't tell hatred from fear.

This illustration is awkwardly compressed, but authors well in control of their craft can move easily from one area of knowledge to another. In the first scene of *War and Peace*, Tolstoy describes Anna Scherer:

> To be an enthusiast had become her social vocation, and sometimes even when she did not feel like it, she became enthusiastic in order not to disappoint the expectations of those who knew her. The subdued smile which, though it did not suit her faded features, always played around her lips, expressed as in a spoiled child, a continual consciousness of her charming defect, which she neither wished, nor could, nor considered it necessary to correct.

In two sentences Tolstoy tells us what is in Anna's mind, what her acquaintances expect of her, what she looks like, what suits her, and what she can and cannot do; and he offers a general reflection on spoiled children.

The omniscient voice is the voice of the classical epic ("And Meleager, far-off, knew nothing of this, but felt his vitals burning with fever"), of the Bible ("So the Lord sent a pestilence upon Israel; and there fell seventy thousand men"), and of most nineteenth-century novels ("Tito put out his hand to help him, and so strangely quick are men's souls that in this moment, when he began to feel that his atonement was accepted, he had a darting thought of the irksome efforts it entailed"). But it is one of the manifestations of modern literature's movement downward in class from heroic to common characters, and from external action to psychological action, that authors of realistic fiction have largely avoided the godlike stance of the omniscient author and restricted themselves to fewer areas of knowledge.

Limited Omniscience

The *limited omniscient* viewpoint is one in which the author may move with some, but not all, of the omniscient author's freedom. The most commonly used form of the limited omniscient point of view is one in which the author can see events objectively and also has access to the mind of one character, but *not* to the minds of the others, nor to any explicit powers of judgment. Limited omniscience is particularly useful for the short story because it very quickly establishes the point-of-view character or *means of perception*. The short story is so compressed a form that there is rarely time or space to develop more than one consciousness. Staying with external observation and one character's thoughts helps control the focus and avoid awkward point-of-view shifts. A further advantage of limited omniscience is that it mimics our individual experience of life, that is, our own inability to penetrate the minds and motivations of others, which can lead to the kinds of conflicts or struggles for connection that inspire much fiction.

Limited omniscience is also frequently used for the novel, as in Gail Godwin's *The Odd Woman*.

> It was ten o'clock on the evening of the same day, and the permanent residents of the household on the mountain were restored to routines and sobriety. Jane, on the other hand, sat by herself in the kitchen, a glass of Scotch before her on the cleanly wiped table, going deeper and deeper into a mood she could recognize only as unfamiliar. She could not describe it; it was both frightening and satisfying. It was like letting go and being taken somewhere. She tried to trace it back. When, exactly, had it started?

It is clear here that the author has limited her omniscience. She is not going to tell us the ultimate truth about Jane's soul, nor is she going to define for us the unfamiliar mood that the character herself cannot define. The author has the facts at her disposal, and she has Jane's thoughts, and that is all.

The advantage of the limited omniscient voice is immediacy. Here, because we are not allowed to know more than Jane does about her own thoughts and feelings, we grope with her toward understanding. In the process, a contract has been made between the author and the reader, and this contract must not now be broken. If at this point the author should step in and answer Jane's question "When, exactly, had it started?" with "Jane was never to remember this, but in fact it had started one afternoon when she was two years old," we would feel it as an abrupt and uncalled-for *authorial intrusion*. Nevertheless, within the limits the author has set herself, there is fluidity and a range of possibilities.

The Objective Author

As an objective author, you restrict your knowledge to the external facts that might be observed by a human witness: to the senses of sight, sound, smell, taste, and touch. In the story "Hills Like White Elephants," Ernest Hemingway reports what is said and done by a quarreling couple, both without any direct revelation of the characters' thoughts and without comment.

> "What should we drink?" the girl asked. She had taken off her hat and put it on the table.
> "It's pretty hot," the man said.
> "Let's drink beer."
> "Dos cervezas," the man said into the curtain . . .
> The woman brought two glasses of beer and two felt pads. She put the felt pads and the beer glasses on the table and looked at the man and the girl. The girl was looking off at the line of hills. They were white in the sun and the country was brown and dry.

In the course of this story we learn, entirely by inference, that the girl is pregnant and that she feels herself coerced by the man into having an abortion. Neither pregnancy nor abortion is ever mentioned. The narrative remains clipped, austere, and external. What does Hemingway gain by this pretense of objective reporting? The reader is allowed to discover what is really happening. The characters avoid the subject, prevaricate, and pretend, but they betray their real meanings and feelings through gestures, repetitions, and slips of the tongue. The reader, focus directed by the author, learns by inference, as in life, so that we finally have the pleasure of knowing the characters better than they know themselves.

Second Person

First and third persons are most common in literature; the *second person* remains an idiosyncratic and experimental form, but it is worth mentioning because several contemporary authors have been attracted to its possibilities.

Han Kang's novel *Human Acts* has recurring sections in the second person, illustrating how a reader is made into a character through this technique.

"Looks like rain," you mutter to yourself.

What we do if it really chucks it down?

You open your eyes so that only a slender chink of light seeps in, and peer at the gingko trees in front of the Provincial Office. As though there, between those branches, the wind is about to take on visible form. As though the raindrops suspended in the air, held breath before the plunge, are on the cusp of trembling down, glittering like jewels.

When you open your eyes properly, the trees' outlines dim and blur. You're going to need glasses before long. . . . Perhaps your sight's now as bad as it's going to get, and you'll be able to get away without glasses after all?

Here the author makes you, the reader, into the character by assigning you specific characteristics and reactions, and thereby—assuming that you go along with her characterization—pulls you deeper and more intimately into the story.

Some writers choose second person to depict trauma, as its slight sense of detachment mutes possible melodrama and mirrors the sense of shock; others may use it to make a highly individual experience feel more universal.

> *What I really want is that intimacy in which the reader is under the impression that he isn't really reading this; that he is participating in it as he goes along.*
> *—Toni Morrison*

The second person is the basic mode of the story only when a character is referred to as *you*. When one character addresses "you" in letter or monologue, that narrative is still told by the "I" character. When an omniscient author addresses the reader as *you* (*You will remember that John Doderring was left dangling on the cliff at Dover*), this is called "direct address" and does not alter the basic third-person mode of the piece. Only when "you" becomes an actor in the drama, so designated by the author, is the story or novel written in second person.

Unlike third or first person, second person draws attention to itself, and it can also be difficult to maintain—it's easy to slip back into third or first person. Also, some readers may resist second person because they don't identify with the character they are supposed to be in the story. (*You're going to need glasses before long.*) It is unlikely that the second person will ever become a major mode of narration as the first and third person are, but for precisely that reason you may find it an attractive experiment.

First Person

A story is told in the first person when one of its characters relates the story's action and events. The term "narrator" is sometimes loosely used to refer to any teller of a tale, but strictly speaking a story has a narrator only when it is told in the first person by one of the characters. This character may be the protagonist, the I telling *my* story, in which case that character is a *central narrator*; or the character may be telling a story about someone else, in which case he or she is a *peripheral narrator*.

In either case it's important to indicate early which kind of narrator we have so that we know who the story's protagonist is, as in the first paragraph of Paul Beatty's *The Sellout*:

> This may be hard to believe, coming from a black man, but I've never stolen a thing. Never cheated on my taxes or at cards. Never snuck into the movies or failed to give back the extra change to a drugstore cashier indifferent to the ways of mercantilism and minimum-wage expectations. I've never burgled a house. Held up a liquor store.

The focus here is immediately thrown on the I of the story, and we now expect that I to be the central character whose desires and decisions impel the action. Here is an even more insistent example, in Lauren Groff's "Ghosts and Empties," of an I on whom we infer the trouble of the story will surely fall:

> I have somehow become a woman who yells, and because I do not want to be a woman who yells, whose little children walk around with frozen, watchful faces, I have taken to lacing on my running shoes after dinner and going out into the twilit streets for a walk,

leaving the undressing and sluicing and reading and singing and tucking in of the boys to my husband, a man who does not yell.

In contrast to these self-directed narratives, the opening lines of Amy Bloom's "Silver Water" establish Violet as a peripheral narrator, an observer and protector of her sister, Rose, who is brought alive through the description of her marvelous singing voice:

> My sister's voice was like mountain water in a silver pitcher; the clear, blue beauty of it cools you and lifts you up beyond your heat, beyond your body. After we went to see *La Traviata*, when she was fourteen and I was twelve, she elbowed me in the parking lot and said, "Check this out." And she opened her mouth unnaturally wide and her voice came out, so crystalline and bright that all the departing operagoers stood frozen by their cars, unable to take out their keys or open their doors until she had finished, and then they cheered like hell.
>
> That's what I like to remember and that's the story I told to all of her therapists. I wanted them to know her, to know that who they saw was not all there was to see.

The central narrator is always, as the term implies, at the center of the action; the peripheral narrator may be in virtually any position other than the center. He or she may be the second most important character in the story (as is Violet) or may appear to be a bystander for much of the story. It is even possible to make the first-person narrator plural, as William Faulkner does in "A Rose for Emily," where the story is told by a narrator identified only as one of "us," the people of the town in which the action has taken place; or as in recurring sections of Scott Blackwood's *We Agreed to Meet Just Here*.

> This is what we imagined the night Odie disappeared: he and Ruth had a fight over the chemotherapy, Odie saying he didn't see the point and Ruth doing what she always did when distressed, driving to the fish market for prawns to sauté with a green mango curry.

Notice how indirect dialogue and summary are used to suggest the-kind-of-thing-that-usually-happened, and therefore the kind of thing "we" could guess at.

That a narrator may be either central or peripheral, that a character may tell either his or her own story or someone else's, is both commonly assumed and obviously logical. But the author and editor Rust Hills, in *Writing in General and the Short Story in Particular*, takes interesting and persuasive exception to this idea. When point of view fails, Hills argues, it is always because the perception we are using for the course of the story is different from that of the character who is moved or changed by the action. Even when a narrator seems to be a peripheral observer and the story is "about" someone else, in fact it is the narrator who is changed, and must be, in order for us to be satisfied by our emotional identification with him or her.

> This, I believe, is what will always be the case in successful fiction: that either the character moved by the action will be the point-of-view character, or else the point-of-view character will *become* the character moved by the action. Call it Hills' Law.

Obviously, this view does not mean we have to throw out the useful fictional device of the peripheral narrator. Hills uses the familiar example of *The Great Gatsby* to illustrate his meaning. Nick Carraway as a peripheral narrator observes and tells the story of Jay Gatsby, but by the end of the book it is Nick's life that has been changed by what he has observed. Likewise, Gish Jen's story "No More Maybe" begins by making clear that the focus is to be on the narrator's in-laws:

> Since my mother-in-law came to visit America she is quite busy. First she has to eat many blueberries. Because in China they are expensive! While here they are comparatively cheap. Then she has to breath the clean air. My husband, Wuji, and I have lived here for five years, so we are used to the air. But my mother-in-law has to take many fast walks. Breathing, breathing. Trying to clean out her lungs, she says, trying to get all the healthy oxygen inside her. She also has to look at the sky.

Yet by the end of the story it is the narrator who is in tears, because she sees that her in-laws' aging, which she has been busy satirizing, can have only one outcome.

Anton Chekhov (as paraphrased by Tobias Wolff) cautioned, "The narrator cannot escape the *consequences* of the story he is telling. If he does, it's not a story. It's an anecdote, a tale, or something else."

Central or peripheral, a first-person narrator is a character, so it's vital to remember that she or he has all the limitations of a human being and cannot be omniscient. The narrator is confined to reporting what she or he could realistically know. More than that, although the narrator may certainly interpret actions, deliver dictums, and predict the future, these remain the fallible opinions of a human being. We are not bound to accept them as we are bound to accept the interpretations, truths, and predictions of the omniscient author. You may want us to accept the narrator's word, and then the most difficult part of your task, and the touchstone of your story's success, will be to convince us to trust and believe the narrator. On the other hand, it may be an important part of your purpose that we should reject the narrator's opinions and form our own. If the answer to *Who speaks?* is *a child, a bigot, a jealous lover, an animal, a schizophrenic, a murderer, a liar*, the implications may be that the narrator speaks with limitations we do not necessarily share. To the extent that the narrator displays and betrays such limitations, she or he is an *unreliable narrator*, a phenomenon that is discussed later in the chapter, under the heading "At What Distance?"

TO WHOM?

In choosing a point of view, the author implies an identity not only for the teller of the tale but also for the intended audience. To whom is the story being told?

The Reader

Most fiction is addressed to a literary convention, "the reader." When we open a book, we tacitly accept our role as a member of this unspecified audience and don't pause to ask, Why are you telling me all this? The most common assumption of the tale-teller, whether omniscient author or narrating character, is that the reader is an open and amenable Everyman, and that the telling needs no justification.

> My mother died at the moment I was born, and so for my whole life there was nothing standing between myself and eternity; at my back was always a bleak, black wind. I could not have known at the beginning of my life that this would be so; I only came to know this in the middle of my life, just at the time when I was no longer young and realized that I had less of some of the things I used to have in abundance and more of some of the things I had scarcely had at all.
>
> —Jamaica Kincaid, *The Autobiography of My Mother*

The use of point of view is to bring the reader into immediate and continuous contact with the heart of the story and sustain him there. Point of view is the proscenium, the transparent window through which the reader views the story.
—Tom Jenks

Another Character

On the other hand, the story may be told to *another character*, or *characters*, in which case we as readers "overhear" it; the teller of the tale does not acknowledge us even by implication.

In the *epistolary* novel or story, the narrative consists entirely of letters written from one character to another, or between characters. The recipient of the letter may be a stranger or a close friend or relative, like the near-annual readers of *The Christmas Letters*, by Lee Smith.

> First, my apologies for not writing a Christmas letter last year (for not returning calls, for not returning letters, etc.). The fact is, for a long time I couldn't do anything. Not a damn thing. Nothing. I was shell-shocked, immobilized. This was followed by a period when I did *too many things*. Marybeth, who has been through it, wrote to me about this time, saying, "Don't make any big decisions"— very good advice, and I wish I'd followed it. Instead, I agreed to

163

a separation agreement, then to a quick no-fault divorce, then to Sandy's plan of selling the house P.D.Q. I just wanted everything *over with*—the way you feel that sudden irresistible urge to clean out your closet sometimes.

Or the convention of the story may be that of a monologue, spoken aloud by one character to another:

> Those are the offices and these are the cubicles. That's my cubicle there, and this is your cubicle. This is your phone. Never answer your phone. Let the Voicemail System answer it. This is your Voicemail System Manual. There are no personal phone calls allowed. We do, however, allow for emergencies. If you must make an emergency phone call, ask your supervisor first. If you can't find your supervisor, ask Phillip Spiers, who sits over there. He'll check with Clarissa Nicks, who sits over there. If you make an emergency phone call without asking, you may be let go.
> —Daniel Orozco, "Orientation"

Again, the possible variations are infinite: the narrator may speak in intimate confessional to a friend or lover, or may present his case to a jury or a mob; she may be writing a highly technical report on the welfare situation, designed to hide her emotions; he may be pouring out his heart in a love letter he knows (and we know) he will never send. Robin Hemley's "Reply All" is written entirely in emails.

In any of these cases, the convention employed is the opposite of that employed in a story told to "the reader." The listener as well as the teller is involved in the action; the assumption is not that we readers are there but that we are not. We are eavesdroppers, with all the ambiguous intimacy that position implies.

Just as often, I find myself writing about disturbing or socially questionable acts and states of mind that have no real basis in my life at all, but which, I am afraid, people will quite naturally attribute to me when they read what I have written.
—Michael Chabon

The Self

An even greater intimacy is implied if the character's story is as secret as a diary or as private as a mind, addressed to *the self* and not intended to be heard by anyone inside or outside the action.

In a *diary* or *journal*, the convention is that the thoughts are written but not expected to be read by anyone except the writer. Here is an entry from the private diary kept by a campaign manager in my novel *The Buzzards*:

> August 11
>
> One day I will throttle that woman. Delicious fantasies of wringing a chicken's neck—no bird she more resembles. Yet the comparison misleading and the product of my own will. Must not be taken in by it.
>
> I looked up this afternoon to see her in the patio of the Booker T. Secondary School in Shreveport, in full view through the double doors—reporters with Alex in the cafeteria could have seen her by taking two steps backward.

The character here is clearly using his diary to vent his feelings and does not intend it to be read by anyone else. Still, he has deliberately externalized his secret thoughts.

Interior Monologue

Because the author has the power to enter a character's mind, the reader also has the power to eavesdrop on that character's thoughts. Overheard thoughts are generally of two kinds, of which the more common is *interior monologue*, the convention being that we follow the character's thoughts in their sequence.

> I must organize myself. I must, as they say, pull myself together, dump this cat from my lap, stir—yes, resolve, move, do. But do what? My will is like the rosy dustlike light in this room: soft, diffuse, and gently comforting. It lets me do . . . anything . . . nothing. My ears hear what they happen to; I eat what's put before me; my eyes see what blunders into them; my thoughts are not

catalog or a television commercial as long as you can also contrive to give it the form of a story.

Form is important to point of view because the form in which a story is told indicates the degree of self-consciousness on the part of the teller; this will in turn affect the language chosen, the intimacy of the relationship, and the honesty of the telling. A written account will imply less spontaneity, on the whole, than one that appears to be spoken aloud, which in turn suggests less spontaneity than thought. A narrator writing a letter to his grandmother may be less honest than he is when he tells the same facts aloud to his friend.

Certain relationships established by the narrative between teller and audience make certain forms more likely than others, but almost any combination of answers is possible to the questions *Who speaks? To whom? In what form?* If you are speaking as an omniscient author to the literary convention of "the reader," we may assume that you are using the convention of "written story" as your form. But you might say:

> Wait, step over here a minute. What's this in the corner, stuffed
> down between the bedpost and the wall? Is that a dust rag or—is it?
> A pair of underpants?

If you do this, you slip at least momentarily into the different convention of the spoken word—the effect is that we are drawn more immediately into the scene—and the point of view of the whole is slightly altered. A central narrator might be thinking, and therefore "talking to herself," while actually angrily addressing her thoughts to another character. Conversely, one character might be writing a letter to another but letting the conscious act of writing deteriorate into a betrayal of his own secret thoughts. Any complexities such as these will alter and inform the total point of view.

....

AT WHAT DISTANCE?

As with the chemist at her microscope and the lookout in his tower, fictional point of view always involves the *distance*, small or great, of the perceiver from the thing perceived. Distance may be *temporal* or *spatial*, involving a literal distance from the events narrated.

> That spring, when I had a great deal of potential and no money at all, I took a job as a janitor. That was when I was very young and spent money very freely, and when, almost every night, I drifted off to sleep lulled by sweet anticipation of that time when my potential would suddenly be realized and there would be capsule biographies of my life on the dust jackets of many books.
>
> —James Alan McPherson, "Gold Coast"

I was extremely nervous about writing a character of another race. I'd never tried it before, and worried, as well I might have, that it would come off as some white guy writing about his idea of what it might be like to be a black woman . . . so I went ahead and did it.

—Michael Cunningham

Here, the distance is one of decades, the point of view that of the narrator regarding his younger self. We are invited to identify with the older writing self, and mockingly clued in to the fact that the sweet anticipation of potential has not been borne out.

By closing the literal distance between the reader and the subject, an intangible distance can be closed as well, as in this passage from my novel *Raw Silk*:

> Her face was half an inch from my face. The curtain flapped at the open window and her pupils pulsed with the coming and going of the light. I know Jill's eyes; I've painted them. They're violent and taciturn . . . a detonation under glass.

Authorial distance, sometimes called *psychic distance*, is the degree to which we as readers feel, on the one hand, intimacy and identification with and, on the other hand, detachment and alienation from the characters. A sense of distance may be increased through the use of abstract nouns, summary, typicality, and apparent objectivity. Such techniques, which in other contexts might be seen as writing flaws, are employed purpose-fully in the following passage to detach readers from characters in a se-ries of details that amount to historical sweep.

> It started in the backyards. At first the men concentrated on heat and smoke, and on dangerous thrusts with long forks. Their wives gave them aprons in railroad stripes, with slogans on the front— HOT STUFF, THE BOSS—to spur them on. Then it began to get all mixed up with who should do the dishes, and you can't fall back on paper plates forever, and around that time the wives got tired of making butterscotch brownies and Jell-o salads with grated carrots and baby marshmallows in them and wanted to make money instead, and one thing led to another.
>   —Margaret Atwood, "Simmering"

Conversely, closeness and sympathy can be achieved by concrete detail, scene, a character's thoughts, and so forth.

> She dreams she does not already have three children. A squeeze around the flowers in her hands chokes off three and four and five years of breath. Instantly she is ashamed and frightened in her superstition. She looks for the first time at the preacher, forces humility into her eyes, as if she believes he is, in fact, a man of God. She can imagine God, a small black boy, timidly pulling the preacher's coattail.
>   —Alice Walker, "Roselily"

Or a combination of techniques may make us feel simultaneously sym-pathetic and detached—a frequent effect of comedy—as in this example:

> I'm a dishwasher in a restaurant. I'm not trying to impress anybody. I'm not bragging. It's just what I do. It's not the glamorous job people make it out to be. Sure, you make a lot of dough and everybody looks up to you and respects you, but then again there's a lot of responsibility. It weighs on you. It wears on you. Everybody wants to be a dishwasher these days, I guess, but they've got an idealistic view of it.
>   —Robert McBrearty, "The Dishwasher"

As author you may ask us to identify completely with one character and totally condemn another. One character may judge another harshly while you as author suggest that we should qualify that judgment. If there is also a narrator, that narrator may think himself morally superior while behind his back you make sure that we will think him morally deficient. In that case, you have created a *moral distance* in the narration, and an *unreliable narrator*.

Here is a first-person narration in which a woman, imperious and sour, tells her story from her point of view:

> I have always, always, tried to do right and help people. It's a part of my community duty and my duty to God. But I can tell you right now, you don't never gets no thanks for it! . . .
>
> Use to be a big ole fat sloppy woman live cross the street went to my church. She had a different man in her house with her every month! She got mad at me for tellin the minister on her about all them men! Now, I'm doin my duty and she got mad! I told her somebody had to be the pillar of the community and if it had to be me, so be it! She said I was the pill of the community and a lotta other things, but I told the minister that too and pretty soon she was movin away. Good! I like a clean community!
>
> —J. California Cooper, "The Watcher"

We mistrust every judgment this woman makes, but we are also aware of an author we do trust, manipulating the narrator's tone to expose her. The outburst is fraught with ironies, but because the narrator is unaware of them, they are directed against herself. We can hear that interference is being dressed up as duty. When she brags in cliché, we agree that she's more of a pill than a pillar. When she appropriates biblical language— "so be it!"—we suspect that even the minister might agree. Punctuation itself, the self-righteous overuse of the exclamation point, suggests her inappropriate intensity. It occurs to us we'd probably like the look of that "big ole fat sloppy" neighbor, and we know for certain why that neighbor moved away.

In this case the narrator is wholly unreliable, and we're unlikely to accept any judgment she could make. But it is also possible for a narra-

171

tor to be reliable in some areas of value and unreliable in others. Mark Twain's Huckleberry Finn is a famous case in point. Here Huck has decided to free his friend Jim, and he is astonished that Tom Sawyer is going along with the plan.

> Here was a boy that was respectable, and well brung up; and had a character to lose; and folks at home that had characters; and he was bright and not leather-headed; and knowing and not ignorant; and not mean, but kind; and yet here he was, without any more pride, or rightness, or feeling, than to stoop to this business, and make himself a shame, and his family a shame, before everybody.
> I couldn't understand it, no way at all.

The extended irony in this excerpt is that slavery should be defended by the respectable, the bright, the knowing, the kind, and those of character. We reject Huck's assessment of Tom as well as the implied assessment of himself as worth so little that he has nothing to lose by freeing a slave. Huck's moral instincts are better than he himself can understand. (Notice, incidentally, how Huck's lack of education is communicated by word choice and syntax and how sparse the misspellings are.) So author and reader are in intellectual opposition to Huck the narrator, but morally identify with him. Similarly reliable "unreliable" narrators, whose distorted views reveal a strangely accurate portrait of the social institutions that confine them, include Chief Bromden, the narrator of Ken Kesey's *One Flew Over the Cuckoo's Nest*, and the "hysterical" wife and patient, forbidden to write, who relates Charlotte Perkins Gilman's 1892 story "The Yellow Wallpaper."

Given enough time, for most writers, point-of-view choices become intuitive. You hear a voice, and you follow.
—Elizabeth Strout

The unreliable narrator—who has become one of the most popular characters in modern fiction—is far from a newcomer to literature and in fact predates fiction. Every drama contains characters who present their own cases, and from whom we are partly or wholly distanced in one area or another. So we admire Oedipus's intellect but are exasperated by his lack of intuition, we identify with Othello's morality but mistrust his logic, we trust Mr. Spock's brain but not his heart. As these examples suggest, the unreliable narrator often presents us with an example of consistent inconsistency and always presents us with dramatic irony, because we always "know" more than he or she does about the characters, the events, and the significance of both.

Distance and the Author-Reader Relationship

The one relationship in which there must not be any distance, however, is between author and reader.

It is a frustrating experience for many beginning (and established) authors to find that, whereas they meant the protagonist to appear sensitive, their readers find him self-pitying; whereas the author meant her to be witty, the readers find her vulgar. When this happens there is a failure of authorial or psychic distance: the author did not have sufficient perspective on the character to convince us to share his or her judgment. I recall one class in which a student author had written, with excellent use of image and scene, the story of a young man who fell in love with an exceptionally beautiful young woman, and whose feelings turned to revulsion when he found out she had had a mastectomy. The most

You are going to write about that incident. You are the main character in the story. But . . . you are going to disguise things in a big way.
—Ira Wood

vocal feminist in the class loved this story, which she described as "the exposé of a skuzzwort." This was not, from the author's point of view, a successful reading of his story. He had meant for the young man in the story to be seen as a sympathetic character.

A writer may also create either distance or closeness through the use of time, space, tone, and irony. A story that happened long ago in a faraway land, told by a detached narrator, won't feel the same as one happening in present tense, told by one of the characters. A story's tone and use of irony are also indications of how the reader should view the characters and their situations. For example, in Daniel Orozco's story "Orientation," quoted on page 164, we can't help but view the office workers from a distance because of the narrator's tone, and that tone remains flat as the distance increases:

> Amanda Pierce also has a husband, who is a lawyer. He subjects her to an escalating array of painful and humiliating sex games, to which Amanda Pierce reluctantly submits. She comes to work exhausted and freshly wounded each morning, wincing from the abrasions to her breasts, or the bruises on her abdomen, or the second-degree burns on the backs of her thighs.

Choosing and *controlling* the psychic distance that best suits a given story is one of the most elusive goals a writer pursues. The good news for novice writers feeling overwhelmed by all of these considerations is that point-of-view choices, like plot and theme, are seldom calculated and preplanned. Rather, point of view tends to evolve organically as a story develops, and you can usually trust intuition to guide you through several drafts. It is when a story is well under way that analysis of its specific point-of-view issues becomes most useful, and the feedback of other writers may be of particular value.

....

CONSISTENCY: A CAUTION

In establishing the story's point of view, you make your own rules, but having made them, you must stick to them. Your position as a fiction writer is analogous to that of a poet, who may choose whether to write free verse or a ballad stanza. If the poet chooses the stanza, then he or she is obliged to rhyme. Similarly, once you signal a point of view to the reader, you are obliged to stick with it. Beginning writers of prose fiction are often tempted to shift viewpoint when it is both unnecessary and disruptive for readers.

> Leo's neck flushed against the prickly weave of his uniform collar. He concentrated on his buttons and tried not to look into the face of the bandmaster, who, however, was more amused than angry.

This is an awkward point-of-view shift: having felt Leo's embarrassment with him, we are suddenly asked to leap into the bandmaster's feelings.

The shift can be corrected by moving instead from Leo's mind to an observation he might make:

> Leo's neck flushed against the prickly weave of his uniform collar. He concentrated on his buttons and tried not to look into the face of the bandmaster, who, astonishingly, was smiling.

The rewrite is easier to follow because we remain in Leo's mind as he observes that the bandmaster is not angry. It further serves to imply that Leo fails to concentrate on his buttons, and so intensifies his confusion.

Apart from the use of significant detail, there is no more important skill for a writer of fiction to grasp than this, the control of point of view. Sometimes it may be hard simply to recognize that your narrative has leaped from one point of view to another—often, in workshop, students are troubled by a point-of-view shift in someone else's story but can't spot one in their own. In other cases there's a healthy desire to explore every possibility in a scene, and a mistaken sense that this can't be done without changing point of view. Indeed, some practiced and skillful writers break this rule of *consistency in point of view* to original and inventive effect. Yet the general rule holds, and a writer shows his amateurism in unintended and ineffective point of view shifts. Once established, point of view constitutes a contract between author and reader, and it will be difficult to break the contract gracefully. If you have restricted yourself to the mind of James Lordly for five pages, as he observes the actions of Mrs. Grumms and her cats, you will violate the contract by suddenly dipping into Mrs. Grumms's mind to let us know what she thinks of James Lordly. We are likely to feel misused, and likely to cancel the contract altogether, if you then suddenly give us the thoughts of the cats.

....

A WORD ABOUT APPROPRIATION

In the early decades of the twenty-first century there has been an outcry about *cultural appropriation*—writing about, and especially from the point of view of, persons of another race, gender, or ethnicity. What right have these, especially middle-class, especially Western, especially white, especially male writers to write about the lives and desires, fears and hopes of people whose experience is totally other—especially blacks, Muslims, victimized women, immigrants—people who have been colonized, conquered, ghettoized, and discriminated against?

The questions are deep and many. There exists, without doubt, the phenomenon of cultural *theft*, where the unacknowledged and unrewarded arts of one culture are exploited for fame and money (minstrels, blaxploitation films, mother-in-law jokes; and Elvis? hip-hop?). There are also serious attempts to learn from other cultures and bring them to a larger audience, or to bridge cultures (Ladysmith Black Mambazo, cool jazz, *Black Panther*). The difference is often difficult to parse, and particularly so in fiction, where it is the specific intent of the story to *inhabit another mind*, a mind that is not the author's but nevertheless a product of the author's. This intent, deliberately and of its nature empathetic, can be distorted, and the result can be crude and demeaning. If it is so, it is bad art, or not art. It must be called out and condemned.

But the empathetic effort is both necessary and urgent. *We need to imagine each other.* As the world becomes more interracial and interethnic, more and more writers will need to imagine themselves more and more deeply into the minds and lives of a multipopulated society. Playwright Lynn Nottage, in her declared desire to dismantle the "white male gaze," set her Pulitzer Prize–winning drama *Sweat* in the steel mills of Reading, Pennsylvania. There, in order to represent the issues of racial and class difference, she could not do otherwise than write from the viewpoint of white as well as black, male as well as female, immigrant as well as native. Annie Proulx, in order to write about the devastation of American forests in *Barkskins*, had to "become" several dozen French trappers, Native Americans, powerful axe-handlers, hard-nosed exploiters, and savvy businesswomen to represent the sweep of the history. These necessities are immemorial requirements of the imaginative art. The "appropriation" and representation of other minds is, and will

> *Of course, there are ancillary advantages to writing fiction. You get to leave your body, for instance, so you can have experiences that a person with your physical characteristics couldn't actually have.*
> —Deborah Eisenberg

POINT OF VIEW: A SUMMARY

WHO SPEAKS?

Third person: Author editorial omniscient limited omniscient objective	*Second person:* Author	*First person:* Character central narrator peripheral narrator

TO WHOM?

Third person: Reader	*Second person:* "You" as character as reader-turned-character	*First person:* Self or: another character

IN WHAT FORM?

	Story, monologue, letter, journal, interior monologue, stream of consciousness, etc.	

AT WHAT DISTANCE?

Complete identification   to   complete opposition between speaker and reader (in time, space, intelligence, morality, diction, sanity, etc.)

become increasingly, the business of writers seeking to imagine their truth. Yet the questions will continue to be asked and the charge of appropriation raised until that mythic future in which the experience of all people is shared and equal.

In the meantime, on the flawed planet we inhabit, there can be, it seems to me, only one way forward, which is to embrace a proposition parallel to the concept of free speech: that the imagination is by its nature free and cannot be censored. As with speech, the writer's imagination can have no boundary imposed except in cases of threat, hate, or sedition. She is free to imagine anyone, anywhere, in the past, the future, or a time that never could exist; he may set his fiction in a country he has never seen or a town he has passed through only once. And then, as with free speech, the imagination may be critiqued: *this rings true, you got that wrong, you caught it exactly, you don't understand, how could you know that?, your imagining is too feeble.* The writer's only obligation to the imagination is, perpetually, to *imagine better.*

....

SUGGESTED STORIES
"Rape Fantasies"
   Margaret Atwood
"Gryphon"
   Charles Baxter
"Jealous Husband Returns in Form of Parrot"
   Robert Olen Butler
"Story"
   Lydia Davis
"Hills Like White Elephants"
   Ernest Hemingway
"Who's Irish?"
   Gish Jen
"Love and Lethe"
   Samuel Beckett
"Orientation"
   Daniel Orozco
"Victory Lap"
   George Saunders
"The Excursion"
   Joy Williams

WRITING PROMPTS
1. Write down a patently false statement about yourself: *I have a pet snake* or *I take my feet off at night* or *I cleared two million in the heist last week*—the farther from the truth the better. Carry on about it. Begin to develop the personality of a person of whom this statement

would be true. You probably won't write a great story out of this prompt, but you may feel more imaginative freedom than you do when the "I" you start from is yourself.

2. Write a scene about the birth or death of anything (person, plant, animal, machine, scheme, passion). Use all five areas of knowledge of the *editorial omniscient author*. Be sure to give the thoughts of more than one character, tell us something about at least one character that she or he doesn't realize, include the past or future, and deliver a universal truth.

3. Take any scene you have previously written and recast it from another point of view, altering not just the *person* but the means of perception, so that we have an entirely different perspective on the events.

4. Write a scene in the *second person*, in which you ask the reader to become a fool, a bigot, a criminal, or some other unsavory type. Try to convince the reader to go along.

5. Write a scene from the point of view of anything nonhuman— animal, vegetable, mineral, mythic monster, angel. Try to imagine yourself into the terms, frame of reference, morals, and language that this creature would use.

6. Write a scene from the point of view of a character whose views we totally reject.

8: Is and Is Not

COMPARISON

METAPHOR AND SIMILE

Every reader reading is a self-deceiver: We simultaneously "believe" a story and know that it is a fabrication. Our belief in the reality of the story may be so strong that it produces physical reactions—tears, trembling, sighs, gasps, a headache. At the same time, as long as the fiction is working for us, we know that our submission is voluntary, that we have, as Samuel Taylor Coleridge pointed out, *suspended disbelief*. "It's just a movie," says the exasperated father as he takes his shrieking six-year-old out to the lobby. For the father the fiction is working; for the child it is not.

Simultaneous belief and awareness of illusion are present in both the content and the craft of literature, and what is properly called artistic pleasure derives from the tension of this *is* and *is not*. The content of a plot, for instance, tells us that something happens that does not happen, that people who do not exist behave in such a way, and that the events of life—which we know to be random, unrelated, and unfinished—are necessary, patterned, and come to closure. Pleasure in artistry comes precisely when the illusion rings true without destroying the knowledge that it is an illusion.

The techniques of every art offer us this tension of things that are and are not alike. This is true of poetry, in which rhyme is interesting because *tend* sounds like *mend* but not exactly like. It is true of music, whose interest lies in variations on a theme. And it is the fundamental nature of metaphor, from which literature derives.

Metaphor is the literary device by which we are told that something is, or is like, something that it clearly is not, or is not exactly, like. It is a way of showing, in that it particularizes the essential nature of one thing by comparing it to another. A good metaphor surprises us with the unlikeness of the two things compared while at the same time convincing us of the truth of the likeness. In the process it may also illuminate the meaning of the story and its theme. A bad metaphor fails to surprise or convince or both—and so fails to illuminate.

Types of Metaphor and Simile

The simplest distinction between kinds of comparison, and usually the first one grasped by beginning students of literature, is between *metaphor* and *simile*. A simile makes a comparison with the use of *like* or *as*, a metaphor without. Though this distinction is technical, it is not trivial, for a metaphor demands a more literal acceptance. If you say, "A woman is a rose," you ask for an extreme suspension of disbelief, whereas "A woman is like a rose" acknowledges the artifice in the statement.

In both metaphor and simile, the resonance of comparison is in the essential or abstract quality that the two objects share. When a writer speaks of "the eyes of the houses" or "the windows of the soul," the comparison of eyes to windows contains the idea of transmitting vision between the inner and the outer. When we speak of "the king of beasts," we don't mean that a lion wears a crown or sits on a throne (although in children's stories the lion often does precisely that, in order to suggest a primitive physical likeness); we mean that king and lion share abstract qualities of power, position, pride, and bearing.

In both metaphor and simile a physical similarity can yield up a characterizing abstraction. So if "a woman" is either "a rose" or "like a rose," the significance lies not in the physical similarity but in the essential qualities that such similarity implies: slenderness, suppleness, fragrance, beauty, color—and perhaps the threat of thorns.

Every metaphor and simile I have used so far is either a cliché or a dead metaphor (a metaphor so familiar that it has acquired a new meaning). Each may at one time have surprised with its aptness, but the surprise is long since gone. I wished to use familiar examples in order to clarify that *resonance of comparison depends on the abstractions conveyed in the likeness of the things compared.* A good metaphor reverberates with the essential; this is the writer's principle of choice.

So Flannery O'Connor, in "A Good Man Is Hard to Find," describes the mother as having "a face as broad and innocent as a cabbage." A soccer ball is roughly the same size and shape as a cabbage; so is a schoolroom globe; so is a street lamp. But if the mother's face were as broad and innocent as any of these things, she would be a different woman altogether. A cabbage is also rural, heavy, dense, and cheap, and so conveys a whole complex of abstractions about the woman's class and men-

Unless you are at home in the metaphor, unless you have had your proper poetical education in the metaphor, you are not safe anywhere.
—Robert Frost

tality. There is, on the other hand, no innocence in the face of Shrike, in Nathanael West's *Miss Lonelyhearts*, who "buried his triangular face like a hatchet in her neck."

Sometimes the aptness of a comparison is achieved by taking it from an area of reference relevant to the thing compared. In *Dombey and Son*, Charles Dickens describes the ships' instrument maker, Solomon Gills, as having "eyes as red as if they had been small suns looking at you through a fog." The simile suggests a seascape, whereas in *One Flew Over the Cuckoo's Nest*, Ken Kesey's Ruckly, rendered inert by shock therapy, has eyes "all smoked up and gray and deserted inside like blown fuses." But the metaphor may range further from its original, though the abstraction conveyed must still strike us as strongly and essentially appropriate. William Faulkner's Emily Grierson in "A Rose for Emily" has "haughty black eyes in a face the flesh of which was strained across the temple and about the eyesockets as you imagine a lighthouse-keeper's face ought to look." Miss Emily has no connection with the sea, but the metaphor reminds us not only of her sternness and self-sufficiency, but also that she has isolated herself in a locked house. The same character as an old woman has eyes that "looked like two pieces of coal pressed into a lump of dough," an image that domesticates her, robs her of her light.

Both metaphors and similes can be *extended*, meaning that the writer continues to present aspects of likeness in the things compared.

> There was a white fog . . . standing all around you like something solid. At eight or nine, perhaps, it lifted as a shutter lifts. We had a glimpse of the towering multitude of trees, of the immense matted jungle, with the blazing little ball of sun hanging over it—all perfectly still—and then the white shutter came down again, smoothly, as if sliding in greased grooves.
> —Joseph Conrad, *Heart of Darkness*

Notice that Conrad moves from a generalized image of "something solid" to the specific simile "as a shutter lifts"; reasserts the simile as a metaphor, "then the shutter came down again"; and becomes still more specific in the extension "as if sliding in greased grooves."

Also note that Conrad emphasizes the dumb solidity of the fog by comparing the larger natural phenomenon with the smaller manufactured object. This is a technique that contemporary writers have used to effects both comic and profound, as when Frederick Barthelme in *The Brothers* describes a young woman "with a life stretching out in front of her like so many unrented videos" or a man's head "bobbing like an enormous Q-Tip against the little black sky."

In a more usual metaphoric technique, the smaller or more ordinary image is compared with one more significant or intense, as in this example from Louise Erdrich's "Matchimanito," where the narrator invokes the names of Anishinabe Indians dead of tuberculosis:

> Their names grew within us, swelled to the brink of our lips, forced our eyes open in the middle of the night. We were filled with the water of the drowned, cold and black—airless water that lapped against the seal of our tongues or leaked slowly from the corners of our eyes. Within us, like ice shards, their names bobbed and shifted.

A *conceit*, which can be either metaphor or simile, is a comparison of two things radically and startlingly unlike—in Samuel Johnson's words, "yoked by violence together." A conceit is as far removed as possible from the purely sensuous comparison of "the eyes of the potato." It compares two things that have very little or no immediately apprehensible similarity, and so it is the nature of the conceit to be long. The author must explain to us, sometimes at great length, why these things can be said to be alike. When John Donne compares a flea to the Holy Trinity, the two images have no areas of reference in common, and we don't understand. He must explain to us that the flea, having bitten both the poet and his lover, now has the blood of three souls in its body.

The conceit is more common to poetry than to prose because of the density of its imagery, but it can be used to good effect in fiction. In *The Day of the Locust*, Nathanael West uses a conceit in an insistent devaluation of love. The screenwriter Claude Estee says:

> Love is like a vending machine, eh? Not bad. You insert a coin and press home the lever. There's some mechanical activity inside the bowels of the device. You receive a small sweet, frown at yourself in the dirty mirror, adjust your hat, take a firm grip on your umbrella and walk away, trying to look as though nothing had happened.

"Love is like a vending machine" is a conceit; if the writer didn't explain to us in what way love is like a vending machine, we'd founder trying to figure it out. So he goes on to develop the vending machine in images that suggest not "love" but seamy sex. The last image—"trying to look as though nothing had happened"—has nothing to do with the vending machine; we accept it because by this time we've fused the two ideas in our minds.

Dead Metaphors

At the opposite end of the scale is the *dead metaphor*, one so familiar that it has in effect ceased to be a metaphor; it has lost the force of the original comparison and acquired a new definition. Fowler's *Modern English Usage* uses the word "sift" to demonstrate the dead metaphor, one that has "been used so often that speaker and hearer have ceased to be aware that the words used are not literal.

Thus, in *the men were sifting the meal* we have a literal use of *sift*; in *Satan hath desired to have you, that he may sift you as wheat*, *sift* is a live metaphor; in *the sifting of evidence*, the metaphor is so familiar that it is about equal chances whether *sifting* or *examination* will be used, and that a sieve is not present to the thought.

English abounds in dead metaphors. *Abounds* is one, where the overflow of liquid is not present to the thought. When a person *runs* for office, legs are not present to the thought, nor is an arrow when we think of someone's *aim*, nor are hot stones when we go through an *ordeal*. There is a residual resonance from the original metaphor but no pointless effort on the part of the mind to resolve the tension. English is fertile with metaphors (including *fertile* in this sentence, and the *eyes* of those potatoes) that have died and been resurrected as idiom, a "manner of speaking." It is scarcely possible to speak in English without using dead metaphors, a fact that makes it especially difficult for adults to learn as a second language.

The metaphor is perhaps one of man's most fruitful potentialities. Its efficacy verges on magic, and it seems a tool for creation which God forgot inside one of His creatures when He made him."
—*José Ortega y Gasset*

Linguist and philospher Steven Pinker, in *The Language Instinct*, demonstrates the ubiquity of dead metaphor as he illustrates how we try to speak of language as if "ideas are objects, sentences are containers, and communication is sending":

> We "gather" our ideas to "put" them "into" words, and if our verbiage is not "empty" or "hollow," we might "convey" or "get" these ideas "across" "to" a listener, who can "unpack" our words to "extract" their "content."

Similarly, my heroine in *Raw Silk*, trying to communicate in English in Japan, discovers the difficulties of dead metaphor as idiom:

> Are you put out, do you put out, I put him out, he put me up, he put it off, you are put off, put 'er there, he put in, he put it in, he put it to

185

me; put 'em up. I wonder that anybody learns English, including the English.

Metaphoric Faults to Avoid

Comparison is not a frivolity. It is, on the contrary, the primary business of the brain. Some eighteenth-century philosophers spoke of the human mind as a *tabula rasa*, a "blank slate" on which sense impressions are recorded, compared, and grouped. Now we're more likely to speak of the mind as a computer "storing" and "processing" "data."

What both metaphors acknowledge is that comparison is the basis of all learning and all reasoning. When a child burns his hand on the stove and hears his mother say, "It's hot," and then goes toward the radiator and again hears her say, "It's hot," the child learns not to burn his fingers. The implicit real-life comparison is meant to convey a fact, and it teaches a mode of behavior. By contrast, the goal of literary comparison is to convey not a fact but a perception, and thereby to enlarge our scope of understanding. When we speak of "the flames of torment," our impulse is comprehension and compassion.

> *Metaphor was the clay the great physicists used to mold new theories of the universe. Einstein first talked of trains and clocks, then expanded the images to weave time and space into a single fabric.*
> *—Jack Hart*

Nevertheless, metaphor is a dirty word in some critical circles, because of the strain of the pursuit. Clichés, mixed metaphors, and similes that are inept, unapt, obscure, or done to death mar good prose and tax the patience of the most willing reader. If a metaphor is too familiar it operates as an abstraction rather than a particularizing detail. If it is too far-fetched, it calls attention to the writer rather than the meaning and causes a hiccup in the reader's involvement. A good metaphor fits so neatly that it fuses to and illuminates the meaning. Generally speaking, where metaphors are concerned, less is more and, if in doubt, don't.

Notice now, the preceding paragraph is full of dead metaphors, all giving the weight of an object or action to an idea: *strain, pursuit, done to death, mar, tax, operates, far-fetched, calls, fits, fuses,* and *illuminates.* Each has acquired a new meaning and so settles into its context with minimal strain. But at the same time the metaphoric echoes of these concrete words make them more interesting than their abstract synonyms: *used too many times . . .* , *make the prose less interesting . . .* , and so forth. I have used one live metaphor, "a hiccup in the reader's involvement," and I'll leave it there to defend itself.

Certainly there are more *don'ts* than *dos* to list for the writing of metaphor and simile, because every good comparison is its own justification by virtue of being apt and original.

To study good metaphor, read. In the meantime, avoid the following:

Cliché metaphors are so familiar that they have lost the force of their original meaning. They are inevitably apt comparisons; if they were not, they wouldn't have been repeated often enough to become clichés. But such images fail to surprise, and we blame the writer for this expenditure of energy without a payoff. Or, to put it a worse way:

Clichés are *the last word* in bad writing, and *it's a crying shame* to see all you *bright young things* spoiling your *deathless prose* with phrases as *old as the hills*. You must *keep your nose to the grindstone,* because *the sweet smell of success* comes only to those who *march to the tune of a different drummer.*

It's a sad fact that at this stage of literary history, you may not say that eyes are like pools or stars, and you should be very wary of saying that they flood with tears. These have been so often repeated that they've become shorthand for emotions (attraction in the first and second instances, grief in the third) without the felt force of those emotions. Anytime you as a writer record an emotion without convincing us to feel that emotion, you introduce a fatal distance between author and reader. Therefore, neither may your characters be hawk-eyed or eagle-eyed, nor may they have ruby lips or pearly teeth or peaches-and-cream complexions or necks like swans or thighs like hams. Let them not shed single tears or freeze like deer caught in headlights. And putting the cliché in quotation marks to signal that you know it's a cliché does not excuse it; it just makes blatant your failure of invention. If you sense—and you may—that the moment calls for the special intensity of metaphor, you may have to sift through a whole stock of clichés that come readily to mind. Or it may be time for freewriting and giving the mind room to play. Sometimes your internal critic may reject as fantastic the comparison that, on second look, proves fresh and apt.

In any case, *pools* and *stars* have become clichés for *eyes* because they capture and manifest something essential about the nature of eyes. As long as eyes continue to contain liquid and light, there will be a new way of saying so. And a metaphor freshly pursued can even take advantage of the shared writer-reader consciousness of familiar images. Here William Golding, in *The Inheritors*, describes his Neanderthal protagonist's first tears, which mark his evolution into a human being:

> There was a light now in each cavern, lights faint as the starlight reflected in the crystals of a granite cliff. The lights increased, acquired definition, brightened, lay each sparkling at the lower edge of a cavern. Suddenly, noiselessly, the lights became thin crescents, went out, and streaks glistened on each cheek. The lights appeared again, caught among the silvered curls of the beard. They hung, elongated, dropped from curl to curl and gathered at the lowest tip. The streaks on the cheeks pulsed as the drops swam down them, a great drop swelled at the end of a hair of the beard, shivering and bright. It detached itself and fell in a silver flash.

In this sharply focused and fully extended metaphor of eyes as caverns, Golding asks us to draw on a range of familiar light imagery: starlight, crystal, the crescent moon, silver. The light imagery usually associated with eyes attaches to the water imagery of tears, though neither eyes nor tears are named. There is a submerged acknowledgment of cliché, but there is no cliché; Golding has reinvested the familiar images with their comparative and emotional force.

In both serious and comic writing, consciousness of the familiar can be a peripheral advantage if you find a new way of exploiting it. Although you may not say her eyes are like pools, you may probably say *her eyes are like the scummy duck pond out back*, and we'll find it comic partly because we know the cliché is lurking under the scum.

Cliché can be useful as a device, however, for establishing authorial distance from a character or narrator. If the author tells us that Rome wasn't built in a day, we're likely to think the author has little to contribute to human insight; but if a character says so, in speech or thought, the judgment attaches to the character rather than to the author.

In Phil Klay's "Money as a Weapons System," a young foreign service officer blunders in Iraq because he hasn't learned the military-political jargon with which things are "accomplished." At one point he receives boxes of baseball uniforms and an email from a "Representative Goodwin" who is also "the mattress king of northern Kansas" and who proposes to pacify Iraqis by having the boys taught to play.

> What I'm saying is, you've got to change the CULTURE first. And what's more AMERICAN than baseball, where one man takes a stand against the world, bat in hand, ready to make history, every moment a one-on-one competition. Batter versus pitcher. Runner versus first baseman. . . . And YET!!! It's a team sport! You're nothing without the team!!!!
>
> . . . It's like we say in the mattress business. SUCCESS = DRIVE + DETERMINATION + MATTRESSES.

In the bittersweet denouement of the story, paralleling these cliches in his actions, the officer learns how to get what he wants by faking a photograph of children at the plate.

Far-fetched metaphors are the opposite of clichés: they surprise but are not apt. As the dead metaphor far-fetched suggests, the mind must travel too far to carry back the likeness, and too much is lost on the way. When such a comparison does work, we speak laudatorily of a "leap of the imagination." But when it does not, what we face is in effect a failed conceit: the explanation of what is alike about these two things does not convince. Very good writers in the search for originality sometimes fetch too far. Ernest Hemingway's talent was not for metaphor, and on the rare occasions that he used a metaphor, he was likely to strain. In this passage from A Farewell to Arms, the protagonist has escaped a firing squad and is fleeing the war.

Always surprised on these days when the mind makes her shotgun, metaphoric leaps for reasons I've never been able to trace. Remembered that Wang Wei said a thousand years ago, "Who knows what causes the opening and closing of the door?"

—Jim Harrison

You had lost your cars and your men as a floorwalker loses the stock of his department in a fire. There was, however, no insurance. You were out of it now. You had no more obligation. If they shot floorwalkers after a fire in the department store because they spoke with an accent they had always had, then certainly the floorwalkers would not be expected to return when the store opened again for business. They might seek other employment; if there was any other employment and the police did not get them.

Well, this doesn't work. We may be willing to see the likeness between stock lost in a department store fire and men and cars lost in a military retreat, but "they" *don't* shoot floorwalkers as the Italian military shot defeated line officers. And although a foreign accent might be a disadvantage in a foreign war, it's hard to see how a floorwalker could be killed because of one, although it might make it hard for him to get hired in the first place, if . . . The mind twists trying to find any illuminating or essential logic in the comparison of a soldier to a floorwalker, and fails, so that the protagonist's situation is trivialized in the attempt.

Mixed metaphors are so called because they ask us to compare the original image with things from two or more different areas of reference: *As you walk the path of life, don't founder on the reefs of ignorance.* Life can be a path or a sea, but it cannot be both at the same time. The point of the metaphor is to fuse two images in a single tension. The mind is adamantly unwilling to fuse three.

Separate metaphors or similes that are too close together, especially if they come from areas of reference very different in value or tone, disturb in the same way the mixed metaphor does. The mind doesn't leap; it staggers.

They fought like rats in a Brooklyn sewer. Nevertheless her presence was the axiom of his heart's geometry, and when she was away you would see him walking up and down the street dragging his cane along the picket fence like an idle boy's stick.

Any of these metaphors or similes might be acceptable by itself, but *rats*, *axioms*, and *boys' sticks* connote three different areas and tones, and two sentences cannot contain them all. Pointed in too many directions, a reader's attention follows none. Writers are sometimes tempted to mix metaphors and then apologize for it in some such phrase as "to mix the metaphor" or "if I may be permitted a mixed metaphor." It doesn't work. Don't apologize and don't mix.

Obscure and overdone metaphors falter because the author has misjudged the difficulty of the comparison. The result is either confusion or an insult to the reader's intelligence. In the case of obscurity, a similarity in the author's mind isn't getting onto the page. One student described the spines on a prickly pear cactus as being "slender as a fat man's fingers." I was completely confused by this. Was it ironic, meaning the spines weren't slender at all? Ah no, he said, hadn't I noticed how startling it was when someone with a fleshy body had bony fingers and toes? The trouble here was that the author knew what he meant but had left out the essential abstraction in the comparison, the startling quality of the contrast: "the spines of the fleshy prickly pear, like slender fingers on a fat man."

Too much of any of these devices makes for ridiculous reading—and the line is thin between too much and just enough. Here's one good guideline: If readers start noticing cause more than consequence, it's probably too much.

—Paula LaRocque

In this case, the simile was underexplained. It's probably a more common impulse—we're so anxious to make sure the reader gets it—to explain the obvious. In the novel *Raw Silk*, I had the narrator describe quarrels with her husband, "which I used to face with my dukes up in high confidence that we'd soon clear the air. The air can't be cleared now. We live in marital Los Angeles. This is the air—polluted, poisoned." A critic friend pointed out to me that anybody who didn't know about LA smog wouldn't get it anyway, and that all the last two words did was ram the comparison down the reader's throat. He was right. "The air can't be cleared now. We live in marital Los Angeles. This is the air." The rewrite is much stronger because it neither explains nor exaggerates, and the reader can enjoy supplying the metaphoric link.

Metaphors using *topical references*, including brand names, esoteric objects, or celebrity names, can work as long as a sense of the connection is given; don't rely for effect on knowledge that the reader may not have. To write, "The group looked a lot like the Pussy Riot" is to make the young Russians do your job—and if the reader happens to be a Beethoven buff, or is reading your story twenty years from now, there may be no way of knowing what the reference refers to. "They had the hard beat and in-your-face political courage of Pussy Riot" will convey the sense even for someone who doesn't follow the news. Likewise, "She was as beautiful as Theda Bara" may not mean much to you, whereas if I say, "She had the saucer eyes and satin hair of Theda Bara," you'll get it, close enough.

....

ALLEGORY

Allegory is a narrative form in which comparison is structural rather than stylistic. An allegory is a continuous fictional comparison of events, in which the action of the story represents a different action or a philosophical idea. The simplest illustration of an allegory is a fable, in which, for example, the race between the tortoise and the hare is used to illustrate the philosophical notion that "the race is not always to the swift." Such a story can be seen as an extended simile, with the original figure of the comparison suppressed: the tortoise and the hare represent types of human beings, but people are never mentioned and the comparison takes place in the reader's mind. George Orwell's *Animal Farm* is a less naive animal allegory, exploring ideas about corruption in a democratic society. Muriel Spark's *The Abbey* is a historical allegory, representing, without any direct reference to Richard Nixon, the events of Nixon's presidential tenure through allegorical machinations in a nunnery. The plots of such stories are self-contained, but their significance lies in the reference to outside events or ideas.

Allegory is a tricky form. In the hands of Dante, John Bunyan, Edmund Spenser, John Keats, Franz Kafka, Henrik Ibsen, and Samuel Beckett, it has yielded works of the highest philosophical insight. But most allegories seem to smirk. A naive philosophical fable leads to a simple-minded idea that can be stated in a single phrase; a historical allegory relies on our familiarity with, for example, the Watergate scandal or the tribulations of the local football team, and so appeals to a limited and insular readership.

....

SYMBOL

A symbol differs from metaphor and simile in that it need not contain a comparison. A symbol is an object or event that, by virtue of association, represents something more or something other than itself. Sometimes an object is invested arbitrarily with such meaning, as a flag represents a nation and patriotism. Sometimes a single event stands for a whole complex of events, as the crucifixion of Christ stands as well for resurrection and redemption. Sometimes an object is invested with a complex of qualities through its association with the event, like the cross itself. These symbols are not metaphors; the cross represents redemption but is not similar to redemption, which cannot be said to be wooden or T-shaped. In "Everything That Rises Must Converge" by Flannery O'Connor, the protagonist's mother encounters a black woman wearing the same absurd hat of which she has been so proud. The hat can in no way be said to "resemble" desegregation, but in the course of the story it comes to represent the tenacious nostalgia of gentility and the aspirations of the new black middle class, and therefore the unacknowledged "converging" of equality. Nevertheless, most literary symbols, including this one, do in the course of the action derive their extra meaning from some sort of likeness on the level of emotional or ideological abstraction. The hat is not "like" desegregation, but the action of the story reveals that both women are able to choose such a hat and buy it; this is a concrete example of equality, and so represents the larger concept of equality.

Margaret Drabble's novel The Garrick Year recounts the disillusionment of a young wife and mother who finds no escape from her situation. The book ends with a family picnic in an English meadow and the return home.

> On the way back to the car, Flora dashed at a sheep that was lying in the path, but unlike all the others it did not get up and move:

it stared at us instead with a sick and stricken indignation. Flora passed quickly on, pretending for pride's sake that she had not noticed its recalcitrance; but as I passed, walking slowly, supported by David, I looked more closely and I saw curled up and clutching at the sheep's belly a real snake. I did not say anything to David: I did not want to admit that I had seen it, but I did see it, I can see it still. It is the only wild snake that I have ever seen. In my book on Herefordshire it says that that part of the country is notorious for its snakes. But "Oh, well, so what," is all that one can say, the Garden of Eden was crawling with them too, and David and I managed to lie amongst them for one whole pleasant afternoon. One just has to keep on and to pretend, for the sake of the children, not to notice. Otherwise one might just as well stay at home.

The sheep is a symbol of the young woman's emotional situation. It does resemble her, but only on the level of abstractions: sickness, indignation, and resignation to the fatal dangers of the human condition. There is here a metaphor that could be expressed as such (*she was sick and resigned as the sheep*), but the strength of the symbol is that such literal expression does not take place: we let the sheep stand in the place of the young woman while we reach out to the larger significance.

A symbol may also begin as and grow from a metaphor, so that it finally contains more qualities than the original comparison. In John Irving's novel *The World According to Garp*, the young Garp mishears the word "undertow" as "under toad" and compares the danger of the sea to the lurking fantasies of his childish imagination. Throughout the novel the "under toad" persists, and comes symbolically to represent all the submerged dangers of ordinary life, ready to drag Garp under just when he thinks he is swimming under his own power. Likewise, the African continent in *Heart of Darkness* is dark like the barbaric reaches of the soul; but in the course of the novella we come to understand that darkness is shot with light and light with darkness, that barbarity and civilization are inextricably intermixed, and that the heart of darkness is the darkness of the heart.

One important distinction in the use of literary symbols is between a symbol of which the character is aware and which therefore "belongs" to him or her, and symbols of which only writer and reader are aware, which therefore belong to the work. This distinction is often important to characterization, theme, and distance. In the passage from *The Garrick Year*, the narrator is clearly aware of the import of the sheep, and her awareness suggests her intelligence and the final acceptance of her situation; the result is that we identify with her in recognizing the symbol. The mother in "Everything That Rises Must Converge," on the other hand, does not recognize the hat as a symbol, and this distances us from her perception. She is merely disconcerted and angered that a black woman can dress in the same style she does, whereas for author and reader the coincidence symbolizes a larger convergence.

When characters are aware of their own symbols, that awareness can develop and define relationship. In Lisa Halliday's *Asymmetry*, a woman in her twenties and her much older, famous lover betray in their banter his wide experience and unwillingness to commit, and her resentment yet, nevertheless, acceptance of the situation:

"I love you," purred Alice.

"You love Vicodin is what you love. We're out of film." He went to the closet.

"What else have you got in there?"

"You don't wanna know."

"Yes I do."

"More girls. Tied up."

"How many?"

"Three."

"What are their names? . . . Let me guess. Katie and . . . Emily? Is Emily in there?"

"Yep."

"And Miranda?"

"That's right"

"Those girls are incorrigible."

"Incorrigible," he repeated, as though she had made up the word.

Sometimes the interplay between these types of symbol—those recognized by the characters and those seen only by writer and reader—can enrich the story in scope or irony. In *The Inheritors*, Golding's Neanderthal tribe has its own religious symbols—a root, a grave, shapes in the ice cap—that represent its life-cycle worship. But in the course of the action, flood, fire, and a waterfall recall biblical symbols that allow the reader to supply an additional religious interpretation, which the characters would be incapable of doing. Likewise the exchange above may represent the novel's title, *Asymmetry*, as a metaphor not, or not yet, acknowledged by the characters. Again, in "Everything That Rises Must Converge," the mother sees her hat as representing, first, her taste and pride and, later, the outrageousness of black presumption. For the reader it has the opposite and ironic significance, as a symbol of equality.

Symbols are subject to all the same faults as metaphor: cliché, strain, obscurity, obviousness, and overwriting. For these reasons, and because the word "symbolism" also describes a particular late nineteenth-century movement in French poetry, with connotations of obscurity, dream, and magical incantation, *symbolism* as a method has sometimes been treated with scorn in the hard-nosed contemporary canon, while prose that is flat, spare, and plain has been praised as more truthful.

Yet is seems to me incontrovertible that the writing process is inherently and by definition symbolic. In the structuring of events, the creation of character and atmosphere, the choice of object, detail, and language, you are selecting and arranging toward the goal that these elements should signify more than their mute material existence. If this were not so, then you would have no principle of choice and might just as well write about any other set of events, characters, and objects. If you so much as say, "as innocent as a cabbage," the image is minutely symbolic, not a statement of fact but selected to mean something more and something other than itself.

People constantly function symbolically. We must do so because we rarely know exactly what we mean, and if we do we are not willing to express it, and if we are willing we are not able, and if we are able we are not heard, and if we are heard we are not understood. Words are unwieldy and unyielding, and we leap past them with intuition, body language, tone, and symbol. "Is the oven supposed to be on?" he asks.

He is only peripherally curious about whether the oven is supposed to be on. He is really complaining: *You're scatterbrained and extravagant with the money I go out and earn.* "If I don't preheat it, the muffins won't crest," she says, meaning: *You didn't catch me this time! You're always complaining about the food and God knows I wear myself out trying to please you.* "We used to have salade niçoise in the summertime," he recalls, meaning: *Don't be so damn triumphant. You're still extravagant, and you haven't got the class you used to have when we were young.* "We used to keep a garden," she says, meaning: *You're always away on weekends and never have time to do anything with me because you don't love me anymore; I think you have a mistress.* "What do you expect of me!" he explodes, and neither of them is surprised that ovens, muffins, salads, and gardens have erupted. When people say "we quarreled over nothing," this is what they mean—they quarreled over symbols.

....

THE OBJECTIVE CORRELATIVE

But the conflict in a fiction cannot be "over nothing," and as a writer you must search for concrete external manifestations that are adequate to the inexpressible feeling. In *The Sacred Wood*, T. S. Eliot used the term "objective correlative" to describe this process and this necessity:

> The only way of expressing emotion in the form of art is by finding an "objective correlative"; in other words, a set of objects, a situation, a chain of events which shall be the formula of that particular emotion; such that when the external facts, which must terminate in sensory experience, are given, the emotion is immediately invoked.

Some critics have argued that Eliot's *objective correlative* is no more than a synonym for *symbol*, but the term and its definition make several important distinctions:

1. An "objective correlative" contains and evokes an *emotion*. Unlike many other sorts of symbols—scientific formulae, notes of music, the letters of the alphabet—the purpose of artistic symbol is to invoke emotion.

2. Some kinds of symbol—religious or political, for example—also arouse emotion, but they do so by virtue of one's acceptance of a general community of belief not specific to the context in which that symbol is used. The wine that represents the blood of Christ will evoke the same general emotion in Venice, Buenos Aires, and New York. But an artistic symbol arouses an emotion specific to the work and does not rely on sympathy or belief outside that work. Mentioning the wine of the Communion ceremony in a story cannot be relied on to produce religious emotion in the reader; indeed, the author may choose to make it arouse some other emotion entirely.

3. The elements of a story are interrelated in such a way that the specific objects, situation, and events produce a specific emotion. The "romance" and "pity" invoked by *Romeo and Juliet* are not the same romance and pity invoked by *Anna Karenina* or *Gone with the Wind*, because the external manifestations in each work (which, being external, "terminate in sensory experience") define the nature of the emotion.

4. The objects, situation, and events of a particular work contain its particular effect; conversely, if they do not contain the desired emotional effect, that effect cannot be produced in that work, either by its statement in abstractions or by appeal to outside symbols. The "objective" sensory experience (objects, situation, events) must be "co-relative" to the emotion, each corresponding to the other, for that is the only way of expressing emotion in the form of art.

When literary symbols fail, it is most often in this difficult and essential mutuality. In a typical example, we begin the story in the room of a dying woman alone with her collection of perfume bottles. The story ranges back over her rich and sensuous life, and at the end we focus on an empty perfume bottle. It is meant to move us at her death, but it does not. Yet the fault is not in the perfume bottle. Presumably a perfume bottle may express mortality as well as a hat may express racial equality. The fault is in the use of the symbol, which has not been integrated into the texture of the story. As Bonnie Friedman puts it in *Writing Past Dark*, "Before a thing can be a symbol it must be a thing. It must do its job as a thing in the world before and during and after you have projected your meaning all over it." In the case of the perfume bottle we would need to be convinced, perhaps, of the importance this woman placed on scent as essence, need to know what part the collection has played in the conflicts of her life, perhaps need to see her fumbling now toward her favorite, so that we could emotionally equate the spilling or evaporation of the scent with the death of her own spirit.

A symbolic object, situation, or event may err because it is insufficiently integrated into the story, and so seems to exist for its own sake rather than to emanate naturally from the characters' lives. It may err because the objective correlative is inadequate to the emotion it is supposed to evoke. Or it may err because it is too heavy or heavy-handed; that is, the author keeps pushing the symbol at us, nudging us in the ribs to say, Get it? In any of these cases we will say that the symbol is artificial—a curious word in the critical vocabulary, analogous to the charge of a formulaic plot, since art, like form, is a word of praise. All writing is "artificial," and when we charge it with being so, we mean that it isn't artificial enough, that the artifice has not concealed itself so as to give the illusion of the natural, and that the artificer must go back to work.

....

SUGGESTED STORIES
"Lost in the Funhouse"
    John Barth
"San"
    Lan Samantha Chang
"The Crane Child"
    David Leavitt
"The Ones Who Walked Away from Omelas"
    Ursula K. Le Guin
"Menagerie"
    Charles Johnson
"Before the Change"
    Alice Munro
"Underground Women"
    Jesse Lee Kercheval

"Eyes of a Blue Dog"
  Gabriel García Márquez
"Wolf of White Forest"
  Anthony Marra
"Signs and Symbols"
  Vladimir Nabokov

WRITING PROMPTS

1. Comb through your journal to find clichés. In each case, replace them with concrete details or more original similes or metaphors.
2. Write two one-page scenes, each containing an extended metaphor. In one, compare an ordinary object to something of great size and significance; in the other, compare a major thing or phenomenon to something smaller and more mundane.
3. List all the clichés you can think of to describe a pair of eyes. Then write a paragraph in which you find a fresh new metaphor for eyes.
4. Write your own interpretation of a fairy tale, setting it in the present to construct an allegory. How might you incorporate the ideas of contemporary technology, politics, relationships, or other social concerns, and still keep recognizable the core of the tale?
5. Let an object smaller than a breadbox symbolize hope, redemption, or love to the central character. Let it symbolize something else entirely to the reader.
6. Take any dead metaphor and write a serious or comic scene that reinvests the metaphor with its original comparative force. (*Sifting the evidence: the lawyer uses a colander, a tea strainer, two coffee filters, and a garlic press to decide the case.*) Try one of these, or make up your own:
   - Bus terminal
   - Reality show
   - Don't spoil your lunch
   - Nothing but net
   - Deadline
   - Broken home

9: Play It Again, Sam

REVISION AND THEME

"Talent is a long patience," Anton Chekhov said, an acknowledgment that the creative process is not all inventive and extends far beyond the first heated rush. Corrective, critical, nutritive, and fostering, revision is a matter of rendering a story the best that it can be. William C. Knott, in *The Craft of Fiction*, cogently observes that "anyone can write; only the writers can rewrite. Here is where the job gets done, where the crucial struggle is fought. And no one can do it for you."

....

RE-VISION

Revising is a process more dreaded than dreadful. The resistance to rewriting is, if anything, greater than the resistance to beginning in the first place. Yet chances are that once you have committed yourself to a first draft, you'll be unable to leave it in an unfinished and unsatisfying state. You'll be *unhappy* until it's right. Making it right will involve a second commitment, to seeing the story fresh and creating it again with the advantage of "re-vision." All the methods of shaping, enriching, and enlivening fiction discussed throughout this book implicitly concern this revision. Alice Munro, in the introduction to her *Selected Stories*, describes the risk, the readiness, and the reward. It is, she says, precisely when you think it is finished that

> the story is in the greatest danger of losing its life. . . . It does what I intended, but it turns out that my intention was all wrong. . . . I go around glum and preoccupied, trying to think of ways to fix the problem. Usually the right way pops up in the middle of this.
>
> A big relief, then. Renewed energy. Resurrection.
>
> Except that it isn't the right way. Maybe a way to the right way. Now I write pages and pages I'll have to discard. . . . Out they go. But by this time I'm on the track. . . . I just have to keep trying till I find the best way of getting there.

Everything that needs to be said has already been said. But since no one was listening, everything must be said again.
—André Gide

To find the best way of getting there, you may have to "see again" more than once. The process of revision involves external and internal insight. You'll need your conscious critic, your creative instinct, and readers you trust. You may need each of them several times, not necessarily in that order. A story gets better not just by polishing and refurbishing, not just by improving a word choice here and an image there, but by taking risks with the structure, re-envisioning, being open to new meaning itself. Annie Dillard uses the metaphor of knocking out "a bearing wall" for the revising writer's sacrifice of the very aspect of the story that inspired its writing. Extreme as it sounds, this is an experience familiar to many accomplished writers:

> The part you must jettison is not only the best-written part; it is also, oddly, that part which was to have been the very point. It is the original key passage, the passage on which the rest was to hang, and from which you yourself drew the courage to begin.
> —Annie Dillard, *The Writing Life*

Worry It and Walk Away
To write your first draft, you banished the internal critic. Now make the critic welcome. Revision is work, but you may find you can concentrate

on the work for much longer than you could play at freedrafting. It has occurred to me that writing a first draft is very like tennis or softball— I have to be psyched for it. Energy level up, alert, on my toes. A few hours is all I can manage, and at the end of it I'm wiped out. Revision is like careful carpentry, and if I'm under a deadline or just determined to get this thing crafted and polished, I can be good for twelve hours of it.

> *It doesn't have to be calm and clear-eyed. You just have to not give up.*
>
> *—David Mamet*

The first round of rewrites is probably a matter of letting your misgivings surface. Focus for a while on what seems awkward, overlong, undeveloped, flat, or flowery. Tinker. Tighten. Sharpen. More important at this stage than finishing any given page or phrase is getting to know your story in order to open it to new possibilities. You will also get tired of it; you may feel stuck.

Then put it away. Don't look at it for a matter of days or weeks— until you feel fresh on the project. In addition to getting some distance on your story, you're mailing it to your unconscious, not deliberately working out the flaws but temporarily letting them go. Rollo May, in *The Courage to Create*, describes what frequently happens next:

> Everyone uses from time to time such expressions as, "a thought pops up," an idea comes "from the blue" or "dawns" or "comes as though out of a dream," or "it suddenly hit me." These are various ways of describing a common experience: the breakthrough of ideas from some depth below the level of awareness.

It is my experience that such realizations occur over and over again in the course of writing a short story or novel. Often I will believe that because I know who my characters are and what happens to them, I know what my story is about—and often I find I'm wrong, or that my understanding is shallow or incomplete.

In the first draft of my novel *Cutting Stone*, for instance, I opened with the sentence, "It took a hundred and twelve bottles of champagne to see the young Poindexters off to Arizona." A page later one character whispered to another that young Mr. Poindexter had "consumption."

I worked on this book for a year (taking my characters off to Arizona where they dealt with the desert heat, thirst, alcoholism, loss of religion, and the development of mining interests and the building trade) before I saw the connection between "consumption" and "champagne." When I understood that simple link, I understood the overarching theme—surely latent in the idea from the moment it had taken hold of me—between tuberculosis, spiritual thirst, consumerism, and addiction, all issues of "consumption."

When you are despairing, walk away from your work. Take out a blank sheet of paper and write down three things that have already happened that day for which you are grateful. Remember how luminous you are; reflect on all the people who believe in you. Then get back to work.

—Frances Ya-Chu Cowhig

It might seem dismaying that you should see what your story is about only after you have written it. But try it; you'll like it. Nothing is more exhilarating than the discovery that a complex pattern has lain in your mind ready to unfold.

In the early stages of revision, both the worrying and the walking away are necessary. Perhaps it is bafflement itself that plunges us into the unconscious space where the answer lies.

Criticism and the Workshop

Once you have thought your story through, drafted it, and worked on it to the best of your ability, someone else's eyes can help to refresh the vision of your own. The trick to making good use of criticism is to be utterly selfish about it. Be greedy for it. Take it all in. Ultimately you are the laborer, the arbiter, and the boss in any dispute about your story, so you can afford to consider any problem and any solution. Most of us feel not only committed to what we have put on the page but defensive on its behalf—wanting, really, to be told only that it is a work of genius or, failing that, to find out that we have gotten away with it. Therefore, the first exigency of revision is that you learn to hear, absorb, and accept criticism.

"Revising is like cutting your own hair," says novelist Robert Stone: while you may sense the need for improvement, it's hard to get right what you can never entirely see for yourself. This is the major advantage of a workshop—your fellow writers may not be able to tell you how to style the material in the way that best suits the story, but they can at least hold up the mirror and also offer a more distanced perspective. Wise professionals rely on the help of an agent or editor at this juncture (although even the wisest still smart at censure), and most count on regular feedback from other writers in regular meetings. So if a workshop is not available to you, start your own. You can always ask other writers, put a notice in the local paper or on social media. Meeting face to face is always best, but online groups can also flourish.

How to assimilate so many opinions, let alone choose what is useful? First, give special consideration to the comments of those two or three workshop members with whose responses you have generally agreed before. However, the best criticism—or at any rate the most useful—simply points out what you had already sensed for yourself but had hoped to get away with. As Flannery O'Connor put it, with typical bluntness, in fiction "you can do anything you can get away with, but nobody has ever gotten away with much."

It used to be popular to speak of "constructive criticism" and "destructive criticism," but these are misleading terms suggesting that positive remarks are useful and negative criticism useless. In practice the opposite is usually the case. You're likely to find that the most constructive thing a reader can do is say I don't believe this, I don't follow this, I don't understand this, pointing to precisely the passages that made you uneasy. This kind of laying-the-finger-on-the-trouble-spot produces an inward groan, but it's also satisfying; you know just where to go to work. Often the most destructive thing a reader can do is offer you a positive suggestion—Why don't you have him crash the car?—that is irrelevant to your vision of the story. Be suspicious of praise that is too extravagant, of blame that is too general. If your impulse is to defend the story or yourself, still the impulse. Behave as if bad advice were good advice, and give it serious consideration. You can reject it after you have explored it for anything of use it may offer.

Workshop members often voice sharply divided responses to a manuscript, a situation that may confuse and frustrate the author. Algonquin Books editor Duncan Murrell advises that workshop writers pay close attention to the parts of their work that make readers stumble, but disregard most of the solutions those readers suggest. . . . Good readers have a gut level understanding that something's wrong in a story, but they're often unclear about what it is, or what to do about it. Yet once pointed to the weak sections, authors almost always come up with better solutions than anything a reader or an editor can offer. . . . The trick is to bite your lip when readers tell you how to fix your story, while noting the passages that need repair.

Indeed, while the author may or may not benefit from peer critique, everyone else in the workshop does, for the practice of thinking through and articulating responses to a story's challenges eventually makes all participants more objective critics of their own work. You will notice that the more specific the criticism you offer—or receive—the more useful it proves and the less it stings; similarly, the more specific the praise of "what works," the more likely it is to reinforce good habits—and to be believed.

> *Art is not difficult because it wishes to be difficult, but because it wishes to be art.*
> *—Donald Barthelme*

After several months with the experience of the workshop, you'll find that you can critique a story within your own imagination, knowing who would say what, with whom you would agree, and what you already know to be true.

Within a day or two of the workshop, novelist-playwright Michelle Carter advises, the author should try to "re-hear criticism," that is, to assess what it is readers are responding to, which may not be apparent from the suggested "fix." For example, if a number of readers suggest changing the story's point of view from third person to first, Carter might reinterpret that to mean that the narrator seems too remote from the characters—not that first-person narration is literally a better choice, but that readers want a more immediate experience of the main character's emotional dilemma.

Similarly, if readers want "to know more about Character X," the best response is not necessarily to sprinkle in more facts and backstory. What they actually want may be a greater understanding of the character's motivations or a closer rendering of crucial moments.

Be tough with yourself, Carter urges, even when you realize that criticism is based on a misreading. Rarely is misinterpretation solely the mistake of the reader: ask what awkwardness of writing or false emphasis might have led to that skewed reading. Novelist Wally Lamb reinforces this point:

> Often I think we let the writer get away with too much. If the writing is unclear, we'll read it a second time and make it clear to ourselves and then let the writer off the hook, when, in fact, the writing has to stand for itself. . . . You want to work on the writing until it is good enough that the writer doesn't have to be in the room explaining and interpreting.

Kenneth Atchity, in A Writer's Time, advises compulsory "vacations" at crucial points in the revising process, in order to let the criticism cook until you feel ready, or impatient, to get back to writing. So once again, walk away, and when you feel that you have acquired enough distance from the criticism and the story to see it anew, go back to work. Make notes of your plans, large and small. Talk to yourself in your journal about what you want to accomplish and where you think you have failed. Let your imagination play with new images or passages of dialogue. Always keep a hard or digital copy of each draft so that you can go back to it if you later want to—and then be ruthless rewriting the next. Eudora Welty advised cutting apart printed pages and pinning them back together so that they can be easily rearranged. I like to use the whole surface of the kitchen table as a cut-and-tape board before I cut-and-paste on the computer. Some people can keep the story in their heads and do their rearranging directly on the screen—which in any case has made the putting-back-together process a mechanical matter.

Revision Questions

As you plan the revision and as you rewrite, you will know (and your critics will tell you) what problems are unique to your story. There are also general, almost universal, pitfalls that you can avoid if you ask yourself the following questions:

Why should the reader turn from the first page to the second? Does the first sentence, paragraph, page introduce real tension? If it doesn't, you have probably begun at the wrong place. If you can't find a way to introduce tension on the first page, you may have to question whether you have a story after all.

Is there unnecessary summary? It is a common impulse to try to cover too much ground. Cut down on summary and unnecessary flashback. These dissipate energy and lead you to tell rather than show. How much *necessary* information can be conveyed through dialogue, dress or gesture, a brief thought?

Is it original? Almost every writer thinks first, in some way or other, of the familiar, the usual, the given. This character is a stereotype, that emotion is too easy, that phrase is a cliché. First-draft mistakes are inevitable, but letting the inert choice stand is a way of being dishonest. A good writer will comb the work for clichés and labor to find the exact, the honest, and the fresh.

Is it clear? Although ambiguity and mystery provide some of our most profound pleasures in literature, beginning writers are often unable to distinguish between mystery and muddle, ambiguity and sloppiness. You may want your character to be rich with contradiction, but we need to be oriented on the simplest level of reality before we can share your imaginative world. Where are we? When are we? Who are they? How do things look? What time of day or night is it? What's the weather? What's happening?

Is it self-conscious? Probably the most famous piece of advice to the rewriter is William Faulkner's "kill all your darlings." When you are carried away with the purple of your prose, the music of your alliteration, the hilarity of your wit, the profundity of your insights, chances are that you are having a better time writing than the reader will have reading. No reader will forgive you, and no reader should. Just tell the story. The style will follow of itself if you just tell the story.

Where is it too long? Most of us, and even the best of us, write too long. We are so anxious to explain every nuance, cover every possible aspect of

character, action, and setting that we forget the necessity of stringent selection. In fiction, and especially in the short story, we want sharpness,
economy, and vivid, telling detail. More than necessary is too much.
I have been helped in my own tendency to tell all by a friend who went
through a copy of one of my novels, drawing a line through the last sentence of about every third paragraph. Then in the margin he wrote, again
and again, "Hit it and get out." That's good advice for anyone.

Are there too many scenes? Many novice writers, especially if a story is
developed from a real experience, are tempted to give each turn of plot
or change of setting a new scene when several could be fused to better
effect. One night they're tender and the next they quarrel? Could the spat
come right after the cuddle, and raise either the comedy or the tension
level, or both? This is hard but sound advice: *Tell your story in the fewest
possible scenes.* It may seem impossible to cut or fuse, but often there's
a way if you give it enough thought.

Is the language fresh? Is there a way to sharpen the imagery, the dialogue, the setting? Are the characters alive? Could they be a little brighter,
darker, more intense, more present to us?

Where is the story undeveloped in character, action, imagery, theme? In any
first, second, or third draft of a manuscript there are likely to be necessary passages sketched, skipped, or
skeletal. What information is miss- **The better I get, the harder it is.**
ing, what actions incomplete, what **—Christopher Coake**
motives obscure, what images in-
exact? Where does the action occur so abruptly that it loses its emotional
force? Is the crisis presented as a scene?

Where is it too general? Originality, economy, and clarity can all be
achieved through the judicious use of significant detail. Learn to spot
general, vague, and fuzzy terms. Be suspicious of yourself anytime you
see nouns like *someone* or *everything*, adjectives like *huge* or *handsome*, adverbs like *very* or *really*. Seek instead a particular thing, a particular size,
an exact degree.

Although the dread of "starting over" is a real and understandable
one, chances are that the rewards of revising will startlingly outweigh
the pains. Sometimes a character who is dead on the page will come to

life through the addition of a few lines of dialogue or the re-seeing of details. Sometimes a turgid or tedious paragraph can become sharp with a few judicious cuts. Sometimes dropping page one and putting page seven where page three used to be can provide a skeleton to an otherwise limp story. And sometimes, often, perhaps always, the difference between an amateur rough cut and a publishable story is in the struggle at the rewriting stage.

Here are a couple of devices to try. If you've been writing your story on a computer, retype at least one full draft, making both planned and spontaneous changes as you go. The computer's abilities can tempt us to take a "fix-it" approach to revision, but jumping in and out of the text to correct problems can result in a revision that reads like patchwork. Rather, the effect of even small changes should ripple through the story, and this is more likely to happen if the writer reenters the story as a whole by literally rewriting it from start to finish.

Write two or three revisions of a story draft, focusing on a different issue each time. You might zero in on the motivations of a character whose behavior and dialogue don't yet ring true; or you might simply focus on using setting to reflect emotion or threading physical activity through dialogue scenes. Focusing on a single goal lets you concentrate your efforts—yet other developments will naturally occur in response to the single-focus changes.

In an interview in *Conversations on Writing Fiction*, novelist and teacher Jane Smiley says she asks her student writers to confront their own sets of "evasions," the counterproductive "rituals which don't actually allow them to spend time with or become engaged with their chosen themes or characters." For example, many people find conflict hard to handle in real life and therefore avoid it, often for good reason. Yet many of us sidestep conflict in our fiction too, even knowing its necessity in driving a character toward a defining crisis. If this sounds like an evasion you've experienced, take a look back at places in the story where explosive scenes *should* happen—places where characters ought to confront or defend. Are these, in fact, all-out scenes? Or do your characters neatly sidestep the conflict and retreat to their private thoughts? Does another character too conveniently knock at the door?

Taking refuge in the making of metaphors, however vivid, rather than clearly depicting what *is*, may be another form of evasion, perhaps reflecting a writer's lack of confidence in the interest of his or her material.

Spiraling off into the weird and random may reflect a similar lack of confidence or indecision; overly clever, bantering dialogue that strains to entertain may reflect a desire to dazzle, while avoiding the harder search for the voice and speech that is both realistic and revealing of character.

Evasions may be easier to observe in others' work at first, so you might want to ask a trusted friend or workshop mate to help you recognize the evasions in your own stories. As you revise and encounter points of resistance—those places you hesitate to go further or become more specific—ask yourself, Is this right for the story or is it simply my comfortable habit?

....

THEME

Asking the Big Question: What Have I Written?
How does a fiction mean?

Imaginative writing is ultimately a hybrid creature, one part wanting wild flight, the other thrilling to the harness. In a piece of literary criticism, your goal is to say as clearly and directly as possible what you mean. In fiction, your goal is to make people and make them do things and, ideally, never to "say what you mean" at all. Theoretically, an outline can never harm a paper for a literature class: this is what I have to say, and I'll say it through points A, B, and C. But if a writer sets out to write a story to illustrate an idea, the fiction will almost inevitably be

A good novel begins with a small question and ends with a bigger one.
—Paula Fox

thin. Even if you begin with an outline, as many writers do, it will be an outline of the action and not of your "points." You may not know the meaning of the story until the characters begin to tell you what it is. You'll begin with an image of a person or a situation that seems vaguely to embody something important, and you'll learn as you go what that something is. Likewise, what you mean will emerge in the reading experience and take place in the reader's mind, "not," as the narrator says of Marlow's tales in *Heart of Darkness*, "inside like a kernel but outside, enveloping the tale which brought it out."

But early or late in the revision process, you may find yourself impelled by, under pressure of, or interested primarily in your theme. It will seem that you have set yourself this lonely, austere, and tortuous task because you do have something to say. At this point you will, and you should, begin to let the sorting-comparing-cataloging neocortex of your brain go to work on the stuff of your story. Rather than "putting in a theme," you'll be looking back to see what you've already, mostly subconsciously, been doing all along. John Gardner describes the process in *The Art of Fiction*.

> Theme, it should be noticed, is not imposed on the story but evoked from within it—initially an intuitive but finally an intellectual act on the part of the writer. The writer muses on the story idea to determine what it is in it that has attracted him, why it seems to him worth telling. Having determined . . . what interests him— and what chiefly concerns the major character . . . he toys with various ways of telling his story, thinks about what has been said before about [his theme], broods on every image that occurs to him, turning it over and over, puzzling it, hunting for connections, trying to figure out—before he writes, while he writes, and in the process of repeated revisions—what it is he really thinks. . . . Only when he thinks about a story in this way does he achieve not just an alternative reality or, loosely, an imitation of nature, but true, firm art—fiction as serious thought.

So, theme is what your story is about. But that is not enough, because a story may be "about" a dying samurai or a quarreling couple or two kids on a trampoline, and those would not be the themes of those stories. A story is also "about" an abstraction, and if the story is significant, that abstraction may be very large; yet thousands of stories are about love, other thousands about death, and still other thousands about both love and death, and to say this is to say little about the theme of any of them.

We might better understand theme if we ask questions like What does this story say about what it's about? What does it tell us about the idea or abstraction that seems to be contained in it? What attitudes or judgments does it imply? Above all, how do the elements of fiction contribute to our experience of those ideas and attitudes in the story?

How Fictional Elements Contribute to Theme
Whatever the idea and attitudes that underlie the theme of a story, that story will bring them into the realm of experience through its particular and unique pattern. Theme involves emotion, logic, and judgment, all three—but the pattern that forms the particular experience of that theme is made up of every element of fiction this book has discussed: the arrangement, shape, and flow of the action, as performed by the characters, realized in their details, seen in their atmosphere, from a unique point of view, through the imagery and the rhythm of the language.

The process of discovering the theme of your story, worrying the story until its theme reveals itself, connections occur, images recur, a pattern emerges—is more conscious than readers know, beginning writers want to accept, or established writers are willing to admit. It has become a popular—cliché—stance for writers to claim that they haven't the faintest idea what they mean in their

> *Some people say that you should write what you know, but I am driven to write what I learn.*
>
> *—Abby Geni*

writing. *Don't ask me; read the book. If I knew what it meant, I wouldn't have written it. It means what it says.* When an author makes such a response, what it indicates is not that there are no themes, ideas, or meanings in the work but that these are not separable from the pattern of fictional experience in which they are embodied.

But beginning critics also resist. Students irritated by the analysis of literature often ask, How do you know she did that on purpose? How do you know it didn't just happen to come out that way? The answer is that you don't. But what is on the page is on the page. An author, no less than a reader or critic, can see an emerging pattern, and the author has both the possibility and the obligation of manipulating it. When you have put something on the page, you have two possibilities, and only two: you may cut it or you are committed to it.

A Revision Narrative

Again, I can only illustrate this labor of revision and discovery from my own experience. As I write this, I am still in the process of revising a novel, *Indian Dancer*. The novel tells the story of a girl born in Belgium in 1930, who escapes to England during the Second World War and later emigrates to America. Most of the novel deals with her adolescent and adult life, but after I had written many of the later scenes, it seemed to me that the novel should begin with an image of that childhood escape, which affects everything she later does. I felt "inspired" when I woke up one morning and tapped out this:

> *If you haven't surprised yourself, you haven't written.*
> *—Eudora Welty*

> Always,
>   she retained one image from the boat, too fleeting for a memory but too substantial for a dream, like a few frames clipped from a kinetoscope. She was standing in the stern, embraced from behind by a woman who was wrapping her in rough blanket stuff. Her shoes and the hem of her coat above her knees were wet. She knew that the woman was kind, but the smell of anxiety and too many nights' sweat filled her with dark judgment. There was no moon at all, which was the point, but all the same she could watch the wake of the boat widening behind them. She also knew, in a cold, numbed way, that her father was bleeding on the shore, but what presented itself as monstrous was the wake, dark and glutinous, ever spreading toward the land, as if she herself were a speck being washed from a wound. *I will never go back. I will never.* This was experienced as grief, not yet a vow.

After a day or so I felt this was melodramatic—that "dark judgment," her father "bleeding on the shore," the "monstrous" and "glutinous" sea. I noticed that "kinetoscope" stuck out like a piece of show-off research.

I thought there should be more sense of the woman trying to help her, and of the others on the boat. The past tense also troubled me. If she "always retained," then wouldn't the memory be in the present?

> Always,
>
> also, she is standing in the stern, embraced from behind by a woman who swaddles her in coarse blanket stuff. Her shoes and the hem of her coat above her knees are wet. There is no moon—which is the point—but all the same she can see the wake widening in the Channel, and close beside her on the deck the boy who broke his shin, the bone stub moving under the flesh like a tongue in a cheek. The man—his father?—still has the boy's mouth stuffed with a forearm of loden coat to keep him from crying out, although they are far enough from shore that the oars have been shipped and the motor roped into life. It sputters like a heart. Behind her the people huddle—you can't tell heroes from refugees—over flasks of tea and Calvados whose fireapple smell flings up on the smell of sea. She will never see any of these people again. The woman's armpit cups her chin, old wet wool and fear. She knows unflinchingly that her father has been left behind. What presents itself as monstrous is the wake—dark, glutinous—which seems to be driving them from the land on its slubbed point as if the boat is a clot being washed from a wound.
>
> *I will never go back. I will never.* This is experienced as grief, not yet a vow.

I fiddled with this a lot, still dissatisfied with its tone, which seemed to set the book on a loftier course than I intended, but it was several months before it struck me that *the woman should tell this scene.* I think it was the image of the boy's broken bone "like a tongue in a cheek" that gave me the first hint of the woman's voice. She was a British woman; I imagined her as working class, one of the accidental heroes of the Resistance, a practical, solid sort. This revelation must have occurred to me on an airplane (the disembodied feeling of airplanes *always* sets me writing) because I scribbled my notes on a page of a yellow pad (shown on page 216).

Now I started over, putting the scene back in chronological order but always chasing the woman's voice, also reading up on the period and

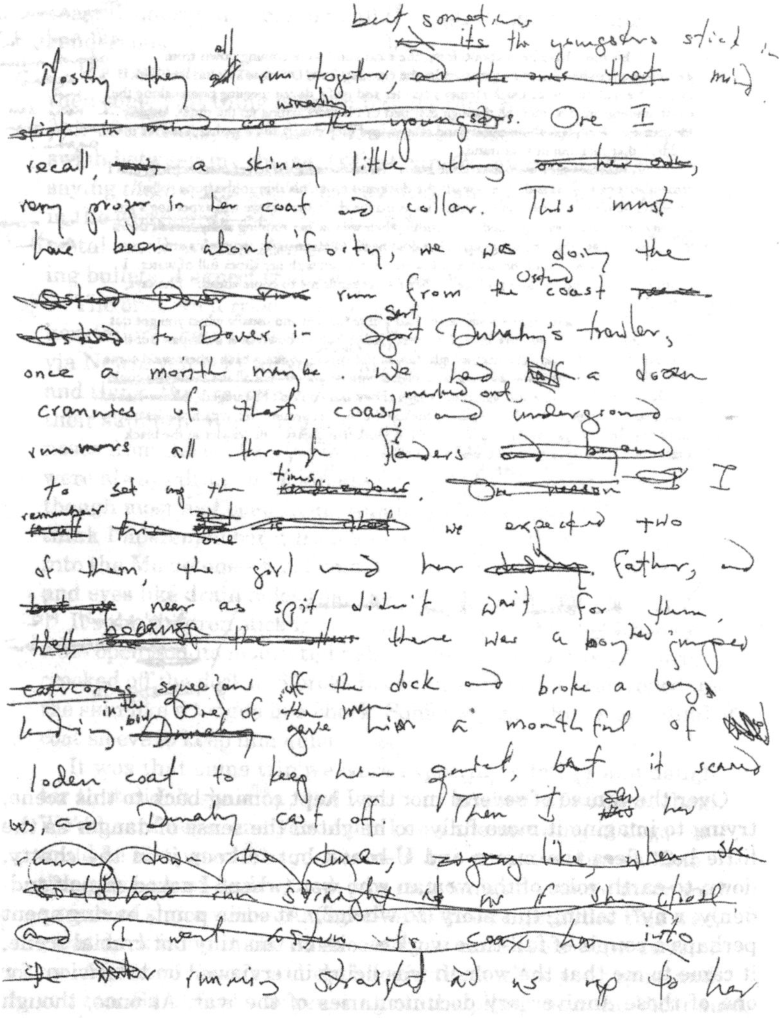
Mostly they all run together, but sometimes the youngsters stick in mind. One I recall, a skinny little thing, very proper in her coat and collar. This must have been about 'forty, we was doing the run from the Ostend coast to Dover in Sgt Dunahy's trawler, once a month maybe. We had a dozen crannies of that coast marked out and underground runners all through Flanders to set up the times. I remember one we expected two of them, the girl and her father, and near as spit didn't wait for them. There was a boy'ed jumped squealing off the dock and broke a leg landing in the bow. One of the men gave him a mouthful of loden coat to keep him quiet, but it scared us, and Dunahy cast off. Then I saw her running straight at us up to her

the events of the war, checking out British expressions with my son who lives in London.

Over the course of several months I kept coming back to this scene, trying to imagine it more fully, to heighten the sense of danger as the little boat flees the mines and U-boats, but to keep it in the chatty, down-

This must have been about 'forty, the Vicar and I were coming down from Teddington maybe once a month to make the crossing from Dover to Ostend and back again. We had the use of Duck Henley's trawler and half a dozen meeting points along the coast, underground runners all through that part of Flanders setting up the times. ~~Usually I~~ ~~they came on foot, talk about misery and scared, and~~ they mostly run together, only it's the children that stick out in your mind.

~~Sometimes they were that dumb brave. There were babies never made a peep, and~~ I remember one boy landed squeejaw off the dock and broke his shin so the bone rolled under his skin like a tongue in a cheek. It was maybe the same trip we was expecting a girl and her father and nearly pushed off without when we saw her running ~~all by herself~~ down the rocks, straight into the water up to her coat hem. O'Hannaughy swung his arm signalling her to go round the dock and lowered her down with her shoes full of water. I wrapped her up and she says po-faced, "My Father sends me to come ahead." She says, "My fah-zer."

What I remember ~~about her~~ is, we had a little bunsen and usually when you got out far enough to rope the motors alive, they were glad to hunker down over a cuppa. But this one didn't leave the stern six, maybe eight hours of crossing, looking back where we'd come from. ~~It was black dark—we always picked nights with no moon—but all the same you could see the wake.~~ Very polite she was in her soggy shoes, but couldn't be budged. ~~I knew not to talk about her father.~~ And I remember I tucked the blanket around her, which she let me, and I thought the way we must have looked to God, that greasy little trawler in the black ~~water~~, like a clot being washed ~~out of~~ a wound.

[handwritten margin notes:] They came in all sorts, talk about misery & scared. I never said a one of them again.

or maybe another.

[handwritten below:] in the ~~black~~ dark ~~with no moon~~.

arrives not. He ~~keeps looking but~~ is ~~not able to~~

---

to-earth voice of the woman who was—when? I asked myself suddenly; why?—telling this story—to whom? At some point, having spent perhaps a couple of full-time work weeks on this tiny but crucial scene, it came to me that the woman was being interviewed on television, for one of those anniversary documentaries of the war. At once, though I do not describe the scene of the interview, I could see and hear her more clearly.

The book now begins this way:

Transit: Ostend–Dover

All that spring and summer we brought back boatloads of the refugees. The Vicar organized us. They didn't mind I was a woman because I was able-bodied. We travelled down from Teddington once a month to make the crossing, and we had the use of Duck Henley's trawler and half a dozen meeting points along the Flemish coast. Underground runners all through Belgium setting up the rendezvous.

It's a wonder what you remember. Great swollen blanks, and then some daft thing bobs up like flotsam. Such as, I'd never worn a pair of trousers, and what I couldn't get used to was the twill going swish between my thighs. Is that camera running? Don't show me saying *thighs*, will you? Anyway, that and the smells. Tar, old fish in the wet boards. Seasick, of course. And off your own skin a bit of metal smell, with a sourness like fireworks. When they say "sweating bullets" I expect that's what they mean.

The ones we ferried came in every sort—rich man, poor man, tinker, tailor. I never saw a one of them again. Now and then I cross via Newhaven over to Normandy for the shopping, and I look around and think: they're not so different, take away their pocket books and their sunburn. What struck me, in Teddington everybody got raw noses from the cold and spider veins from the fire, but those ones were always drained-looking like they hadn't been out of doors, although most had been living rough or walking nights. You probably think I misremember it from a newsreel—not that we ever made it into the Movietone—but I said it at the time: every one of them gray, and eyes like drain holes that the color washed right down.

It's the children stick in your mind—a wee tiddler with its eyes wide open and its mouth tight shut. I remember one boy landed crooked off the dock and broke his shin, so the bone stub rolled under the skin like a tongue in a cheek. Somebody gave him a mouthful of coat sleeve to keep him quiet.

It was that same trip we were expecting a father and daughter that didn't show up, and we about pushed off without them. We'd heard dogs, and you never knew the meaning of dogs—it could be the patrols, or just somebody's mutt in a furore. One thing I've never understood, you pick a night with no moon and a piece of shore without a light—a disused lighthouse this was, great dark lump

in the dark—and you can't see a whit, *can not see*. And then there's
a click, like, in the back of your eyes, and you can. Sandiford was
pressing off the piling, and the Vicar said, *no, steady on*. Duck was
reluctant—you couldn't know when the boy would yell out—and
then he felt it too and had them put up the oars. The waves were
thick as black custard, and the black shore, and now, click! there's
this girl, maybe ten or twelve, gawky little tyke, slogging straight into
the water up to her coat hem. Sandiford swung his arm signaling
her to go round the dock and fetched her down with her shoes full of
water. She's got one hand done up in a fist against her collar bone.
I wrapped her up, and she says po-faced, "My father arrives not.
I arrive alone." She says, "My fah-zer." I knew better than to ask.

From there across—you understand, nobody said *U-boats*.
Nobody said *mines*. Mostly you didn't keep an eye out, except
for Duck and Sandiford whose job it was, because you were
superstitious you would call them up. All the same that's what was
in everybody's mind. You just hoped the kiddies didn't know the
odds.

What I remember is, we had a little paraffin stove, and usually
when you got out far enough to rope the motors into life, they were
all glad to settle down over a cuppa. But this one didn't leave the
stern maybe eight hours of rough crossing, looking back where
we'd come from in the dark. She held that one hand tight as lockjaw,
and I thought she had some money in there, maybe, or a bit of
jewelry, something she'd been told to keep from harm. You'd think
you wouldn't be curious under the circumstances, but eight hours
is a long time to be standing, your mind must be doing something.
I remember I tucked the blanket tighter around her and held it
there, which she let me, and for most of the way we just stood till it
was lightening a little down by the horizon. She dozed, I thought.
She sagged against me and bit by bit her hand relaxed over the top
of the blanket. There was nothing in it. Not a thing. I cupped it in
my own and chafed it back to life a little. And I thought the way we
must have looked to God, that greasy little trawler in the black wake,
like a clot being washed from a wound.

My folder of drafts of this passage now runs to forty pages, excessive and obsessive perhaps, but it is after all the beginning of the book and must be right. I have noticed over the years that my digging at, fiddling with, scratching away at a scene will often turn up something much more fundamental than a new image or a livelier verb. In this case, I gradually realized that the reason the scene must be in somebody else's voice is that *the heroine does not remember it.* Traumatized by her flight, she cannot recall witnessing her father's death until she is nearly fifty years old. When I realized that, I understood much better what story I was telling and how the plot could be shaped and resolved. I had the delicious chance to let my heroine see the television documentary in the 1980s—in a twenty-year-old rerun—and let that chunk of interview, which contained the reader's first view of her, finally jog her memory.

> *You can make a fresh start with your final breath.*
> *—Bertolt Brecht*

A Last Word

A child learns to draw one circle on top of another, to add two little triangles at the top and a curved line at the bottom, and from this particular pattern of marks emerges a creature of an altogether different nature: a cat! The child draws one square on top of another and connects the corners—and has made three dimensions where there are only two! And although these are simple tricks that can be taught and learned, they partake of the nature of creativity, in which several elements are joined to produce not merely a whole that is greater than the sum of its parts, but a whole that is something altogether other. The fusion of elements into a unified pattern is the nature of creativity—from the sprouting of an onion to the painting of *Guernica*. At the conception of a human fetus or a short story, there occurs the conjunction of two unlike things, cells or images, that have never been joined before. Around this conjunction other cells, other images and ideas accumulate in a deliberate pattern. That pattern is the unique being of the creature, and if the pattern does not cohere, it miscarries or is stillborn.

In the organic unity of a work of literature concrete image is not separate from character, which is revealed in dialogue and point of view, which may be illuminated by simile, which may reveal theme, which is contained in plot as water is contained in an apple. No one can tell you how to achieve this, nor if you achieve it will you be able to explain very clearly how you have done so. A good critic can show you where a metaphor does or does not illuminate character, where character does or does not ring true in an action. But the critic cannot tell you how to make the character breathe. You achieve that only through identifying what to cut and what to commit to, in the hope that you may arrive at an organic story, one that cannot be reduced to a theme but embodies one.

In the unified pattern of a fiction there is also something to which the name of "magic" may be given, where one empty word is placed upon another and tapped with a third, and a flaming scarf or a long-eared hope is pulled out of the tall black heart. The most magical thing about this magic is that once the trick is explained, it is not explained, and the better you understand how it works, the better it will work again.

Ideas are not new, but the form in which they are expressed is constantly renewed, and new forms give life to what used to be called the eternal verities. An innovative writer tries to forge, and those who follow try to perfect, forms that so fuse with meaning that form itself expresses.

....

SUGGESTED STORIES
"Ad Infinitum"
  John Barth
"The Library of Babel"
  Jorge Luis Borges
"The Mandelbrot Set"
  Janet Burroway
"Ralph the Duck"
  Frederick Busch
"Cathedral"
  Raymond Carver

"The Babysitter'
  Robert Coover
"Town and Country"
  Nadine Gordimer
"Mobius the Stripper"
  Gabriel Josipovici
"Runaway"
  Alice Munro
"A Man Told Me the Story of His Life"
  Grace Paley

WRITING PROMPTS

1. One of your stories has been accepted for publication on the condition that you cut it by 25 percent. Figure out your word count goal and edit toward it. Be both aggressive and picky. Cut expendable words, fuse two scenes, do away with this paragraph. Can you get there? Is the story better for it?
2. If you did the postcard story on page 152, go back to it now and rewrite it as a full eight- to ten-page story. Develop the characters, give us their dialogue, escalate the conflict, intensify the crisis.

The four prompts below are arranged in order of ascending difficulty. The first is easiest, and likely to produce a bad story. If the story is good, you will have done something more difficult than it asked for (gold star). The second should produce better work. If you choose to do one of the last two, you may already have doomed yourself to the writing craft and will be very poor for a few years while you work out the place that writing will have in your life.

3. Take a simple but specific political, religious, scientific, or moral idea; it should be possible to state it in a single sentence. Write a short story that illustrates the idea. Do not state the idea, but we should understand what it is, and we should also experience it.
4. Take as your title a common proverb or maxim, such as *power corrupts* or *walk softly and carry a big stick* or *haste makes waste*. Write a story that makes the title ironic.

5. Identify a belief that you hold profoundly and passionately. Write a story that explores an instance in which it does not hold true.
6. Write the story that you've wanted to write all term but did not write because you knew it was too big for you and you would fail. You may fail. Write it anyway.

Acknowledgments

There have been so many contributors, reviewers, users, and friends to *Writing Fiction* over the course of ten editions that it would be neither desirable nor possible to mention them all by name. Elizabeth and Ned Stuckey-French have been unalterably generous with their time, their expertise, and their friendship. Colleagues and students at the Florida State University, Northwestern University, and the Iowa Writers' Workshop have lent suggestions, ideas, prompts, and wise words. The book has also benefited from members and activities of the Association of Writers and Writing Programs, including its publications *The Writer's Chronicle* and *Pedagogy Papers*, from the "Art of Fiction" interviews in the *Paris Review*, from the *Glimmer Train* supplement "Writers Ask," and from *Poets & Writers* and Chicago Dramatists. Rosellen Brown and Sandi Wisenberg were large-hearted in introducing me to the literary life of Chicago, including especially my writing group, PerSisters.

For this edition, I am especially grateful for the farsighted and intelligent way my editor Mary Laur has shepherded the book into its new pasture at University of Chicago Press, and for the smart counsel of intellectual property director Laura Leichum, manuscript editor Joel Score, and promotions manager Lauren Salas. And I'm also grateful for the thoughtful responses of reviewers Miles Harvey and Scott Blackwood, and for the fine design work inside and out of this edition by Rich Hendel and Zoe Norvell. I am every day sustained in life and thought by my husband Peter Ruppert.

Index